MW01629946

Authoritative Parenting

Authoritative Parenting

*Synthesizing Nurturance and Discipline
for Optimal Child Development*

**Edited by Robert E. Larzelere,
Amanda Sheffield Morris, and Amanda W. Harrist**

American Psychological Association • Washington, DC

Published by
American Psychological Association
750 First Street, NE
Washington, DC 20002
www.apa.org

To order
APA Order Department
P.O. Box 92984
Washington, DC 20090-2984
Tel: (800) 374-2721; Direct: (202) 336-5510
Fax: (202) 336-5502; TDD/TTY: (202) 336-6123
Online: www.apa.org/pubs/books
E-mail: order@apa.org

In the U.K., Europe, Africa, and the Middle East, copies may be ordered from
American Psychological Association
3 Henrietta Street
Covent Garden, London
WC2E 8LU England

Typeset in Goudy by Circle Graphics, Inc., Columbia, MD

Printer: Edwards Brothers, Inc., Ann Arbor, MI
Cover Designer: Mercury Publishing Services, Rockville, MD

The opinions and statements published are the responsibility of the authors, and such opinions and statements do not necessarily represent the policies of the American Psychological Association.

Library of Congress Cataloging-in-Publication Data

Authoritative parenting : synthesizing nurturance and discipline for optimal child development / edited by Robert E. Larzelere, Amanda Sheffield Morris, and Amanda W. Harrist. — 1st ed.
    p. cm.
  Includes bibliographical references and index.
  ISBN 978-1-4338-1240-8 — ISBN 1-4338-1240-1 1. Parenting. 2. Child psychology.
3. Child development. I. Larzelere, Robert E. II. Morris, Amanda Sheffield. III. Harrist,
Amanda W.

  HQ755.8.A968 2013
  649'.1—dc23
                                        2012019477

British Library Cataloguing-in-Publication Data

A CIP record is available from the British Library.

Printed in the United States of America
First Edition

DOI: 10.1037/13948-000

CONTENTS

CONTRIBUTORS

Brian K. Barber, PhD, Department of Child and Family Studies, University of Tennessee, Knoxville

Diana Baumrind, PhD, Institute of Human Development, University of California, Berkeley

Heidi Beebe, MA, Department of Psychology, University of California, Riverside

Lisha Bullard, PhD, Department of Psychology, Wichita State University, Wichita, KS

Timothy A. Cavell, PhD, Department of Psychology, University of Arkansas, Fayetteville

Ronald B. Cox Jr., PhD, Department of Human Development and Family Science, Oklahoma State University, Stillwater

Michael M. Criss, PhD, Department of Human Development and Family Science, Oklahoma State University, Stillwater

Lixian Cui, MS, Department of Human Development and Family Science, Oklahoma State University, Stillwater

Tamara Del Vecchio, PhD, Department of Psychology, St. John's University, Queens, NY

Mary Gauvain, PhD, Department of Psychology, University of California, Riverside

Amanda W. Harrist, PhD, Department of Human Development and Family Science, Oklahoma State University, Stillwater

Carolyn S. Henry, PhD, Department of Human Development and Family Science, Oklahoma State University, Stillwater

Laura Hubbs-Tait, PhD, Department of Human Development and Family Science, Oklahoma State University, Stillwater

Robert E. Larzelere, PhD, Department of Human Development and Family Science, Oklahoma State University, Stillwater

Sabina Low, PhD, Department of Psychology, Wichita State University, Wichita, KS

Jelani Mandara, PhD, Department of Human Development and Social Policy, Northwestern University, Evanston, IL

Christy Marvin, MA, Department of Psychology, Wichita State University, Wichita, KS

Amanda Sheffield Morris, PhD, Department of Human Development and Family Science, Oklahoma State University, Tulsa

Susan M. Perez, PhD, Department of Psychology, University of North Florida, Jacksonville

Andrea Reed, PhD, Department of Psychology, Wichita State University, Wichita, KS

Lynn Schrepferman, PhD, Department of Psychology, Wichita State University, Wichita, KS

James Snyder, PhD, Department of Psychology, Wichita State University, Wichita, KS

Nadia Sorkhabi, PhD, Department of Child and Adolescent Development, San Jose State University, San Jose, CA; Institute of Human Development, University of California, Berkeley

Laurence Steinberg, PhD, Department of Psychology, Temple University, Philadelphia, PA

Marissa Wachlarowicz, MA, Department of Psychology, Wichita State University, Wichita, KS

Mingzhu Xia, PhD, Department of Child and Family Studies, University of Tennessee, Knoxville

ACKNOWLEDGMENTS

This book was truly a team effort based on Diana Baumrind's ground-breaking work on authoritative parenting. She not only developed the authoritative synthesis throughout her productive career but also stimulated many others to build on that foundation in various ways during recent decades—examples include the authors of this book's chapters, who summarize their current thinking about authoritative parenting from years of relevant parenting research. Several chapter authors also provided helpful feedback on other chapters, but none more than Carolyn S. Henry and Laura Hubbs-Tait. They incorporated all the chapters into their concluding synthesis and often provided very helpful critiques of each version of those chapters.

Marjorie Lindner Gunnoe, Leslie Leve, and Duane Rudy provided excellent critical reviews of earlier versions of several chapters. Beth Hatch of the American Psychological Association shaped our initial efforts into a much improved final version. Finally, we would like to thank the Department of Human Development and Family Science of Oklahoma State University (OSU) for supporting the 2010 OSU Chautauqua on Parenting, the mini-conference that first brought these outstanding scholars together to celebrate and build on Diana Baumrind's career-long efforts to combine the best of a wide range of parenting perspectives into the authoritative parenting synthesis.

Authoritative Parenting

INTRODUCTION

MICHAEL M. CRISS AND ROBERT E. LARZELERE

During recent decades, American parents have become increasingly ambivalent about how firmly they should discipline their children. Part of this confusion can be attributed to the wide range of parenting advice in popular books, which often have reflected transient fads more than scientific evidence. The most important change in recent generations may be the trend away from strict authoritarian parenting to more child-centered discipline. As psychologist Diana Baumrind saw that trend developing in the 1960s, she began her famous research on parenting styles, which concluded that optimal parenting combined responsiveness (e.g., nurturance) and demandingness (e.g., control) rather than choosing one over the other (Baumrind, 1989). The classic textbook summary of her parenting styles consists of the four quadrants defined by responsiveness and demandingness (see Figure 1). Her original parenting prototypes were *authoritarian* (low responsiveness, high demandingness), *permissive* (high responsiveness, low demandingness), and *authoritative* parenting

DOI: 10.1037/13948-001
Authoritative Parenting: Synthesizing Nurturance and Discipline for Optimal Child Development,
Robert E. Larzelere, Amanda Sheffield Morris, and Amanda W. Harrist (Editors)

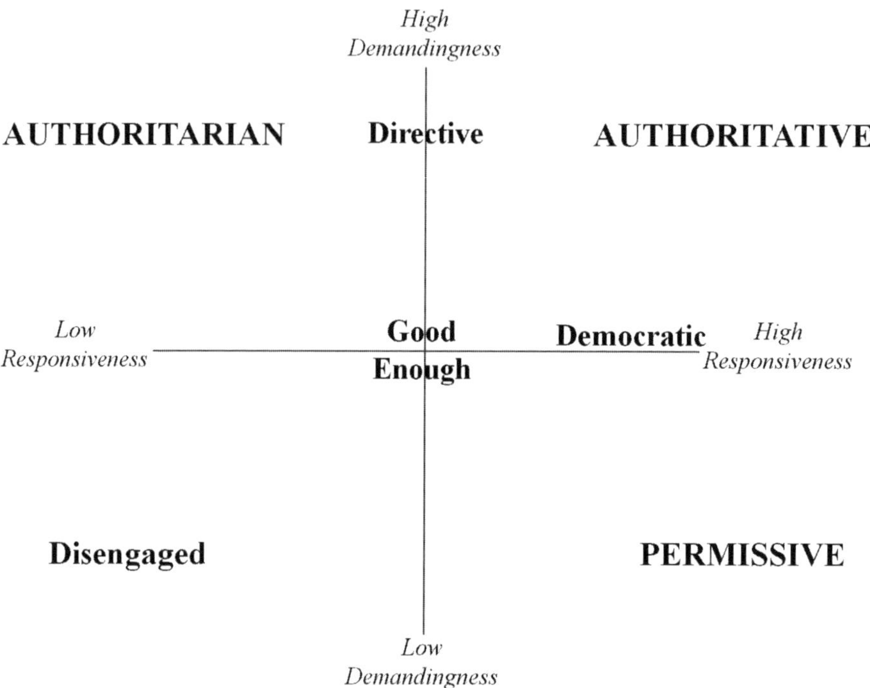

Figure 1. Baumrind's seven parenting styles.

(high responsiveness, high demandingness). Because few parents fit those prototypes exactly, Baumrind expanded her parenting patterns to include parents low on both dimensions (*disengaged*) and those who are average on one or both dimensions (e.g., *directive, good enough,* and *democratic;* Baumrind, 1989; Baumrind, Larzelere, & Owens, 2010).

As she recounts in this book, Baumrind's typological approach emphasizes the gestalt notion that both responsiveness and demandingness have to be understood in the context of the overall parenting pattern, not investigated as disembodied parenting dimensions. Baumrind's main contribution is her assertion that although responsiveness is crucial for optimal parenting, it does not negate the role of demandingness. The role of demandingness in the socialization process, in contrast, has been much more controversial than responsiveness and, as such, is emphasized more in this book. Varying perspectives on optimal demandingness have led to what Baumrind (see also Chapter 1, this volume) calls *definitional drift.* On the other hand, Figure 1 is simplistic in implying that authoritative and authoritarian parents are equivalent on demandingness. In Baumrind's own research (Baumrind et al., 2010; see Chapter 1), they are equivalent only on confrontive discipline. Authoritative parents impose more maturity demands than authoritarian parents but avoid types of power assertion used by authoritarian parents, such as verbal hostility, psychological control, severe physical punishment, and arbitrary discipline. Parenting experts have made other qualitative and quantitative distinctions between how authoritative and authoritarian parents implement demandingness, differences that are reflected across the chapters in this book. Although the authoritative combination of responsiveness and demandingness has consistently been associated with optimal child outcomes (e.g., Baumrind et al., 2010; Steinberg, 2001), future research still needs to clarify the distinctive characteristics of authoritative demandingness and how it can best be integrated with supportive responsiveness.

Although numerous ideas, fads, and theories about parenting have come and gone, Baumrind's seminal work has had an enduring impact on the field for more than 4 decades. Hers is widely recognized as the leading typological approach to parenting (e.g., Parke & Buriel, 2006). In addition to its longevity, her theory on authoritative parenting has influenced a variety of individuals from a wide range of disciplines, including students, researchers, practitioners, parenting educators, clinicians, and educators. For instance, her work has influenced a generation of clinical interventions for children with disruptive behaviors (see, e.g., Chapter 8, this volume). Moreover, Baumrind has taught generations of parents that they can have high expectations for their children's behavior while remaining warm and responsive.

There has been an extensive body of empirical research focusing on Baumrind's parenting dimensions, and her theory has been widely summarized in introductory textbooks on child development and parenting. However, the present book is the first scholarly book on authoritative parenting by leading researchers. As such, its purpose is to summarize the most important current parenting research relevant to authoritative parenting, including research on its three unresolved issues as noted by Parke and Buriel (2006). First, the specific mechanisms that account for the effectiveness of authoritative parenting are addressed in several chapters that pinpoint and expand the aspects of responsiveness and demandingness that are particularly helpful or harmful for important child outcomes. Second, Sorkhabi and Mandara (see Chapter 5) address another unresolved issue by exploring how the effects of authoritative parenting vary across cultures. Finally, Morris, Cui, and Steinberg (see Chapter 2) and Larzelere, Cox, and Mandara (see Chapter 4) explore the third issue of whether the positive outcomes associated with authoritative parenting are due to parent or child effects.

The chapters not only summarize the current research relevant to authoritative parenting but also clarify its distinctive attributes in important ways. Examples include the relevance of psychological control and of cultural variations in authoritative parenting and equally effective approximations to it. Several chapters supplement Baumrind's recent research by suggesting different ways to distinguish appropriate from counterproductive types of demandingness. Other authors summarize how authoritative parenting is related to emotion socialization, adolescent negotiations for increasing autonomy, cognitive development, and treatments to reduce aggression. Overall, this book incorporates research on authoritative parenting that has been conducted with diverse samples (e.g., clinical and nonclinical, fathers and mothers, younger and adolescent children, urban and rural) in North America and around the world.

This book is divided into four sections. Part I covers the history and current state of authoritative parenting research. Baumrind (see Chapter 1) provides needed clarification of her original definition of authoritative parenting to correct what she sees as a drift away from its original distinctive combination of demandingness and responsiveness. She also provides a fascinating overview of the philosophical, theoretical, and political influences that shaped the development of her theory. Baumrind differentiates confrontive behavioral control, as typically used by authoritative parents, from coercive and psychological control, which are more typical of authoritarian parents. Next, Morris et al. (see Chapter 2) summarize three important developments in the parenting style literature since the seminal work of Darling and Steinberg (1993). They first discuss components of authoritative parenting, including emotion-related parenting and distinctions between effective and ineffective types of parental control. Second, they discuss bidirectional effects between parents and children, including new physiological bases for child temperament. Finally, they propose that parenting can best be understood within a set of interconnected dynamic systems that include intraindividual processes, the larger family as a system, and the immediate environment and overall culture.

In Part II, authors distinguish harmful from appropriate types of demandingness, including how demandingness can support disciplinary reasoning and autonomy development in various cultural contexts. Barber and Xia (see Chapter 3) build on Baumrind's conceptualization of parental control by updating the distinction between psychological control and behavioral control. They argue that appropriate control helps children negotiate the fundamental duality of developing individual autonomy while coordinating their own interests with societal expectations and needs. Barber and Xia also summarize the substantial recent progress in clarifying the fundamental characteristics of psychological control. They assert that research on behavioral control has failed to make similar progress partly because of insufficient attention to the nonlinearity and contextual variations of its effects. Larzelere et al. (see Chapter 4) explain how authoritative parenting combines reasoning and power assertion in responding to perceived misbehavior in young children. Using Bell's control system model (Bell & Harper, 1977), they argue that the power-assertive skills emphasized in parent management training can support the disciplinary reasoning and negotiation emphasized in child development research. This integrative model suggests how contingent power assertion can support milder verbal discipline and then be phased out. It also implies that skillful use of verbal disciplinary responses can enhance moral internalization and reduce the need for power assertion. Sorkhabi and Mandara (see Chapter 5) conclude that a combination of nurturance and control is optimal in all cultures, but cultures vary in the specific manifestations and balance of those dimensions. What looks too authoritarian in one culture may approximate authoritative parenting fairly well in its own cultural context. What is crucial is that the parenting pattern is *perceived* by children in that cultural context as both responsive and appropriately demanding. Sorkhabi (see Chapter 6) also addresses how parental communication and control work together when adolescents negotiate their increasing need for autonomy, especially in conflicts across various domains (e.g., personal vs. moral domains). She argues that parenting styles influence the extent to which conflicts occur and how adaptive they are for autonomy development. Acknowledging that conflict varies by domain, she posits that the ideal developmental path involves a positive connection between parents and adolescents while supporting the youth's expanding autonomy.

In Part III, authors consider the implications of authoritative parenting for clinical and educational interventions. Cavell, Harrist, and Del Vecchio (see Chapter 7) summarize 10 essential principles in improving parent management training. One of their major themes is that the quality of the parent–child relationship is more important for the long-term success of parenting than are the parental management skills used to curb immediate noncompliance. Consistent with authoritative parenting, they argue that the combination of reliable responsiveness with effective discipline is associated with the best outcomes in clinically referred aggressive children. The application of authoritative parenting to clinical interventions is next discussed by Snyder and colleagues (see Chapter 8), who highlight clinical parenting interventions that focus on children's and parents' emotions. The authors discuss interventions that emphasize emotion socialization of children in ways that are consistent with authoritative parenting. They summarize how parenting interventions, which historically have emphasized contingent behavior management skills, have begun to incorporate aspects of the responsiveness dimension of authoritative parenting into their protocols. Gauvain, Perez, and Beebe (see Chapter 9) review research on the types of social support that are optimal for children's cognitive development. The authors highlight the importance of nurturance, sensitivity to the child's needs, and supportive communication that respects the child's perspective. Authoritative parents encourage autonomy but also hold appropriate maturity demands in both learning and play situations that can be reflected in their effective use of scaffolding. The authors posit that authoritative parenting may be ideal for transferring responsibility for learning from the parent to the child.

In Part IV, the final section of the book, Henry and Hubbs-Tait (Chapter 10) highlight important themes about parenting that have emerged from these chapters. In particular, they identify blueprints for bridging authoritative parenting with other prominent approaches to parenting, review classic and emerging theoretical perspectives on authoritative parenting, and summarize the enrichment of both the responsiveness and demandingness dimensions, including understanding these dimensions within the broader contexts of ongoing parent–child relations and specific sequences of parent–child interactions. They also highlight key implications for research directions and practical applications.

It is our hope that this book advances Baumrind's original aim: to understand and promote optimal ways in which parents can combine responsiveness and demandingness in socializing their children for the best possible outcomes for them and for society. We believe that this book will benefit students and parenting scholars as well as parenting educators, teachers, and ultimately parents and their children themselves.

REFERENCES

Baumrind, D. (1989). Rearing competent children. In W. Damon (Ed.), *Child development today and tomorrow* (pp. 349–378). San Francisco, CA: Jossey-Bass.

Baumrind, D., Larzelere, R. E., & Owens, E. B. (2010). Effects of preschool parents' power assertive patterns and practices on adolescent development. *Parenting: Science and Practice, 10*, 157–201. doi:10.1080/15295190903290790

Bell, R. Q., & Harper, L. V. (1977). *Child effects on adults*. Hillsdale, NJ: Erlbaum.

Darling, N., & Steinberg, L. (1993). Parenting style as context: An integrative model. *Psychological Bulletin, 113*, 487–496. doi:10.1037/0033-2909.113.3.487

Parke, R. D., & Buriel, R. (2006). Socialization in the family: Ethnic and ecological perspectives. In N. Eisenberg, W. Damon, & R. M. Lerner (Eds.), *Handbook of child psychology. Vol. 3: Social, emotional, and personality development* (6th ed., pp. 429–504). Hoboken, NJ: Wiley.

Steinberg, L. (2001). We know some things: Parent–adolescent relationships in retrospect and prospect. *Journal of Research on Adolescence, 11*, 1–19. doi:10.1111/1532-7795.00001

I

THE HISTORY AND CURRENT STATE OF AUTHORITATIVE PARENTING RESEARCH

1

AUTHORITATIVE PARENTING REVISITED: HISTORY AND CURRENT STATUS

DIANA BAUMRIND

In his 2001 presidential address to the Society for Research on Adolescence titled "Some Things We Know: Parent–Adolescent Relationships in Retrospect and Prospect," Laurence Steinberg asserted:

> Studies of American samples show that as a general rule, adolescents fare better when their parents are authoritative, regardless of their racial or social background or their parents' marital status (Steinberg, 1990). This finding has been confirmed in samples from countries around the world that have extreme diversity in their value systems, such as China, Pakistan, Hong Kong, Scotland, Australia, and Argentina. (p. 12)

I am pleased to acknowledge the generous support of the William T. Grant Foundation for my program of research and the consistent support of the Institute of Human Development at the University of California, Berkeley, and of my colleagues, in particular, Nadia Sorkhabi and Steven Kniep. I am appreciative of the interest in my work shown by Marjorie Gunnoe and by Robert E. Larzelere, Amanda S. Morris, and Amanda W. Harrist of the Department of Human Development and Family Science, Oklahoma State University, which evolved into the publication of this volume on authoritative parenting, and of the efforts of the authors of the outstanding chapters contained herein.

DOI: 10.1037/13948-002
Authoritative Parenting: Synthesizing Nurturance and Discipline for Optimal Child Development,
Robert E. Larzelere, Amanda Sheffield Morris, and Amanda W. Harrist (Editors)
Copyright © 2013 by the American Psychological Association. All rights reserved.

Authoritative parenting is marked by a balanced synthesis of two orthogonal dimensions, demandingness and responsiveness, which are described later in this chapter. Among the child attributes that Steinberg (2001) concluded were fostered by authoritative parents are "self-reliance, achievement motivation, prosocial behavior, self-control, cheerfulness, and social confidence" (p. 13). The same constellation of qualities that define the authoritative pattern in parents has been found to characterize effective educators, work supervisors, and coaches in contemporary industrial societies (Bear, 2004; Gregory & Weinstein, 2004; Hughes, 2002; Scarlett, Ponte, & Singh, 2009).

The wide endorsement of authoritative parenting has been accompanied by a definitional drift away from its original meaning. For example, the Authoritative subscale of the Parenting Styles and Dimensions Questionnaire (Robinson, Mandleco, Olsen, & Hart, 1995) consists of four dimensions (Warmth and Involvement, Reasoning/Induction, Democratic Participation, Good Natured/Easy Going), none of which assesses the confrontive control aspect of the demandingness component of the authoritative construct.

One purpose of this chapter is to standardize the meaning of the authoritative parenting pattern by grounding the pattern in its theoretical heritage and expanding on constructs, in particular, confrontive control, that are integral to its definition but sometimes overlooked. I begin this chapter by defining the authoritative prototype, followed by a review of the philosophical and theoretical heritages and social ideology that ground my parent typology. I then distinguish between confrontive and coercive kinds of power assertion, a crucial distinction accounting for the differential effects of authoritative and authoritarian parenting. I then describe my longitudinal program of research by presenting its research strategy and methodology and the research variables and procedures used to test hypotheses concerning the differential effects on child outcomes of contrasting patterns of parental authority. I conclude by summarizing what I consider to be the distinctive features of my longitudinal program of research.

THE AUTHORITATIVE PROTOTYPE DEFINED

A parental *authority* is a person whose expert knowledge and greater ability to protect and lead invests him or her with the power and right to designate behavioral alternatives for his or her progeny. I introduced the term *authoritative* into the parenting lexicon in 1966 to recapture this neutral meaning of an authority and thus dispel the pejorative connotations associated with a parental authority (Baumrind, 1966). With the publication in 1950 of *The Authoritarian Personality*, an influential classic by Adorno, Frenkel-Brunswik, Levinson, and Sanford, the concept of an authority figure had become infused with censorious connotations more appropriate to the authoritarian personality, leading some parents in the American democratic society to question the ethics of parents acting as authority figures to their children. As characterized by Adorno et al. (p. 971), the authoritarian personality is rigid, repressed, conventional, power oriented, and hierarchical, in contrast to the democratic personality, who is warm, flexible, equalitarian, and genuine. As a parent, an authoritarian personality would be expected to be a restrictive, punitive, repressive, and coercive authority figure (in short, authoritarian), in contrast to a democratic personality, who would be expected to be unconditionally accepting, autonomy supportive, and lenient (in short, permissive).

I identified a type of parent in my research who fit neither the authoritarian nor the permissive prototype and whom I labeled *authoritative*. An authoritative parent displays neither the coercive disciplinary style expected of an authoritarian personality nor the indulgent disciplinary style expected of a democratic personality but in contrast to both is responsive and demanding, confrontive and autonomy supportive, affectionate and power assertive. Thus, the authoritative prototype is antithetical both to the permissive prototype characterized by few rules or demands and to the authoritarian prototype characterized by coercive and functionally superfluous control (Baumrind, 1966).

Misunderstanding of parental authority and of the authoritative construct is fostered when parental control and love are represented as opposite ends of the same continuum rather than as two independent dimensions. For example, in her description of the last century of expert advice on child rearing, Hulbert (2003) wrote:

> Though you would never have guessed it from their press, much less from their opposition to each other, the parent-centered ministers and the child-centered mentors professed allegiances to the same cause: "authoritative parenting," an approach that struck a balance between love and control, which was the consensus position in the child development field. Both schools toed the conventional line in distinguishing it from "authoritarian parenting" on the one hand, which they all agreed was overbearing, and "permissive parenting" on the other, which they concurred was indulgent. (p. 335)

This quote from Hulbert (2003), which describes authoritative parenting, represents love and control as a single dimension by equating high control with low love and positioning authoritative parenting midway between love and control. However, authoritative parenting is not an approach that strikes a balance between love and control but an approach that treats love and control as two independent dimensions. In contrast to advocates of child-centered permissiveness, such as Richard Farson (1974) and Alfie Kohn (2005), who treated control and love as a single dimension by equating confrontive behavioral control with rejection and unconditional love with unconditional acceptance, authoritative parents are neither unconditionally accepting nor rejecting. They are high on both control and love, and thus the antithesis of disengaged parenting, which is low on both love and control, not the antithesis of either authoritarian or permissive parenting.

The authoritative style is a syncretic coalition of the beneficial components of the opposing dualities represented by the authoritarian and permissive styles of parenting by being both power assertive and demanding (a mark of authoritarian parenting) and loving and responsive (a mark of permissive parenting). As a syncretic coalition, the authoritative dialectic of high demandingness and responsiveness changes the nature and effect of each component. Although permissive and authoritative parents are both loving, in contrast to permissive parents who are unconditionally accepting, authoritative parents explicitly sanction acts of which they disapprove. Although authoritarian and authoritative parents are both power assertive, in contrast to authoritarian parents, who are coercive as well as confrontive, authoritative parents are responsive and confrontive, but not coercive.

PHILOSOPHICAL AND THEORETICAL HERITAGES OF BAUMRIND'S PARENT TYPOLOGY

In common with the sociocultural approach of Vygotsky (1978), my perspective on parenting reflects a Marxist theoretical heritage (Baumrind, 1978a, 1998). My perspective on socialization reflects the psychological insights of educational theorists like Maria Montessori and group dynamics theorists like Kurt Lewin.

Marxist Dialectical Materialism

Marxist philosophy based on the Hegelian dialectic posits that all phenomena contain opposing forces (*thesis* and *antithesis*), such as agency and communion or firm control and autonomy support, which are reconciled or *synthesized* in optimal functioning. Like the Marxist psychologist Vygotsky (see Chapter 9, this volume), I hold that the ecologically valid way to study children is within their natural environments and that the stages of human development do not unfold naturally but are largely driven by interactions with parents and educators. As a materialist, I hold that human beings must look to themselves and each other, not a supreme being, for guidance so that parents must assume responsibility for shaping the person their child will become (see Vande Kemp, 1995, on Baumrind).

A Marxist approach as it applies to how children should be raised was put into practice by the Soviet educator A. S. Makarenko (1954), who was given the task of rehabilitating homeless delinquent youth after the Russian revolution (see Bronfenbrenner, 1979). Makarenko imposed an orderly regimen and justified his directives with persuasive reasoning. He used socially useful labor as a formative influence on his young charges, whom he guided to become responsible, agentic members of their society. His disciplinary style was authoritative in that he integrated firm control and high maturity demands with love and unconditional commitment. Like Makarenko, I conceive of socialization as character education designed to instill desirable habits of mind and behavior by a synthetic combination of nurturance and reasoning with high standards for achievement and prosocial behavior firmly reinforced.

Educational Theories of Maria Montessori

Nancy Rambusch (1962), a disciple of Maria Montessori, described the way in which authoritative control is used to resolve the tension between personal freedom for children and the need for order in a Montessori classroom:

> The teachers exert an authoritative presence; they may also exert authority in certain circumstances. But the discipline resides in three areas in a Montessori classroom: It resides in the environment itself which is controlled; in the teacher herself who is controlled and is ready to assume an authoritarian role if it is necessary; and from the very beginning it resides in the children. It is a three-way arrangement, as opposed to certain types of American education in which all of the authority is vested in the teacher, or where, in the caricature of permissive education, all of the authority is vested in the children. (pp. 49–50)

Within the American context, a similar philosophy was promoted by John Dewey. According to Rambusch (1962):

> Both Dewey and Montessori feel that interest and discipline are connected and not opposed. Dewey himself decried unrestrained freedom of action in speech, in manners, and lack of manners. He was, in fact, critical of all those progressive schools that carried the thing they call freedom nearly to the point of anarchy. (p. 63)

Like Montessori and Dewey, I view both freedom of action unrestrained by adult authority (unconditional acceptance) and overbearing exercise of adult authority (coercive control) as detrimental to children's development.

Kurt Lewin's Group Dynamics Movement

In a historical overview of the study of socialization, Eleanor Maccoby (1992) described my work contrasting effects of parenting styles as contradistinctive to the work on social climates of Kurt Lewin, who originated the group dynamics movement.

Mentored by Professor Hubert Coffey, a student of Lewin, I completed my doctoral dissertation on structured and unstructured discussion groups of college students at the University of California, Berkeley, in 1955. Lewin and his colleagues (Lewin, Lippitt, & White, 1939) had examined the differential influence of experimentally contrived democratic and autocratic leadership styles on the functioning of group processes: Autocratic leaders made all the decisions and dispensed praise and blame without explaining their criteria; democratic leaders were supportive of group processes by being available as a resource but remaining objective and detached from the group's decisions. Lewin et al. (1939) favored democratic leadership because it gave maximum decision-making power to group members. My own bias favored a "structured" leadership that is less domineering than autocratic leadership but more directive than Lewin et al.'s democratic leadership. Therefore, the leaders of my structured discussion groups were neither democratic nor autocratic.

I (Baumrind, 1955) hypothesized and found that the optimal leadership style, defined by (a) high-quality essays produced by the students and (b) students' written satisfaction with their group leader, was guided by structured leaders. Members of the structured groups tended to model themselves after their assertive group leader rather than relinquish their own independent judgment and autonomy to their leader, as group dynamics theorists predicted they would. My dissertation research on the effects of structured leadership in discussion groups introduced the combined leadership qualities of assertive authority and responsiveness to members' input that reemerged in my research on parental authority as the authoritative prototype.

Prior to my application of group dynamics theory to parenting, Baldwin (1949) and colleagues (Baldwin, Kalhoun, & Breese, 1945) had studied the effects on children of democratic, authoritarian, and laissez-faire parenting. Their democratic model, like Lewin's, was characterized by minimal adult control, objectivity (i.e., detached scientific attitude), and support of the child's input to family decisions. Baldwin and colleagues concluded that democratic parenting was maximally conducive to children's cognitive and social development but also to egoistic self-expression.

My parent typology (Baumrind, 1966) incorporated a feature of Baldwin's democratic model by including as a criterion of optimal parenting the encouragement of children's input to decisions that affect them. But my typology differed from Baldwin's by emphasizing decisive adult leadership in the form of confrontive behavioral control as a mark of the optimal parenting style I labeled *authoritative*. My authoritative parenting pattern was a novel style in that it synthesized the demanding, confrontive, and monitoring features of the autocratic or authoritarian style rejected by Lewin and Baldwin as domineering and retrogressive with the responsive and communicative features of the democratic style they favored.

Unlike Baldwin's earlier typology that made binary distinctions between a democratic parenting style that is responsive and liberal and an authoritarian or autocratic parenting style that is demanding and conservative, Baumrind, Larzelere, and Owens (2010) found more and less desirable forms of demanding child-rearing styles in the distinctive characteristics of authoritative and authoritarian parents (both demanding) and of responsive child-rearing styles in the distinctive characteristics of authoritative and permissive parents (both responsive). Although not defined by social ideology, these parenting styles were expected to differ on social ideology, with strict parents more conservative than lenient parents.

SOCIAL IDEOLOGY REFLECTED IN PARENTING STYLE

Parents' child-rearing styles as well as scholars' child-rearing theories typically reflect their progenitors' social ideology. Writing on the role of moral politics in family life, the sociologist and linguist George Lakoff (1996) proposed that the ideological determinant of parents' child-rearing styles occurred along a conservative–liberal continuum.

Lakoff's Strict Father and Nurturant Parent Metaphors

Lakoff used the metaphors *strict father* and *nurturant parent* to capture fundamental differences in conservative (strict father) versus liberal (nurturant parent) social ideologies, which he theorized guide parents' child-rearing objectives and practices. Lakoff conjectured that authoritarian parents are motivated by conservative ideology and authoritative as well as permissive parents by liberal ideology. The conservative ideology of the strict father affirms parents' responsibility to cultivate obedience and deference to authority as the foundation of children's character. The liberal ideology of the nurturant parent, grounded in Rawls's (1971) theory of justice, affirms children's natural right to self-determination and unconditional acceptance as the basis for children's development of morality and effectance.

Although Lakoff (1996, p. 357) equated the authoritative prototype with the nurturant parent, the authoritative prototype conforms to neither the strict father nor the nurturant parent but shares certain features of each (see, e.g., Baumrind, 1966, 1968, 1971a). Like Lakoff's nurturant parent and Baldwin's democratic parent, the authoritative parent affirms the child's sense of worth, providing an emotional climate of warmth and involvement intended to encourage a child's independence and autonomous self-expression. Like Lakoff's strict father, the authoritative parent affirms parents' responsibility to set standards and firmly enforce demands for achievement and self-control. However, in contrast to the strict father, authoritative parents do not view children and youth as passive recipients of adult wisdom or demand unquestioning obedience. They are issue oriented not obedience oriented, flexible in the way they enforce demands, and like the nurturant parent, warm and willing to negotiate in response to reasoned dissent. However, in contrast to liberal ideologists such as Paul Goodman (1960), John Holt (1974), Alfie Kohn (2005), and A. S. Neill (1964), who claimed for children the right to freedom from adult authority and to have equal input to family decisions, authoritative parents do not think it necessary to first consult their children before setting and enforcing standards and limits. Also, unlike permissive parents, authoritative parents are not distinctively liberal in their social ideology or lenient in their practices (see Baumrind et al. 2010, p. 179, Table 3).

Authoritative Parents Balance Freedom and Control

Parents' incontrovertibly greater control of resources and immensely greater knowledge, experience, and strength can compel obedience and indeed legitimate in the mind of young children parents' right to use their power in disciplinary encounters. During adolescence, as the child assumes more adult responsibilities, authoritative parents increasingly encourage verbal give-and-take and more readily negotiate to resolve conflicts (Baumrind, 1991b, 1991c). Parents' ultimate success in eliciting children's willing compliance depends on parents' readiness to justify their directives so as to enhance their children's growing understanding of their parents' child-rearing objectives.

Authoritative parents regard the rights and responsibilities of parents and children as reciprocal, not equal, reflecting their different social roles and their children's changing competencies and developmental needs. Because authoritative parents value both independence and compliance in their children, they do not conceive of freedom and control in a child-rearing context as antagonistic forces, whereas both authoritarian and permissive parents appear to conceive of children's freedom to think and act autonomously and parents' disciplinary role to enforce firm limits as contradictory objectives. Consistent with their conservative ideology, authoritarian parents view parents' right and responsibility to assert strict control as primary and children's autonomy as secondary. Consistent with their liberal ideology, permissive parents treat parental control as an undesirable counteractive force to children's growth-enhancing motive to act autonomously. Unlike permissive parents, authoritative parents regard children's willingness to comply with directives from parents and teachers as essential for their normal development of self-discipline, personal agency, and moral values.

Unlike authoritarian parents, authoritative parents differentiate between the effects of confrontive control, which they regard as beneficial, and the effects of coercive control, which they regard as detrimental (see Baumrind et al., 2010, p. 178 and p. 179, Table 3).

CONFRONTIVE VERSUS COERCIVE BEHAVIORAL CONTROL

Confrontive control is demanding, firm, and goal-directed, whereas coercive control is intrusive, manipulative, punitive, autonomy undermining, and restrictive (Patterson, 1982). Both confrontive and coercive control of children's behavior are overtly power assertive. However, confrontive control differs from coercive control by being functional (goal oriented) and reasonable (subject to rational justification and negotiation).

The differences between confrontive and coercive behavioral control are crucial to explaining the differential effects of authoritative and authoritarian styles of parenting, both of which differ from permissive parenting by their ready use of confrontive control but differ from each other in their use of coercive control and reason. Authoritative parents use a high level of confrontive control of children's behavior to provide organization and limits and to enforce compliance when a child is defiant, but they seldom use coercive forms of control and are willing to modify their directive on the basis of their child's reasoned objections. Authoritative parents tailor the balance between asserting control and allowing freedom to the resilience, unique temperament, and developmental stage of their child. Authoritarian parents, in contrast to authoritative parents, use control of children's behavior not only to obtain immediate compliance with a specific directive but also to induce their child by coercive means to become more dispositionally compliant.

By *dispositional compliance* I mean internalization of the norm of compliance, resulting in deferential conformity to the directives of a designated authority. Dispositionally compliant children lack agency (i.e., self-assertion, self-determination, and individuation). Behavioral control that is confrontive but not coercive is unlikely to be experienced by children as disaffiliative, or as a threat to their sense of self-determination, and thus to result in dispositional compliance or a defiant demeanor (Baumrind, 1996; Baumrind, Larzelere, & Cowan, 2002; Baumrind et al., 2010).

The differences between the effects of confrontive and coercive control of children's behavior are likely to be overlooked by scholars for whom *control, controlling,* and *power assertion* are pejorative terms. When coercive and confrontive kinds of control are not distinguished, possible differential effects of these two kinds of power assertion cannot be discerned. A high level of any kind of power assertion by parents is often assumed to be intrusive and overcontrolling and thus detrimental. Smith (2010), for example, did not distinguish between coercive and confrontive kinds of control when she created a "controlling maternal behavior summary score" from the mean of intrusiveness and directiveness: Intrusiveness was described as "overstimulating and overcontrolling," and directiveness was defined in part as "allowing for few spontaneously introduced actions from children" (p. 6). Smith foreclosed the possibility of distinguishing between confrontive and coercive forms of controlling behavior by defining controlling as inherently intrusive and restrictive of children's initiative, thus coercive. Similarly, Grolnick and Pomerantz (2009) conceptualized control as "parenting characterized by pressure, intrusion and domination" (p. 165), and guidance as structure. Defined in this way, any control is functionally superfluous and presumptively maladaptive, unlike guidance, which the authors proposed provides beneficial structure.

Smith's (2010) controlling behavior and Grolnick and Pomerantz's (2009) control, like Hoffman's (1960) power assertion, emphasize what I refer to as coercive rather than confrontive kinds of control or power assertion. By Smith's definition of controlling, authoritarian parents are behaviorally controlling but authoritative parents are not behaviorally controlling (because they are not coercive, i.e., restrictive and intrusive). Consequently, the disciplinary style of authoritative parents would not be differentiated from that of permissive parents. However, by my earlier differentiation between coercive and confrontive behavioral control, authoritative parents differ from permissive parents by their use of confrontive power to influence their children and from authoritarian parents by abjuring the use of coercive behavioral control to compel obedience. The kind of power assertion (confrontive, not coercive), not the amount of power assertion, used by authoritative parents is what differentiates authoritative from authoritarian parents. Baumrind et al. (2010) found that whereas confrontive behavioral control was used as much by authoritative as authoritarian parents, coercive behavioral control was used frequently by authoritarian parents but seldom by authoritative parents.

Baumrind et al. (2010) hypothesized and found that power-assertive control of children's behavior that was confrontive but not coercive was associated concurrently and over time with children's prosocial behavior, self-assertiveness, and mental health, confirming earlier findings that the effects of confrontive control are likely to achieve compliance without subduing self-assertiveness (Baumrind, 1971a, 1989, 1991c). Baumrind et al. (2010) referred to coercive behavioral control as *authoritarian-distinctive* power assertion to mark the difference in how and why authoritarian and authoritative parents asserted disciplinary power.

THE FAMILY SOCIALIZATION AND DEVELOPMENTAL COMPETENCE RESEARCH PROGRAM

I designed the Family Socialization and Developmental Competence Research Program (FSP) to test hypotheses concerning the differential effects on children's attributes and behavior from preschool through adolescence of contrasting patterns of parental authority that differ in their socialization practices and ideology. *Patterns of parental authority* are stable constellations of cognitively motivated parental practices.

In the FSP, the effects on children of contrasting parenting patterns and practices at three developmental stages—nursery school, latency, and adolescence—were assessed (Baumrind, 1971a, 1989, 1991c). Measures of mothers and fathers at each time period consisted of between 81- and 174-item Likert-type rating scales, and measures of children consisted of between 72- and 90-item Q sorts supplemented at adolescence by 63 Likert-type items rating scales. Parent ratings were correlated and reduced to manageable clusters of items. Cluster analytic techniques (Tryon & Bailey, 1966) and principal component analyses were applied to these ratings to derive the child and parent variables. At each time period the parenting types were derived by a second-order principal component analysis of the first-order factors for mothers and fathers. The two second-order parenting factors, demandingness and responsiveness, were then extracted and used to derive the parent patterns for the purpose of explaining developmental outcomes by comprehensive measures of family functioning.

Theory and Hypotheses

Socialization is an adult-initiated process by which children and youth, through education, training, and imitation, acquire their culture and the values, skills, knowledge, and habits necessary to function effectively in that culture. The ways children respond to parents' socialization efforts vary in skillfulness and functional adaptability. Compliance with adults' directives solely in response to fear of disapproval or punishment is less skillful and functional than reflective compliance in which the child feels free to suggest an alternative that would coordinate the child's own plans with those of the parent. Noncompliance varies in lack of skillfulness and functional adaptability from impulsive defiance to simple refusal without defiance to initiating negotiations intended to effect a mutually satisfactory compromise.

How parents achieve an adequate level of behavioral compliance without inducing dispositional compliance is an important theme in parent–child interactions and one that differentiates the parenting styles that emerged from my program of research. I hypothesized that the disproportionate emphasis authoritarian parents place on prompt, unquestioning compliance would inhibit children's reflective thought and agentic behavior and instead engender nonreflective compliance or defiance. In contrast to authoritarian parents, authoritative parents provide adolescents with reasons and incentives to comply as well as ways to explain their disobedience when they choose not to comply. I hypothesized that children from permissive and disengaged families would be less capable of functional forms of compliance and noncompliance than children from authoritative families because both kinds of low-demand parents fail to reward children's responses that balance the needs and rights of self and others or to engage children in reflective thought.

Authoritative parents differ from both permissive and authoritarian parents in their interpretation of and response to noncompliance. If challenged, permissive parents are unlikely to enforce compliance with their few demands because they fear their children will perceive confrontation as rejection or become angry. Authoritarian parents, if challenged, threaten punishment and give "because I say so" as a reason for compliance, rather than citing the intended benefits to self and others of obeying the directive. Authoritative parents enforce compliance with their demands, which are functional and, if challenged, justified by reasons at the child's level of understanding.

Research Strategy and Methodology

I designed my research methodology to control confounds, avoid deceptive methods, and maximize inferential and ecological validity (Bronfenbrenner, 1979). To prevent confounding by shared source variance, a common limitation of correlational research in which data for the independent and dependent variables are often obtained from the same source, different trained graduate psychologists rated parents and children within and across data collection waves.

Avoiding Deception

In a series of articles, I argued that the use of deception when obtaining consent or debriefing participants is a violation of the fiduciary obligations of researchers to adequately protect the welfare of research participants and therefore is an unacceptable ethical cost that cannot be justified by the benefits, including better control of confounding factors, which might result from the use of deceptive means when obtaining "informed" consent (Baumrind, 1964, 1971b, 1972b, 1975, 1979, 1985, 1990).

Methodological Issues

To maximize inferential and ecological validity (Bronfenbrenner, 1979), I used naturalistic observation and comprehensive interviews rather than survey-type self-reports or experimental manipulation in contrived settings. Because the unique qualities of families are not reducible to a sum of the properties of their component practices, I used a typological rather than a variable approach to the study of parenting effects.

Inferential and Ecological Validity. *Inferential validity* refers to the applicability of causal inferences made in research settings to the real-life experiences of participants. *Ecological validity* (Bronfenbrenner, 1979) refers to the extent to which research results are representative of conditions in the wider world, which in turn affects a study's inferential validity.

The use of impoverished measures to assess complex constructs compromises a study's inferential and ecological validity. Some investigators (e.g., Fletcher, Darling, Steinberg, & Dornbusch, 1995; Radziszewska, Richardson, Dent, & Flay, 1996) dimensionalized authoritativeness (sometimes with a single survey item, e.g., "My parents ask my opinion, but generally make the decision"; Radziszewska et al., 1996, p. 304). To maximize inferential and ecological validity, the data I used to operationalize parenting patterns and child outcomes consisted of transcribed comprehensive interviews and specimen records of parent–child interactions and child behaviors observed in diverse natural settings.

Typological Versus Variable Analyses. A *typological* approach to parenting treats the family as a complex living system that is more than the sum of its parts, whereas a *variable-centered* approach to parenting reduces molar activities of family members to levels of isolated variables such as warmth, control, and cohesiveness (Darling & Steinberg, 1993; Magnusson, 2001; Mandara, 2003; Waller & Meehl, 1998). A typological approach synthesizes the nomothetic variable-centered and idiographic case-oriented methods.

A parenting pattern (also known as a *type* or *category*) is a gestalt made up of parenting practices that interact in such a way that their joint effect differs from the sum of the individual effects of their component practices. Thus, authoritative parenting as a gestalt is a unique synthesis of antithetical beneficial practices such as autonomy support and confrontive behavioral control. Different parenting patterns (e.g., authoritarian and authoritative) with similar levels of a particular beneficial component variable (e.g., confrontive control) can have very different effects on child outcomes, depending on the level of another, but detrimental, component (e.g., coercive power assertion).

Child Effects. Although I choose to focus on how parents and educators "cause" their children's behavior, I assume that potent child effects on parental behavior exist. As documented in Baumrind et al. (2010), we controlled for early child attributes when analyzing the effects of parents' child-rearing behavior on their children's later functioning because, as Bell (1968) argued, parent–child effects are bidirectional. We also incorporated into the meaning of parental responsiveness the assumption that children by their nature and actions influence parenting behavior. The responsiveness dimension in my study assesses the extent to which parents fit their demands to the unique temperament, bids, and thought processes of each child.

Whether children trust their parents to act in their best interests affects how they will respond to parents' directives and discipline. However, it is one thing to assert that children are active agents who influence the microenvironments that are designed to affect them and quite another to deny, as Judith Harris (1998) has done, that parents have the greater power and the crucial responsibility to design these microenvironments so as to shape their children's behavior and personal attributes (Baumrind, 1993). Many child characteristics, such as an aggressive or shy temperament, which makes children difficult, or a calm and relaxed temperament, which makes children docile, impact parents' child-rearing behaviors and moderate their effects. However, as Hoffman (2000, pp. 144–146) convincingly argued, the greater power and designated roles and responsibilities of parents ensure their continuing influence.

The meaning children ascribe to strict parental control moderates its effects. Attempts to understand that meaning have focused on religion and ethnicity. Gunnoe, Hetherington, and Reiss (2006), for example, hypothesized that the association between parents' authoritarian behavior and adolescents' adjustment would be moderated by the family's religious ideology. They found that fathers' authoritarian behavior in structured family discussions had a less adverse impact in conservative Protestant than in other families, presumably because of community prevalence and endorsement of such parental behavior and demeanor.

Similarly, Ruth Chao (1994) speculated that in Chinese homes where children as well as their parents prioritize school achievement, close supervision (that might be resented as overly intrusive in ideologically liberal homes whose members prioritize personal autonomy) would be accepted as intended to be in their best interests by children and associated with their success. In accord with Chao's speculations, Sophia Chua-Rubenfeld (2011), now 18, in a recent article in the *New York Post* titled "Why I Love My Strict Chinese Mom," wrote in support of her mother, writer and lawyer Amy Chua, that the parenting style of her "tiger mother" (strict, demanding, protective, loving) taught her to be "independent," "who I want to be," and to "pretty much do my own thing." Rather than being intimidated by Chua's assertive parenting, her two daughters emulated their tiger mother's independence and fortitude.

Research Variables and Procedures

The procedures that generated data on preschool children's attributes and parents' child-rearing styles in my longitudinal program of research were pretested in a pilot study (Baumrind, 1967) and are described fully in Baumrind

(1989, 1991c) and Baumrind et al. (2010). Observers' ratings based on lengthy observations in natural settings constitute the major source of data.

Observers' ratings of children's competence and mental health were based on at least 20 hours of observation of the target child on the playground, in the classroom, and with peers outside of school at play. Observers' ratings of parents were based on more than 30 hours of parent interviews and observations of parent–child interactions. Verbatim records of parents' interactions with their target child were made during two or more home visits that took place at the dinner and evening hours, when parent–child conflicts are most likely to occur. Following the home visits, parents were interviewed separately in depth, at which time they were asked to reflect on how the observer's presence affected their normal parent–child interactions. Transcribed comprehensive structured interviews with both parents provided data on parents' child-rearing ideology and rationale for their disciplinary practices. Experimental procedures were used to elicit children's responses to parents' disciplinary efforts. The categorization of parents into family patterns at each time period was the last step at each wave (preschool, middle school, high school) in this process.

Child Outcome Variables: Communion and Agency

At the most general level, the child variables treated as outcomes of parenting practices in the FSP are organized along the orthogonal dimensions of *communion* and *agency*, terms introduced by David Bakan (1966) "to characterize two fundamental modalities in the existence of living forms" (pp. 14–15). These two modalities emerge as orthogonal axes from most factor analyses of competent human behavior (e.g., Baumrind & Black, 1967; Leary, 1957; Lonner, 1980; Wiggins, 1979). Optimal competence requires both the capacity for cooperation and compliance (communion) and for self-determination and constructive dissent (agency). Communion refers to the desire to be of service and to be included and connected in some larger unit of which the individual is a part, whereas agency refers to the drive to distinguish oneself from others by taking initiative and asserting oneself. In my research, communion in children was measured as affiliation with adult (parents and teachers) directives, cooperation with collective (peer group and adult leader) efforts, empathy, and friendliness with peers; agency in children was measured as individuation, self-efficacy, initiative, self-determination, and resistance to peer pressure or adult demands deemed unjust or intrusive.

Optimal Competence: Synthesizing Agency and Communion

Developmental competence and the adaptive nature of compliance and noncompliance can be evaluated by how well both agency and communion are integrated in the child's functioning. An imbalance in the direction of either aspect of social competence signifies dysfunction in the process of social reciprocity between the legitimate claims of the individual on the collective and the collective on the individual. To be optimally competent, children must synthesize the positive aspects of agency and communion, that is, be assertive but not disruptive or defiant and compliant but not submissive or obeisant. The syncretic combination of high levels of communal and agentic attributes in the development of optimal competence reflects the simultaneous necessity of balancing the interests of self and other and the transformation and conservation of established cultural values depending on contexts and circumstances.

Parenting Dimensions: Responsiveness and Demandingness

Socialization for optimal competence requires parents to foster self-confident, autonomous behavior as well as reasonable compliance with adult directives by responding to children's input and unique characteristics as well as by demanding compliance with adult standards of socially approved conduct (Baumrind, 1978b, 1980, 1989). *Responsiveness* refers to parents' emotional warmth and supportive actions that are attuned to children's vulnerabilities, cognitions, and inputs and are supportive of children's individual needs and plans. *Demandingness* has two related components, monitoring and confrontive control, and refers to the claims parents make on their children to become integrated into and contribute to the family unit: *monitoring*, which provides structure, order, and predictability to the child's life; and *control*, which shapes the child's behavior and restrains the child's potentially disruptive agentic expressions. When demandingness and responsiveness are treated as one dimension, as they often are (e.g., see earlier reference to Smith, 2010; Grolnick & Pomerantz, 2009), rather than, correctly, as two orthogonal factors, parents who are highly demanding are presumed to be unresponsive.

Earl Schaefer's (1959, 1965) three intercorrelated parent dimensions—acceptance versus rejection, firm versus lax behavioral control, and psychological autonomy versus psychological control—were the organizing theoretical constructs for the empirical parent clusters that were related to facets of agency and communion in children and adolescents (Baumrind 1971a, 1973, 1991a; Baumrind & Black, 1967) and that differentiate my four prototypic parent patterns. These parent patterns (authoritative, authoritarian, permissive, disengaged) were derived from four quadrants represented by the intersection of the two orthogonal factors responsiveness and demandingness (Baumrind, 1971a).

In common with Brian Barber (see Chapter 3, this volume), I differentiate between the effects of consistent confrontive control of children's behavior and control of children's psychological world. *Behavioral control* is direct, overt, and aimed at inducing compliance with parental directives through the use of limit setting, maturity demands, and monitoring, whereas *psychological control* is indirect, covert, intrusive, and aimed at manipulating the child's psychological world and personal identity through the use of withdrawal of affection and guilt induction (Barber, 1996). As Barber (1996, 2002a, 2002b) and colleagues (Barber, Olsen, & Shagle, 1994) have documented, the detrimental effects on children's sense of autonomy of psychological control are linear and unconditional, whereas, as discussed in an earlier section, the effects on children's competence and mental health of behavioral control are conditional, depending on whether behavioral control is confrontive or coercive.

Baumrind's Parent Typology

My four parent prototypes are distinguished as follows on Schaefer's three dimensions: *Authoritarian* parents are characterized by firm behavioral control, psychological control, and rejection; *permissive* parents are characterized by psychological autonomy, acceptance, and lax behavioral control; *rejecting-neglecting* (also known as *disengaged*) parents are characterized by rejection and lax behavioral control; and *authoritative* parents are characterized by the optimal combination of firm behavioral control, acceptance, and psychological autonomy (Baumrind, 1996).

Just as optimal competence synthesizes rather than sums a high level of both agentic and communal attributes, optimal parenting synthesizes rather than sums a high level of both demanding and responsive practices. Balance between responsive and demanding practices as well as commitment reflected in high allocation of time and resources are necessary ingredients of optimal parenting (Baumrind et al., 2010). Authoritative parents, unlike authoritarian parents, temper high expectations and demands with sensitivity and open communication. In common with permissive parents, authoritative parents allow their children considerable leeway to make their own decisions and to speak freely. By being responsive as well as demanding, authoritative parents avoid the harmful effects of coercive kinds of behavioral control. However, unlike permissive parents and in common with authoritarian parents, authoritative parents are ready to back up their directives with sanctions.

The four prototypic patterns (authoritative, authoritarian, permissive, disengaged) originally identified when the children in the FSP were preschoolers were further differentiated as the children matured. When the children were adolescents (see Baumrind, 1991a, 1991b), two authoritative-like parent patterns were added—the democratic pattern in which parents were medium demanding and, in common with permissive parents, highly responsive and ideologically liberal and the directive pattern in which parents were medium responsive and, in common with authoritarian parents, highly demanding and ideologically conservative.

My research with adolescents identified both liberal and conservative parents whose children were competent (see Baumrind et al., 2010). Adolescents whose parents were democratic (liberal) or directive (conservative) were almost as competent as children whose parents were authoritative (Baumrind, 1991a, 1991b). Unlike their permissive and authoritarian counterparts whose practices were either disproportionately responsive or disproportionately demanding, democratic and directive parents were only moderately imbalanced in their responsive (democratic) or demanding (directive) ratio. Unless manifested by marked imbalance in their responsive or demanding ratio, parents' social ideology did not affect the quality of their parenting practices as assessed by children's competence.

THE AUTHORITATIVE CONSTRUCT RECONSIDERED

The authoritative parenting style, when I introduced it in 1966, was first viewed as iconoclastic because it was antithetical to the permissive parenting style, which was regarded as optimal at that time and in liberal quarters (Lakoff, 1996) still is. Even today many experts who ostensibly endorse authoritative parenting fail to acknowledge that authoritative upbringing is highly demanding as well as highly responsive or incorrectly interpret the responsive component of the authoritative construct to imply unconditional acceptance, thus obscuring the beneficial effects of confrontive control, the distinctive feature that differentiates authoritative from permissive parents.

On the basis of nominations of child psychologists from all walks of life, Wallace E. Dixon Jr. (2003) included my 1971 monograph "Current Patterns of Parental Authority" among the *Twenty Studies That Revolutionized Child Psychology*. However, social science "facts" are contextually contingent, not universal truths. When cultural values and life realities vary, parents' objectives and the specific family processes that are most effective in accomplishing these objectives may also vary. For example, the strict and domineering kinds of control I refer to as coercive, although functionally superfluous and authoritarian—distinctive in middle-class families residing in an ideologically liberal and safe community such as Berkeley, California, might reflect a high level of protective care and thus be perceived as nurturant by children living in dangerous social environments (Deater-Deckard & Dodge, 1997; Mandara, 2006; Mandara & Murray, 2002; Rohner & Britner, 2002). Therefore, my typology should be revisited when applied to populations other than the kinds of families for which it was originally tailored (see Baumrind, 1972a).

The characteristics of my work on parenting that may account for its durability, despite its unrepresentative sample, include attention to definitional clarity and theoretical grounding, differentiation between the meaning and effects of unconditional acceptance and unconditional commitment, differentiation between coercive and confrontive behavioral control to help account for the contrasting effects of authoritarian and authoritative parenting styles, inclusion of agentic and assertive child behavior as a component of optimal competence equal in importance to communal and cooperative behavior, articulation of a guiding philosophy of science to ground my theoretical framework and research strategy, adherence to explicit ethical precepts binding researchers' interactions with human subjects, introduction of balance and commitment as superordinate theoretical parenting constructs, a longitudinal design strengthening causal inference concerning parental effects, reliance on objective sources of data rather than self-reports, avoidance of shared source variance that otherwise could account for the findings, and a focus on child configurations and parenting patterns rather than on isolated child and parent variables.

REFERENCES

Adorno, T. W., Frenkel-Brunswik, E., Levinson, D. J., & Sanford, R. N. (1950). *The authoritarian personality.* New York, NY: Harper & Row.

Bakan, D. (1966). *The duality of human existence: Isolation and communion in Western man.* Boston, MA: Beacon Press.

Baldwin, A. L. (1949). The effect of home environment on nursery school behavior. *Child Development, 20,* 49–62. doi:10.2307/1125606

Baldwin, A. L., Kalhoun, J., & Breese, F. H. (1945). Patterns of parent behavior. *Psychological Monographs, 58*(3, Whole No. 258), 1–75. doi:10.1037/h0093566

Barber, B. K. (1996). Parental psychological control: Revisiting a neglected construct. *Child Development, 67,* 3296–3319. doi:10.2307/1131780

Barber, B. K. (2002a). *Intrusive parenting: How psychological control affects children and adolescents.* Washington, DC: American Psychological Association. doi:10.1037/10422-000

Barber, B. K. (2002b). Reintroducing parental psychological control. In B. K. Barber (Ed.), *Intrusive parenting: How psychological control affects children and adolescents* (pp. 3–13). Washington, DC: American Psychological Association. doi:10.1037/10422-001

Barber, B. K., Olsen, J. E., & Shagle, S. C. (1994). Associations between parental psychological and behavioral control and youth internalizing and externalizing behaviors. *Child Development, 65,* 1120–1136. doi:10.2307/1131309

Baumrind, D. (1955). *Some personality and situational determinants of behavior in a discussion group* (unpublished doctoral dissertation). University of California, Berkeley.

Baumrind, D. (1964). Some thoughts on ethics of research: After reading Milgram's "Behavioral study of obedience." *American Psychologist, 19,* 421–423. doi:10.1037/h0040128

Baumrind, D. (1966). Effects of authoritative parental control on child behavior. *Child Development, 37*, 887–907. doi:10.2307/1126611

Baumrind, D. (1967). Child care practices anteceding three patterns of preschool behavior. *Genetic Psychology Monographs, 75*, 43–88.

Baumrind, D. (1968). Authoritarian vs. authoritative parental control. *Adolescence, 3*, 255–272.

Baumrind, D. (1971a). Current patterns of parental authority. *Developmental Psychology Monographs, 4*(1, Pt. 2), 1–103. doi:10.1037/h0030372

Baumrind, D. (1971b). Principles of ethical conduct in the treatment of subjects: Reaction to the draft report of the Committee on Ethical Standards in Psychological Research. *American Psychologist, 26*, 887–896. doi:10.1037/h0032145

Baumrind, D. (1972a). An exploratory study of socialization effects on Black children: Some Black–White comparisons. *Child Development, 43*, 261–267. doi:10.2307/1127891

Baumrind, D. (1972b). Reactions to the May 1972 draft report of the Ad Hoc Committee on Ethical Standards in Psychological Research. *American Psychologist, 27*, 1083–1086. doi:10.1037/h0033985

Baumrind, D. (1973). The development of instrumental competence through socialization. In A. Pick (Ed.), *Minnesota Symposia on Child Psychology* (Vol. 7, pp. 3–46). Minneapolis: University of Minnesota Press.

Baumrind, D. (1975). Metaethical and normative considerations governing the treatment of human subjects in the behavioral sciences. In E. C. Kennedy (Ed.), *Human rights and psychological research: A debate on psychology and ethics* (pp. 83–102). New York, NY: Crowell.

Baumrind, D. (1978a). A dialectical materialist's perspective on knowing social reality. *New Directions for Child Development, 2*, 61–82. doi:10.1002/cd.23219780206

Baumrind, D. (1978b). Reciprocal rights and responsibilities in parent–child relations. *Journal of Social Issues, 34*, 179–196. doi:10.1111/j.1540-4560.1978.tb01038.x

Baumrind, D. (1979). IRBs and social science research: The costs of deception. *IRB: A Review of Human Subjects Research, 1*(6), 1–4. doi:10.2307/3564243

Baumrind, D. (1980). The principle of reciprocity: The development of prosocial behavior in children. *Educational Perspectives, 19*(4), 3–9.

Baumrind, D. (1985). Research using intentional deception: Ethical issues revisited. *American Psychologist, 40*, 165–174. doi:10.1037/0003-066X.40.2.165

Baumrind, D. (1989). Rearing competent children. In W. Damon (Ed.), *Child development today and tomorrow* (pp. 349–378). San Francisco, CA: Jossey-Bass.

Baumrind, D. (1990). Doing good well. In C. B. Fisher & W. W. Tryon (Eds.), *Ethics in applied developmental psychology: Emerging issues in an emerging field: Vol. 4. Advances in applied developmental psychology* (pp. 17–28). Norwood, NJ: Ablex.

Baumrind, D. (1991a). Adolescent exploratory behavior: Precursors and consequences. In L. P. Lipsitt & L. L. Mitnick (Eds.), *Self-regulation and risk-taking* (pp. 109–142). Norwood, NJ: Ablex.

Baumrind, D. (1991b). Effective parenting during the early adolescent transition. In P. E. Cowan & E. M. Hetherington (Eds.), *Advances in family research* (Vol. 2, pp. 111–163). Hillsdale, NJ: Erlbaum.

Baumrind, D. (1991c). The influence of parenting style on adolescent competence and substance use. *The Journal of Early Adolescence, 11*, 56–95. doi:10.1177/0272431691111004

Baumrind, D. (1993). The average expectable environment is not good enough: A response to Scarr. *Child Development, 64*, 1299–1317. doi:10.2307/1131536

Baumrind, D. (1996). A blanket injunction against disciplinary use of spanking is not warranted by the data. *Pediatrics, 98*, 828–831.

Baumrind, D. (1998). From ought to is: A neo-Marxist perspective on the use and misuse of the culture construct. *Human Development, 41*, 145–165. doi:10.1159/000022575

Baumrind, D., & Black, A. E. (1967). Socialization practices associated with dimensions of competence in preschool boys and girls. *Child Development, 38*, 291–327. doi:10.2307/1127295

Baumrind, D., Larzelere, R. E., & Cowan, P. (2002). Ordinary physical punishment: Is it harmful? Comment on Gershoff (2002). *Psychological Bulletin, 128*, 580–589. doi:10.1037/0033-2909.128.4.580

Baumrind, D., Larzelere, R. E., & Owens, E. (2010). Effects of preschool parents' power assertive patterns and practices on adolescent development. *Parenting: Science and Practice, 10*, 157–201. doi:10.1080/15295190903290790

Bear, G. (2004). *Developing self-discipline and preventing and correcting misbehavior.* Boston, MA: Allyn & Bacon.

Bell, R. Q. (1968). A reinterpretation of the direction of effects in studies of socialization. *Psychological Review, 75*, 81–95. doi:10.1037/h0025583

Bronfenbrenner, U. (1979). *The ecology of human development: Experiments by nature and design.* Cambridge, MA: Harvard University Press.

Chao, R. K. (1994). Beyond parental control and authoritarian parenting style: Understanding Chinese parenting through the cultural notion of training. *Child Development, 65*, 1111–1119. doi:10.2307/1131308

Chua-Rubenfeld, S. (2011, January 18). Why I love my strict Chinese mom. *New York Post.* Retrieved from http://www.nypost.com/p/entertainment/why_love_my_strict_chinese_mom_uUvfmLcA5eteY0u2KXt7hM

Darling, N., & Steinberg, L. (1993). Parenting style as context: An integrative model. *Psychological Bulletin, 113*, 487–496. doi:10.1037/0033-2909.113.3.487

Deater-Deckard, K., & Dodge, K. A. (1997). Externalizing behavior problems and discipline revisited: Nonlinear effects and variation by culture, context, and gender. *Psychological Inquiry, 8*, 161–175. doi:10.1207/s15327965pli0803_1

Dixon, W. E., Jr. (2003). *Twenty studies that revolutionized child psychology.* Upper Saddle River, NJ: Prentice Hall.

Farson, R. (1974). *Birthrights.* New York, NY: Macmillan.

Fletcher, A. C., Darling, N. E., Steinberg, L., & Dornbusch, S. M. (1995). The company they keep: Relation of adolescents' adjustment and behavior to their friends' perceptions of authoritative parenting in the social network. *Developmental Psychology, 3*, 300–310. doi:10.1037/0012-1649.31.2.300

Goodman, P. (1960). *Growing up absurd: Problems of youth in the organized system.* New York, NY: Random House.

Gregory, A., & Weinstein, R. (2004). Connection and regulation at home and in school: Predicting growth in achievement for adolescents. *Journal of Adolescent Research, 19*, 405–427. doi:10.1177/0743558403258859

Grolnick, W. S., & Pomerantz, E. M. (2009). Issues and challenges in studying parental control: Toward a new conceptualization. *Child Development Perspectives, 3*, 165–170. doi:10.1111/j.1750-8606.2009.00099.x

Gunnoe, M. L., Hetherington, E. M., & Reiss, D. (2006). Differential impact of father's authoritarian parenting on early adolescent adjustment in conservative Protestant versus other families. *Journal of Family Psychology, 20*, 589–596. doi:10.1037/0893-3200.20.4.589

Harris, J. R. (1998). *The nurture assumption: Why children turn out the way they do.* New York, NY: Free Press.

Hoffman, M. L. (1960). Power assertion by the parent and its impact on the child. *Child Development, 31*, 129–143. doi:10.2307/1126389

Hoffman, M. L. (2000). *Empathy and moral development: Implications for caring and justice.* New York, NY: Cambridge University Press.

Holt, J. (1974). *Escape from childhood: The needs and rights of children.* New York, NY: Dutton.

Hulbert, A. (2003). *Raising America: Experts, parents, and a century of advice about children.* New York, NY: Knopf.

Hughes, J. N. (2002). Authoritative teaching: Tipping the balance in favor of school versus peer effects. *Journal of School Psychology, 40*, 485–492. doi:10.1016/S0022-4405(02)00125-5

Kohn, A. (2005). *Unconditional parenting: Moving from rewards and punishments to love and reason.* New York, NY: Atria Books.

Lakoff, G. (1996). *Moral politics: What conservatives know that liberals don't.* Chicago, IL: University of Chicago Press.

Leary, T. (1957). *Interpersonal diagnosis of personality: A functional theory and methodology for personality evaluation.* New York, NY: Ronald Press.

Lewin, K., Lippitt, R., & White, R. K. (1939). Patterns of aggressive behavior in experimentally created "social climates." *The Journal of Social Psychology, 10*, 269–299. doi:10.1080/00224545.1939.9713366

Lonner, W. J. (1980). The search for psychological universals. In H. C. Triandis & W. W. Lambert (Eds.), *Handbook of cross-cultural psychology* (Vol. 1, pp. 143–204). Boston, MA: Allyn & Bacon.

Maccoby, E. E. (1992). The role of parents in the socialization of children: An historical overview. *Developmental Psychology, 28,* 1006–1017. doi:10.1037/0012-1649.28.6.1006

Magnusson, D. (2001). The holistic-interactionistic paradigm: Some directions for empirical developmental research. *European Psychologist, 6,* 153–162. doi:10.1027//1016-9040.6.3.153

Makarenko, A. S. (1954). *A book for parents.* (R. Daglish, Trans.). Moscow, Soviet Union: Foreign Languages.

Mandara, J. (2003). The typological approach in child and family psychology: A review of theory, methods, and research. *Clinical Child and Family Psychology Review, 6,* 129–146. doi:10.1023/A:1023734627624

Mandara, J. (2006). The impact of family functioning on African American males' academic achievement: A review and clarification of the empirical literature. *Teachers College Record, 108,* 206–223. doi:10.1111/j.1467-9620.2006.00648.x

Mandara, J., & Murray, C. B. (2002). Development of an empirical typology of African American family functioning. *Journal of Family Psychology, 16,* 318–337. doi:10.1037/0893-3200.16.3.318

Neill, A. S. (1964). *Summerhill.* New York, NY: Hart.

Patterson, G. R. (1982). *A social learning approach to family intervention: Vol. 3. Coercive family process.* Eugene, OR: Castalia Press.

Radziszewska, B., Richardson, J. L., Dent, C. W., & Flay, B. R. (1996). Parenting style and adolescent depressive symptoms, smoking, and academic achievement: Ethnic, gender, and SES differences. *Journal of Behavioral Medicine, 19,* 289–305. doi:10.1007/BF01857770

Rambusch, N. (1962). *Learning how to learn: An American approach to Montessori.* Baltimore, MD: Helicon.

Rawls, J. A. (1971). *A theory of justice.* Cambridge, MA: Harvard University, with Belknap Press.

Robinson, C. C., Mandleco, B., Olsen, F. S., & Hart, H. C. (1995). Authoritative, authoritarian, and permissive parenting practices: Development of a new measure. *Psychological Reports, 77,* 819–830. doi:10.2466/pr0.1995.77.3.819

Rohner, R. P., & Britner, P. A. (2002). Worldwide mental health correlates of parental acceptance–rejection: Review of cross-cultural and intracultural evidence. *Cross-Cultural Research: The Journal of Comparative Social Science, 36*(1), 15–47. doi:10.1177/106939702129146316

Scarlett, W. G., Ponte, I. C., & Singh, J. P. (2009). *Approaches to behavior and classroom management: Integrating discipline and care.* Los Angeles, CA: Sage.

Schaefer, E. S. (1959). A circumplex model for maternal behavior. *The Journal of Abnormal and Social Psychology, 59,* 226–235. doi:10.1037/h0041114

Schaefer, E. S. (1965). A configurational analysis of children's reports of parent behavior. *Journal of Consulting Psychology, 29,* 552–557. doi:10.1037/h0022702

Smith, C. L. (2010). Multiple determinants of parenting: Predicting individual differences in maternal parenting behavior with toddlers. *Parenting: Science and Practice, 10,* 1–17. doi:10.1080/15295190903014588

Steinberg, L. (1990). Autonomy, conflict, and harmony in the family relationship. In S. S. Feldman & G. R. Elliott (Eds.), *At the threshold: The developing adolescent* (pp. 255–276). Cambridge, MA: Harvard University Press.

Steinberg, L. (2001). We know some things: Parent–adolescent relationships in retrospect and prospect. *Journal of Research on Adolescence, 11*(1), 1–19. doi:10.1111/1532-7795.00001

Tryon, R. C., & Bailey, D. E. (1966). The BC TRY computer system of cluster and factor analysis. *Multivariate Behavioral Research, 1,* 95–111. doi:10.1207/s15327906mbr0101_6

Vande Kemp, H. (1995). Diana Baumrind: Researcher and critical humanist. In D. Moss (Ed.), *Humanistic and transpersonal psychology: Historical and biographical sourcebook* (pp. 125–144). New York, NY: Greenwood Press.

Vygotsky, L. S. (1978). *Mind in society: The development of higher psychological processes.* Cambridge, MA: Harvard University Press.

Waller, N. G., & Meehl, P. E. (1998). *Multivariate taxometric procedures: Distinguishing types from continua.* Thousand Oaks, CA: Sage.

Wiggins, J. S. (1979). A psychological taxonomy of trait-descriptive terms: The interpersonal domain. *Journal of Personality and Social Psychology, 37,* 395–412. doi:10.1037/0022-3514.37.3.395

2

PARENTING RESEARCH AND THEMES: WHAT WE HAVE LEARNED AND WHERE TO GO NEXT

AMANDA SHEFFIELD MORRIS, LIXIAN CUI,
AND LAURENCE STEINBERG

Diana Baumrind laid the foundation for over 3 decades of parenting research with her groundbreaking observational study of parenting styles and children's associated outcomes (see Chapter 1, this volume). Baumrind's research on parenting styles indicates that constellations of parenting behaviors characterized as overly lax (*permissive*) or overly strict (*authoritarian*) result in maladaptive outcomes in children and adolescents (e.g., low self-esteem, aggression, difficulties in school). In contrast, a parenting style characterized by moderate levels of control and high levels of warmth (*authoritative*) typically is associated with children who are well adjusted, independent, and successful in school (Baumrind, 1971; Steinberg, Elmen, & Mounts, 1989). Nevertheless, scholars have worked to identify the nuanced parenting behaviors that compose parenting styles and lead to variation in outcomes. In addition, researchers have examined other factors that explain differential effects of parenting, such as child effects (e.g., child temperament, genetics)

DOI: 10.1037/13948-003
Authoritative Parenting: Synthesizing Nurturance and Discipline for Optimal Child Development, Robert E. Larzelere, Amanda Sheffield Morris, and Amanda W. Harrist (Editors)

and the broader social context (e.g., peers, family system, neighborhood, culture).

Trends in parenting research over the past 3 decades inspired by Baumrind's approach can be summarized into three major themes: examining components of parenting style, understanding child effects on parenting, and placing parenting in a broader social context. The purpose of this chapter is to examine and summarize each of these themes, providing some key examples of research and related theories. We present broad research themes and examples of particular studies focused on both children and adolescents rather than a thorough review of the parenting literature (for detailed reviews, see Bugental & Grusec, 2006; Parke & Buriel, 2006). We review the literature in the context of Baumrind's work, emphasizing her influence and how current themes fit within her theoretical framework. We end the chapter with a discussion of new directions in parenting science and provide suggestions for future research and theoretical integration.

EXAMINING COMPONENTS OF PARENTING STYLE

Parenting researchers and practitioners often break apart the components of parenting typologies into specific behaviors, resulting in what Gray and Steinberg (1999) called the "unpacking of parenting styles." For example, popular parenting books stress the importance of emotion coaching and/or appropriate limit setting (e.g., Gottman & Declaire, 1998; Steinberg, 2005b, 2011). Darling and Steinberg (1993) delineated parenting style (emotional climate of the parent–child relationship) from parenting practices (specific socialization behaviors). Similarly, Pettit and Mize (1993) distinguished between socialization style (quality of parent–child interactions) and substance (informational content of interactions). To date, the Darling and Steinberg article has been cited more than 1,400 times (according to Google Scholar data), indicating the importance of such theoretical distinctions. We argue that over the past 2 decades scientists have primarily targeted two dimensions of parenting style: parental control/discipline (see Chapters 3 and 4, this volume) and emotion-related parenting practices (see Chapter 8, this volume). These dimensions correspond with the control and warmth/responsiveness dimensions that have often been used to characterize Baumrind's parenting styles (Maccoby & Martin, 1983).

Parental Control

The dimension of parenting style that has probably received the most direct attention is parental control/demandingness. Baumrind discusses the importance of parents providing firm, authoritative control while maintaining flexibility and not being overly intrusive (see Chapter 1, this volume). There has been a trend over the last several decades for researchers to dissect parental control into various components to better understand the particular parenting practices associated with children's adjustment. Control has been examined in terms of monitoring, disciplinary action, maturity demands, structure, power assertion, psychological control, behavioral control, and various other constructs with similar definitions (e.g., supervision, intrusiveness, overprotectiveness). Nevertheless, research findings consistently support Baumrind's original work indicating the importance of firm parental control that encourages appropriate autonomy granting and considers the child's perspective and input on decision making and rules (Bugental & Grusec, 2006).

Recently, parental monitoring has received a great deal of attention. *Monitoring* refers to parents' awareness of their own attempts to manage children's schedules, peer associations, activities, and physical whereabouts (Peterson & Hann, 1999). In many studies, parental monitoring has been associated with diminished adolescent delinquency, substance use, and deviant peer involvement (e.g., Laird, Criss, Pettit, Dodge, & Bates, 2008). Stattin and Kerr (2000) argued that parental monitoring assessments used in the late 1980s and early 1990s assessed what parents knew about their children (knowledge regarding whereabouts and behavior), not what parents actually did to monitor behavior. They outlined three sources parents used to gain information about their children: child disclosure, parental solicitation, and parental active control (e.g., requiring permission for behavior, rules, demands for information). In their 2000 study and later work, they found that higher levels of parental knowledge were linked to better adjustment. Parental solicitation and control were less strongly linked to parental knowledge than was child disclosure. Importantly, it was child disclosure that significantly predicted less delinquency, depression, and greater self-esteem (Kerr, Stattin, & Burk, 2010), and at least one study has found that parental monitoring (i.e., how hard parents tried to keep track of the adolescent's activities and whereabouts) deters adolescent problem behavior even after taking parental knowledge into account (Fletcher, Steinberg, & Williams-Wheeler, 2004). Research indicates that adolescents naturally disclose information when they have warm, close relationships with their parents and/or perceive their parents to be authoritative (Darling, Cumsile, Caldwell, & Dowdy, 2006). Such findings point to the importance of considering overall parenting style when examining specific behaviors such as disclosure.

Parental control that is emotionally manipulative and includes strategies such as guilt induction, love withdrawal, shaming, inhibiting autonomy, and the invalidation of feelings has been labeled as *psychological control* in the parenting literature (see Chapter 3, this volume). Parents who use this type of control send a message to their children that love and acceptance are contingent on behavior. This is communicated for parents to control the child's behavior and is a powerful way for parents to encourage children to give in to or comply with parental demands. Parents who use this type of control are often overprotective and intrusive in nature, leading to children feeling less independent and incapable of success without parental intervention. Indeed, psychological control has been associated with a host of negative outcomes in numerous studies. Specifically, psychological control has been linked to high levels of child anxiety, depression, delinquency, and aggression, and to low self-esteem (Barber, 1996; Silk, Morris, Kanaya, & Steinberg, 2003). Although much of the work on psychological control has focused on adolescents, several studies including younger children have found that psychological control is positively associated with both internalizing and externalizing problems (Olsen et al., 2002), and it has been found to be particularly detrimental among children with vulnerable temperaments (Morris et al., 2002).

Researchers have argued that psychological control involves parental control over matters that the adolescent perceives as personal in nature. This is in contrast to the more common view of psychological control as an emotionally manipulative parental control technique that stifles independence (see Steinberg, 2005a). Steinberg (2005a) argued that it is ultimately the subjective experience of the adolescent that defines whether a parent is psychologically controlling and that conflicts over matters of personal choice are common during early adolescence, reflecting the individuation process. Thus, future research should consider how adolescents determine whether a parent is being intrusive and how culture and peer norms play a role in such perceptions.

Another form of parental control that is important in parenting research and practice is discipline. Parental discipline and guidance can take on many forms, including power assertion (e.g., removal of privileges, time out), setting rules and limits, encouraging positive behavior, and/or reasoning about wrongdoing (see Grusec & Goodnow, 1994). Broadly, discipline can be thought of as parental control attempts to create an environment that minimizes negative and maximizes positive behavior. Most parents use a variety of disciplinary techniques, and disciplinary tactics typically change as children grow older (e.g., time out in early childhood and removal of privileges in middle childhood and adolescence; Grusec & Goodnow, 1994). It can be argued that the goal of discipline is for children to internalize prosocial moral values and develop optimal social competence and personal agency (Baumrind, 1996; Hoffman, 2001). These outcomes result from repeated parental socialization efforts (Hoffman, 2001).

There is a growing body of literature indicating that inductive discipline (parental discipline involving explanation and reasoning) is associated

with children's prosocial (helping) behavior, empathy, and sympathy (see Eisenberg, Fabes, & Spinrad, 2006). In contrast, an increasing number of studies report links between punitive power assertive techniques and less prosocial behavior and empathy (e.g., Nix et al., 1999). Hoffman (2001) and others have argued that reasoning about misbehavior and encouraging children to consider how behavior affects others (i.e., inductive discipline) likely increase empathy and perspective taking, facilitating the internalization of moral behavior (Eisenberg et al., 2006). In contrast, harsh punishment may result in a fearful response, with subsequent positive behavior stemming from fear of punishment rather than an awareness of how one's behavior affects another (Eisenberg et al., 2006). Moreover, harsh punishment has been associated with negative outcomes in many studies (Bugental & Grusec, 2006). For example, high levels of harsh physical punishment have been found to predict children's externalizing problems even after controlling for previous levels of problem behavior (e.g., Nix et al., 1999). This suggests that harsh discipline increases children's aggressive behavior. There also is evidence, however, that occasional power assertion that is not harsh and is applied to a specific situation in the context of a positive parent–child relationship is not harmful and is sometimes associated with positive outcomes (see Eisenberg et al., 2006; Grusec & Goodnow, 1994).

More research is needed on specific forms of power assertion and their effectiveness (see Chapter 4, this volume). Nevertheless, evidence increasingly suggests that corporal punishment (i.e., physical punishment with the intent to cause pain) has deleterious effects on children (Gershoff & Bitensky, 2007). As Bugental and Grusec (2006) summarized, opponents of corporal punishment argue that it is linked to antisocial behavior and is a potential precursor to physical abuse (Gershoff & Bitensky, 2007). In contrast, Baumrind, Larzelere, and Cowan (2002) believe that occasional mild spanking between the ages of toddlerhood and puberty is a valid socialization tool when done in the context of an authoritative parent–child relationship. Evidence does support a link between corporal punishment and increased child compliance (Gershoff, 2002; Larzelere & Kuhn, 2005). However, despite the difficulty in determining causal patterns (we cannot assign children to spanking or nonspanking families), Gershoff and Bitensky (2007) drew several conclusions regarding the effects of corporal punishment in their review of the spanking literature, which included many longitudinal studies and/or intervention programs aimed at reducing corporal punishment (e.g., Beauchaine, Webster-Stratton, & Reid, 2005). First, children with more behavior problems elicit more corporal punishment. Second, in longitudinal studies, even after controlling for children's previous behavior problems, corporal punishment continues to predict children's aggression and antisocial behavior, suggesting a possible causal link. Third, corporal punishment is associated with eroded parent–child relationship quality, likely because of children's fear and a lack of trust that may result from harsh discipline. Holden (2002) argued that researchers need to consider children's individual responses to corporal punishment and that some children may be more negatively impacted by corporal punishment than others (see also Kochanska, Aksan, & Joy, 2007). Indeed, the message that the child receives during any disciplinary encounter is important, and the child's individual temperament, cognitive development, and the quality of the parent–child relationship all affect how messages are interpreted and internalized (Chao & Aque, 2009). Moreover, cultural norms play a role in children's perceptions of control.

In summary, research indicates that parental monitoring and knowledge (whether obtained through solicitation or child disclosure) are associated with positive outcomes among adolescents, whereas psychological and harsh control are associated with negative outcomes among both children and adolescents. These findings are in line with Baumrind's parenting typologies indicating that lack of control (low monitoring) in permissive parents and negative forms of control used among authoritarian parents (harsh parenting, psychological control) are associated with adjustment difficulties among children and adolescents (see Chapters 1 and 3, this volume). In contrast, authoritative parents use appropriate levels of control within a warm and responsive parent–child relationship. This also supports Baumrind's work on confrontive control, which is more common among authoritative parents, and coercive control, which is more common among authoritarian parents (see Chapter 1, this volume). Authoritative parenting and noncoercive control likely lead to more child and adolescent disclosure and an environment in which children's perceptions and ideas are valued and accepted. Research supports this premise, indicating that within a positive family environment, adolescents are more likely to disclose information and trust their parents (Fletcher et al., 2004; Kerr & Stattin, 2000). Research reviewed also suggests that parental monitoring should be thought of as a social process whereby children actively disclose information in the context of a trusting parent–child relationship. This dynamic relationship perspective applied to the control dimension of parenting has great potential to better inform the understanding of parenting effects.

Another theme that has emerged over the past few decades is the importance of children's perceptions of control. For example, studies indicate that adolescents who interpret parental control as intrusive and negative are more likely to be depressed, break rules, and believe that they are not important to their parents (Kakihara, Tilton-Weaver, Kerr, & Stattin, 2010). These findings suggest that there are negative consequences when children feel overcontrolled. Inductive discipline in childhood may indeed be a precursor to actively engaging children in discussions about misbehavior and discipline, creating an open dialogue leading to adolescent disclosure. However, research is needed to confirm such a premise. Whereas Darling and Steinberg (1993) focused on parents' socialization goals, recent research highlights the need for an understanding of children's and adolescents' interpretation of parents' socialization goals (see Steinberg, 2005a). This focus is likely to yield a better understanding of socialization effects and how they may differ according to context and child characteristics.

Emotion-Related Parenting

In the past few decades, there has been an increased interest in studying the emotional dynamics of the parent–child relationship. Research on the role of emotion in the parent–child relationship has included parents' emotion socialization, dyadic emotion regulation, emotion coaching (see Chapter 8, this volume), and the roles of child temperament (reactivity and regulation) and affective biological systems. Baumrind's original conception of warmth/responsiveness maps onto recent work on parents' responses to children's emotions (responsiveness) and the overall emotional climate of the family, sometimes assessed as emotional expressiveness (warmth). Positive emotion-related parenting practices, such as emotion coaching and parental warmth/responsiveness, have been associated with a number of adjustment outcomes in children and adolescents, such as greater regulation of anger and sadness, better school adjustment, and better socioemotional functioning (Eisenberg, Valiente, & Eggum, 2010; Morris, Silk, Steinberg, Myers, & Robinson, 2007).

Parental socialization of emotion reflects attempts to directly teach children about emotion regulation and expression and the role of emotion in social situations. Emotion socialization also occurs when children observe emotional interactions. Researchers have examined emotion socialization in terms of both parenting style and parenting practices (see Morris et al., 2007). Research indicates that parenting style, or the emotional climate of the family (Darling & Steinberg, 1993), affects children's emotion regulation and expression by providing the emotional foundation of the parent–child relationship. Children with authoritative parents typically are emotionally secure, know what to expect with regard to emotions displayed in the home, and have parents who respond appropriately and consistently to children's emotional displays. In contrast, children of authoritarian or permissive parents often experience a family emotional climate that is negative, coercive, or unpredictable, and children are at risk for becoming highly emotionally reactive or emotionally blunted (see Morris et al., 2007).

Specific parenting practices related to emotion regulation (e.g., labeling emotions, aiding children in responding to emotions) also have a strong impact on the development of emotion management abilities and related outcomes because such practices allow parents to teach children regulatory skills and strategies (Morris et al., 2007, 2011). Gottman and colleagues (e.g., Gottman, Katz, & Hooven, 1997) were among the first to examine particular parenting practices and their link to children's emotion regulation. In particular, they proposed a theory of meta-emotion philosophy that reflects an individual's organized set of beliefs and feelings about emotions. Moreover, Gottman et al. (1997) posited that parents' meta-emotion philosophy is related to the emotion-coaching or emotion-dismissing behaviors that they display in response to children's emotional expressions. When parents engage in emotion coaching, for example, they help children to verbally label emotions, empathize with or validate children's emotions, and help children to problem solve (Gottman et al., 1997, p. 84). In contrast to emotion coaching, a parent can dismiss an emotion or derogate a child for expressing an emotion. Parents' emotion coaching has been linked to children's effective regulatory skills and emotion understanding (Denham, Mitchell-Copeland, Strandberg, Auerbach, & Blair 1997; Gottman, Katz, & Hooven, 1996), whereas parents' emotion-dismissing behaviors have been linked to more emotion regulation difficulties and behavior problems (Lunkenheimer, Shields, & Cortina, 2007).

Further empirical evidence for the importance of emotion-related parenting practices has been found by Eisenberg, Cumberland, and Spinrad (1998), who examined parents' responses to children's sadness and anger to investigate whether punitive or negative responses serve to heighten children's emotional arousal and teach children to avoid rather than understand and appropriately express emotions. In a series of studies, Eisenberg et al. (1998) found that parents' punitive and minimizing reactions to emotions were associated with poor emotion regulation and maladjustment, and problem-focused reactions were associated with better coping and regulation. Studies also indicate that parental responses that are overly emotional and magnify the negative emotion that the child displays are associated with emotion dysregulation and adjustment difficulties (e.g., Silk et al., 2011). These findings are in line with Gottman and colleagues' work (Gottman & Declaire, 1998; Gottman et al., 1997) and highlight the importance of parents' supportive and constructive responses to children's emotional displays.

In addition to simply responding to an emotion, parents may intentionally teach children strategies for regulating and expressing emotions. For example, parents may provide children with specific suggestions for coping with negative emotions (e.g., take a deep breath, think about something else). Observational research indicates that parents' cognitive reframing (reframing the situation in a positive light) and attention refocusing (shifting attention away from an emotionally negative situation) are effective strategies for immediate reduction of children's expressions of anger and sadness, particularly when the children are also engaging in the strategy used (Morris et al., 2011). Developmentally, when children are young, physical comfort aids in emotion management, whereas during preschool and early middle childhood, more cognitive approaches seem to be more beneficial (Morris et al., 2011). As children grow older, parents become less actively involved in children's emotion regulation strategies, with parental attempts to regulate their children's emotions gradually giving way to children's self-regulation (Eisenberg & Morris, 2003), although parents remain an important influence in adolescent emotion regulation by providing emotional support and general guidance (Morris et al., 2007).

Although more research is needed to fully examine emotion socialization within the parenting styles framework, several conclusions can be drawn from the research reviewed. It can be argued that when a child expresses a negative emotion, an authoritative parent acts as an emotion coach, labeling and validating the emotion and problem solving to help the child feel better. Although the authoritative parent is generally accepting of emotions (there are no bad or wrong emotions), the authoritative parent also recognizes the need to sometimes discipline an accompanying behavior (e.g., it is OK to be angry, but it is not OK to hit your sister.). In contrast, the authoritarian parent might disapprove of or punish a child for expressing emotions, whereas the permissive parent might dismiss a child's emotion or allow emotionally driven misbehavior. More nuanced research is needed to support such premises, and empirical research is needed to support the claim that authoritative parents use emotion coaching. Nevertheless, understanding emotion socialization styles is a promising venue for future research (see Gottman et al., 1997).

UNDERSTANDING CHILD EFFECTS

In the early 1980s, Lewis (1981) argued that Baumrind's assessment of firm control reflected children's willingness to obey rather than active parental control. Lewis claimed that children of authoritative parents require less control because they have higher self-esteem and social competence and are well behaved. Her assertions were drawn from attribution theory, which focuses on the importance of internal rather than external control needed for internalization. Similarly, self-determination theory has recently been applied to the study of parenting, stressing the importance of intrinsic motivation rather than extrinsic control in personality development (Joussemet, Landry, & Koestner, 2008; see also Chapter 3, this volume).

Longitudinal studies support Baumrind's assertion that firm control is in fact an influence on child adjustment (see Chapter 1, this volume). However, increasingly, parenting is being viewed as a bidirectional process within the context of the parent–child relationship, and a complete description of the parenting process includes both parent effects and child effects. Research suggests that child characteristics affect the behaviors that children elicit from parents and, as well, that children differentially interpret parenting messages on the basis of past experiences and beliefs (Rothbart & Bates, 2006). For example, siblings in the same family often experience similar parenting behaviors differentially and elicit divergent behaviors from their parents on the basis of their individual characteristics (see Deater-Deckard, 1996). Moreover, child characteristics such as emotional reactivity may exacerbate the effects of negative parenting, whereas adaptive characteristics such as emotion regulation may serve as a protective factor (Morris et al., 2002). Research on how parenting affects children's psychophysiology and vice versa is relatively new, but findings from this recent research consistently indicate that the biological predisposition of the child is an important factor to consider when examining parental socialization.

One question that parenting researchers have grappled with over the past few decades is the relative importance of parenting in child adjustment given that effect sizes are typically small to moderate (Bates, Pettit, Dodge, & Ridge, 1998). A growing body of research indicates that although parenting matters (Collins, Maccoby, Steinberg, Hetherington, & Bornstein, 2000), parenting does not affect all children in the same way or to the same degree. Research suggests that children's individual differences in emotionality and emotion regulation, two commonly studied components of child temperament, are likely major contributors to variation in parental effects (Morris et al., 2002, 2007). Although parents play a direct role in socializing children's emotion regulation, children are biologically predisposed to variation in emotional reactivity and regulatory abilities (Rothbart & Bates, 2006), providing a starting point or range of regulation that is somewhat dispositionally based.

Over the past 20 years, a growing number of studies have examined both child temperament and parenting in the prediction of children's socioemotional adjustment. Results from these studies suggest that parenting accounts for considerably more variance in child outcomes when temperamental characteristics of the child are taken into consideration (Morris et al., 2002). Moreover, children's temperament explains variation in the elicitation of different parenting behaviors from the same parents, and children's interpretation and experiences of parenting are affected by their temperamental makeup (Rothbart & Bates, 2006).

Children with a predisposition toward negative emotionality and emotion dysregulation seem to be particularly vulnerable to the deleterious effects of authoritarian parenting. These children are more likely to experience coercive and hostile interchanges as highly aversive (Rothbart &

Ahadi, 1994). Conversely, reactive and/or dysregulated children may fail to develop difficulties when parents are sensitive and responsive to their emotional swings, as would be the case with authoritative parents. Belsky (2005) argued from an evolutionary perspective that variation in children's susceptibility to parenting evolved to protect children against the deleterious impact of adverse rearing strategies. More recently, scientists have begun to explore the biological underpinnings of children's susceptibility to negative parenting. For example, studies of harsh and insensitive parenting examining gene–environment interactions have found that some children may be genetically more susceptible to parenting influences given children's specific genotype. Specifically, studies indicate that children with a certain dopamine D4 receptor polymorphism (Bakermans-Kranenburg & van IJzendoorn, 2006), a MAO-A polymorphism (Caspi & Moffitt, 2006), and the *rs40184* and *VNTR* polymorphisms of the dopamine transporter gene (Haeffel et al., 2008; Lahey et al., 2011) are more likely to develop problem behaviors in the context of negative parenting. Despite such findings, many gene–environment interactions are in need of replication, and findings may be partially explained by evocative gene–environment correlations—a phenomenon whereby children's genetically influenced traits evoke differential parenting and subsequent adjustment.

Boyce and Ellis (2005) proposed the concept of biological sensitivity to context and argued that heightened stress or emotional reactivity reflects increased biological sensitivity to context and is related to negative health effects in contexts high in adversity but positive health effects in supportive and protective contexts. Many empirical studies seem to confirm this for-better-and-for-worse differential susceptibility model (e.g., Belsky, Bakermans-Kranenburg, & van IJzendoorn, 2007), but more research is needed. Although there are many unsolved theoretical and methodological issues involved in the study of biology–environment interactions, a promising area of future research is to examine children's biological differential susceptibility to the effects of parenting and the role that children's biological susceptibility plays in the parent–child relationship (Ellis & Boyce, 2011). Indeed, evidence is emerging that supports the premise that some children are biologically predisposed to be more or less affected by parenting. Studies find that contextual factors affect children's brain development, the expression of genes, and neural functioning, which in turn affect cognitive, emotional, and social development (Steinberg et al., 2006). Epigenetic studies with animals and humans suggest that parenting behaviors in the first several weeks of life can alter gene functioning in offspring (e.g., Ogren & Lombroso, 2008). The notion that parenting can "turn on" or "turn off" genes has major implications for future research. Studies also suggest that parents' own genetic factors affect parenting, even after controlling for education, mental health, and other familial factors (e.g.,

Bakermans-Kranenburg & van IJzendoorn, 2008). Thus, individual differences in emotionality and children's and parents' genetic makeup provide a window through which to examine future models of parental socialization.

PLACING PARENTING IN A BROADER SOCIAL CONTEXT

The science of parenting has benefited greatly from systemic, contextual, and ecological perspectives on child development. As many social scientists have noted, the parent–child relationship is nested within the family; the family is positioned within the neighborhood; and children and families are impacted by peers, schools, media, and culture (Bronfenbrenner, 1989).

Baumrind's work focused specifically on the parent–child dyad. However, much has been learned about how this dyad fits within and is impacted by broader social systems. Specifically, over the past 20 years, there has been an increased interest in the influence of family structure and system variables, siblings, marital conflict, neighborhood, ethnicity, peers, media, and schools on children's development and the parent–child relationship (Parke & Buriel, 2006). Research on the father–child relationship has burgeoned (Parke, 2002), and a growing number of studies have examined peer and parenting effects within the same study (e.g., Criss, Shaw, Moilanen, Hitchings, & Ingoldsby, 2009). Another hot topic has been the applicability of parenting typologies to parents from various cultural backgrounds. In the next section, we focus on contextual influences that are closely tied to the parent–child relationship.

The Family System

The family systems perspective takes into account mutual influences, or reciprocal processes, that occur between multiple family members and between family subsystems (i.e., parent–child, marital, sibling–sibling; Cox, Paley, & Harter, 2001). Olson et al. (1992) argued that families must balance closeness and individuality, with ideal family functioning consisting of moderate levels of cohesion or closeness and adaptability or flexibility regarding things such as family, rules, limits, and routines. Several studies have examined parenting behavior and family systems variables within the same study, and research supports the premise that family cohesion and adaptability are associated with greater child functioning and more positive parenting (Henry, Robinson, Neal, & Huey, 2006; Houltberg, Henry, & Morris, 2012). Parenting in families with moderate levels of cohesion and adaptability has been found to be more authoritative and less authoritarian in nature (Mupinga, Garrison, & Pierce, 2002). The family system also has been implicated in responses to stress and adaptation. At points of transition, pieces of the system are in flux, and parents must collaborate and adapt to changes and conflicts that occur to stabilize the family (Bugental & Grusec, 2006). In addition, socialization occurs within the overall family system, and this can happen through family myths, stories, rituals, and routines (Parke & Buriel 2006) as well as through observation of subsystem interactions and through family members other than parents (e.g., siblings; Criss & Shaw, 2005).

The concept of coparenting, or joint caregiving, stems from the family systems perspective. McHale, Lauretti, Talbot, and Pouquette (2002) reviewed the coparenting literature and concluded that coparenting can be viewed from a typological approach. They identified three main coparenting patterns: oppositional/hostile-competitive, disconnected/disengaged, and cohesive-engaged/harmonious (p. 141). Oppositional/hostile-competitive parents are imbalanced in their parenting and experience couple distress, whereas cohesive-engaged parents present a unified supportive front with clear rules and limits (McHale et al., 2002). It can be argued that cohesive-engaged parents are authoritative in nature. It is also possible, however, that cohesive-engaged parents may present a unified hostile front and are more authoritarian in nature. This is not the common view of coparenting that has been used in intervention programming and popular press books on parenting after divorce (e.g., Thayer & Zimmerman, 2001), but more research is needed on coparenting and various parenting styles.

The roles of both the father and the mother as well as the quality of the couple relationship are important from a systems viewpoint. Multiple theories have posited why and how the marital couple subsystem affects parent–child relations (Parke & Buriel, 2006), and evidence indicates that marital functioning is related to children's adjustment both directly (e.g., Cummings, Goeke-Morey, & Papp, 2004) and indirectly (Harold & Conger, 1997) through its effects on parenting. The quality of the marital relationship is positively related to the quality of the parent–child relationship (Erel & Burman, 1995), suggesting that supportive marriages are associated with better parenting. Cummings and Wilson (1999) argued that a child's emotional security is derived from family systems processes and that marital conflict damages a child's sense of security because of the stress and anxiety caused by the conflict. Such stress-induced insecurity has been associated with children's internalizing behavior (Davies, Harold, Goeke-Morey, & Cummings, 2002).

Siblings are another important socialization agent in the family system. In the United States, 80% of individuals have at least one sibling, and children today are more likely to grow up with siblings than fathers (Noller, 2005). Studies examining both parent and sibling influences have found that older siblings exert a unique influence on younger siblings' behavior above and beyond parenting (e.g., Snyder, Bank, & Burraston, 2005). This may be due to shared parenting or direct socialization. Research suggests that siblings can be a positive or negative influence (Steinberg & Morris, 2001). For example, younger siblings are more likely to engage in risky or antisocial behavior if they have an older sibling who engages in such behaviors (e.g., East, 1996). Studies also find that the quality of the parent–child relationship influences relations among siblings, and close parent–child relationships are associated with less sibling conflict (e.g., Jodl, Bridges, Kim, Mitchell, & Chan, 1999), whereas negative parent–child relationships are associated with more aggression among siblings and peers (e.g., Criss & Shaw, 2005).

One example of how the overall family system affects development is found in research on the effect of the family environment on pubertal timing. Studies of puberty in girls suggest that negative family factors (e.g., father absence, maternal harsh control, family conflict) are associated with earlier age at menarche (see Susman & Dorn, 2009, for a review). Father absence is typically the indicator of family stress in these studies, but some studies have examined parenting qualities or family disruption (Belsky, Steinberg, et al., 2007; Ellis & Essex, 2007). Also in support of the importance of family effects, even after controlling for maternal age at menarche, one proxy for a genetic explanation (Belsky, Steinberg, et al., 2007), the link between family stress variables and earlier menarche has been established. A variety of explanations have been proposed for this association, all implicating family stress as an important influence on females' developing biological system. Indeed, Ellis, McFadyen-Ketchum, Dodge, Pettit, and Bates (1999) found that the quality of father involvement in the family was the most salient predictor of a daughter's pubertal timing, suggesting that father absence may be the source of stress and/or that the father–daughter relationship is an important protective factor for early pubertal development.

Culture

Researchers have argued that parents develop a style of parenting based to some degree on the context and culture in which they live (e.g., Chao, 1994). Social relationship qualities, expectations, and values may differ across cultures and different ethnic groups. However, a burgeoning number of studies confirm that authoritative parenting benefits children more than any other parenting style across socioeconomic backgrounds, household compositions, and ethnic minority status in U.S. and non-U.S. cultures (Steinberg, 2001). Yet, some studies have found that African American and Asian American children are not as negatively affected by authoritarian parenting as European American children (Steinberg, 2001). Chao (1994) argued that the concepts grounding parenting styles are culturally rooted and that African and Asian Americans might have different cultural values. For example, she highlighted an indigenous Chinese concept of "training" (*Chiao shun* and *Guan*) that indicates parental care, concern, and involvement

(Chao, 1994). Such care is considered positive and fits Chinese cultural and social expectations of parenting behavior but also has some components of authoritarian parenting (highly controlling), as exemplified in so-called tiger mothering (Chua, 2011). Similarly, corporal punishment has been associated with aggression among European Americans but not African Americans in some studies (Deater-Deckard, Dodge, Bates, & Pettit, 1996). To better understand Baumrind's parenting typology, noticing the cultural nuances in parenting behavior is important (see Chapter 5, this volume), and calls for an examination of specific parenting behaviors within the parent–child relationship context, possibly highlighting the need to evaluate children's and adolescents' perceptions of parenting behaviors.

In summary, research suggests that family factors such as cohesion, adaptability, couple conflict, family structure, and sibling relations all affect children's and adolescents' development. Family systems theorists point out the importance of examining the parent–child relationship within the broader family context (e.g., overall family cohesiveness) and stress the need to consider parenting from a coparenting perspective. This is in line with a need for more research on the father–child relationship, which has been growing over the past few decades but is still scant compared with the number of mother–child relationship studies. Research indicates that characteristics of authoritative parenting are beneficial across cultures, and authoritative parenting is associated with better sibling relations. Within the context of a balanced family (moderate cohesion and adaptability), authoritative parenting can be particularly beneficial as its principles are validated and operationalized across multiple subsystems (parent, sibling, coparenting).

NEW DIRECTIONS

The foundation of much of the work we have discussed in this chapter is the seminal research of Diana Baumrind. Her scientific approach to the study of parenting paved the way for studies of parenting practices associated with different forms of control and highlighted the need to consider parental warmth and responsiveness and key emotion variables. Since her work, much has been learned about specific control techniques, child effects on parenting, and the important role of emotion within the parent–child relationship. Baumrind's legacy to parenting science is the important concept that parents combine different aspects of parenting into a coherent form that makes sense to them, given their goals for socialization. These goals are influenced by context, cultural norms, and values. Baumrind's work also suggests that the whole is greater than the sum of its parts and that parenting is best understood in terms of typologies, patterns, or styles.

Why is it important to consider parenting styles in future work? We argue that socialization research often benefits from a typological perspective for multiple reasons. First, typological approaches put specific behaviors in context. As important as it is to consider specific parenting practices, understanding the emotional context that surrounds the behavior is imperative (Darling & Steinberg, 1993). Second, much of parenting involves a careful balance between various relational dimensions (e.g., autonomy vs. control, involvement vs. intrusiveness, warmth vs. enmeshment, acceptance vs. permissiveness). A typological approach allows for the consideration of multiple parenting dimensions within one framework, capturing the whole picture rather than merely specific components. Thus, although much has been learned by "unpacking" parenting, ultimately the components must be "repacked" to provide a sensible perspective on the parenting process. Indeed, approaching parenting from a categorical, typological perspective underscores that parenting is best understood as a constellation of beliefs and goals that provides the foundation for parents' behaviors toward their children. For example, if parents value independence and curiosity and want their children to be well behaved, they will most likely engage in parenting behaviors consistent with authoritative parenting. In contrast, if parents value obedience and authority, they are likely to behave in an authoritarian style. Understanding not only behaviors but also how beliefs and cultural values affect parenting will aid in the understanding of differential socialization effects.

Parke and Buriel (2006) discussed the need to locate families in a network of socialization influences (see also Bronfenbrenner, 1989). We agree and argue that the next generation of parenting research will benefit from using a systems perspective when considering the influence of the parent–child relationship on children's functioning and adjustment. These dynamic socialization systems often involve multiple contexts and may include the examination of gene–environment effects, dyadic regulation, family systems effects on parenting, or parenting effects on children's peer relations and vice versa (Holden, 2010). Currently, most parenting research has focused primarily on one or two interacting systems. However, the next wave of parenting research should consider interacting systems and multiple systems influences (see also Masten, 2007). Research on multiple systems has been limited because of methodological difficulties. Indeed, it is difficult to measure parenting, sibling, peer, marital, and neighborhood qualities in one study. However, with greater statistical advances (e.g., multilevel modeling; Bryk & Raudenbush, 1992), such examinations are possible.

It is evident from the literature reviewed that some next steps for the study of parenting include an examination of the role of biology in parenting and socialization (e.g., epigenetics), children's and adolescents' perceptions of parenting and control messages, family systems variables in parent–child relations, a greater emphasis on fathers, and a greater consideration of possible cultural nuances in parenting. Much of the study of parenting has focused on Western cultures, neglecting to a large extent the majority of the world. Moreover, a great deal of parenting research has come out of developmental science and has not taken a cross-discipline approach. Examining how socialization occurs across multiple levels of analysis in development within a variety of cultural settings is a worthy, although optimistic, goal that likely will benefit from a cross-disciplinary perspective. Technologies have lagged behind conceptual models for examining multiple layers of influence and reciprocity on children (see Masten, 2007). However, methods are improving, and by reaching across disciplines and examining interacting systems, a greater understanding of children's development and socialization is likely to emerge. Such knowledge is needed to better inform prevention and intervention efforts aimed at helping children and parents maximize their developmental potential.

REFERENCES

Bakermans-Kranenburg, M. J., & van IJzendoorn, M. H. (2006). Gene–environment interaction of the dopamine D4 receptor (DRD4) and observed maternal insensitivity predicting externalizing behavior in preschoolers. *Developmental Psychobiology, 48,* 406–409. doi:10.1002/dev.20152

Bakermans-Kranenburg, M. J., & van IJzendoorn, M. H. (2008). Oxytocin receptor (OXTR) and serotonin transporter (5-HTT) genes associated with observed parenting. *Social Cognitive and Affective Neuroscience, 3,* 128–134. doi:10.1093/scan/nsn004

Barber, B. K. (1996). Parental psychological control: Revisiting a neglected construct. *Child Development, 67,* 3296–3319. doi:10.2307/1131780

Bates, J. E., Pettit, G. S., Dodge, K. A., & Ridge, B. (1998). Interaction of temperamental resistance to control and restrictive parenting in the development of externalizing behavior. *Developmental Psychology, 34,* 982–995. doi:10.1037/0012-1649.34.5.982

Baumrind, D. (1971). Current patterns of parental authority. *Developmental Psychology Monographs, 4*(1, Pt. 2), 1–103. doi:10.1037/h0030372

Baumrind, D. (1996). The discipline controversy revisited. *Family Relations, 45,* 405–414. doi:10.2307/585170

Baumrind, D., Larzelere, R. E., & Cowan, P. A. (2002). Ordinary physical punishment: Is it harmful? Comment on Gershoff (2002). *Psychological Bulletin, 128,* 580–589. doi:10.1037/0033-2909.128.4.580

Beauchaine, T. P., Webster-Stratton, C., & Reid, M. J. (2005). Mediators, moderators, and predictors of 1-year outcomes among children treated for early-onset conduct problems: A latent growth curve analysis. *Journal of Consulting and Clinical Psychology, 73,* 371–388.

Belsky, J. (2005). Differential susceptibility to rearing influence: An evolutionary hypothesis and some evidence. In B. Ellis & D. Bjorklund (Eds.), *Origins of the social mind: Evolutionary psychology and child development* (pp. 139–163). New York, NY: Guilford Press.

Belsky, J., Bakermans-Kranenburg, M. J., & van IJzendoorn, M. H. (2007). For better and for worse: Differential susceptibility to environmental influences. *Current Directions in Psychological Science, 16*, 300–304. doi:10.1111/j.1467-8721.2007.00525.x

Belsky, J., Steinberg, L. D., Houts, R. M., Friedman, S. L., DeHart, G., Cauffman, E., & Susman, E. (2007). Family rearing antecedents of pubertal timing. *Child Development, 78*, 1302–1321. doi:10.1111/j.1467-8624.2007.01067.x

Boyce, W. T., & Ellis, B. J. (2005). Biological sensitivity to context: I. An evolutionary-developmental theory of the origins and functions of stress reactivity. *Development and Psychopathology, 17*, 271–301. doi:10.1017/S0954579405050145

Bronfenbrenner, U. (1989). Ecological system theories. *Annals of Child Development, 6*, 187–251.

Bryk, A. S., & Raudenbush, S. W. (1992). *Hierarchical linear models: Applications and data analysis methods*. Thousand Oaks, CA: Sage.

Bugental, D. B., & Grusec, J. E. (2006). Socialization processes. In W. Damon, R. M. Lerner (Series Eds.), & N. Eisenberg (Vol. Ed.), *Handbook of child psychology: Vol. 3. Social, emotional, and personality development* (6th ed., pp. 366–428). Hoboken, NJ: Wiley. doi:10.1002/9780470147658.chpsy0307

Caspi, A., & Moffitt, T. E. (2006). Gene–environment interactions in psychiatry: Joining forces with neuroscience. *Nature Reviews Neuroscience, 7*, 583–590. doi:10.1038/nrn1925

Chao, R. K. (1994). Beyond parental control and authoritarian parenting style: Understanding Chinese parenting through the cultural notion of training. *Child Development, 65*, 1111–1119. doi:10.2307/1131308

Chao, R. K., & Aque, C. (2009). Interpretations of parental control by Asian immigrant and European American youth. *Journal of Family Psychology, 23*, 342–354. doi:10.1037/a0015828

Chua, A. (2011). *Battle hymn of the tiger mother*. New York, NY: Penguin.

Collins, W. A., Maccoby, E. E., Steinberg, L., Hetherington, E. M., & Bornstein, M. H. (2000). Contemporary research on parenting: The case for nature and nurture. *American Psychologist, 55*, 218–232. doi:10.1037/0003-066X.55.2.218

Cox, M. J., Paley, B., & Harter, K. (2001). Interparental conflict and parent–child relations. In J. Grych & F. Fincham (Eds.), *Interparental conflict and child development* (pp. 249–272). New York, NY: Cambridge University Press. doi:10.1017/CBO9780511527838.011

Criss, M. M., & Shaw, D. S. (2005). Sibling relationships as contexts for delinquency training in low-income families. *Journal of Family Psychology, 19*, 592–600. doi:10.1037/0893-3200.19.4.592

Criss, M. M., Shaw, D. S., Moilanen, K. L., Hitchings, J. E., & Ingoldsby, E. M. (2009). Family, neighborhood, and peer characteristics as predictors of child adjustment: A longitudinal analysis of additive and mediation models. *Social Development, 18*, 511–535. doi:10.1111/j.1467-9507.2008.00520.x

Cummings, E. M., Goeke-Morey, M. C., & Papp, L. M. (2004). Everyday marital conflict and child aggression. *Journal of Abnormal Child Psychology, 32*, 191–202. doi:10.1023/B:JACP.0000019770.13216.be

Cummings, E. M., & Wilson, A. (1999). Contexts of marital conflict and children's emotional security: Exploring the distinction between constructive and destructive conflicts from the children's perspective. In M. J. Cox & J. Brooks-Gunn (Eds.), *Conflict and cohesion in families: Causes and consequences* (pp. 105–129). Mahwah, NJ: Erlbaum.

Darling, N., Cumsile, P., Caldwell, L. L., & Dowdy, B. (2006). Predictors of adolescents' disclosure to parents and perceived parental knowledge: Between- and within-person differences. *Journal of Youth and Adolescence, 35*, 667–678. doi:10.1007/s10964-006-9058-1

Darling, N., & Steinberg, L. (1993). Parenting style as context: An integrative model. *Psychological Bulletin, 113*, 487–496. doi:10.1037/0033-2909.113.3.487

Davies, P. T., Harold, G. T., Goeke-Morey, M. C., & Cummings, E. M. (2002). Child emotional security and interparental conflict. *Monographs of the Society for Research in Child Development, 67*, i–v. doi:10.1111/1540-5834.00205

Deater-Deckard, K. (1996). Within family variability in parental negativity and control. *Journal of Applied Developmental Psychology, 17*, 407–422. doi:10.1016/S0193-3973(96)90034-9

Deater-Deckard, K., Dodge, K. A., Bates, J. E., & Pettit, G. S. (1996). Physical discipline among African American and European American mothers: Links to children's externalizing behaviors. *Developmental Psychology, 32*, 1065–1072. doi:10.1037/0012-1649.32.6.1065

Denham, S. A., Mitchell-Copeland, J., Strandberg, K., Auerbach, S., & Blair, K. (1997). Parental contributions to preschoolers' emotional competence: Direct and indirect effects. *Motivation and Emotion, 21*, 65–86. doi:10.1023/A:1024426431247

East, P. L. (1996). The younger sisters of childbearing adolescents: Their attitudes, expectations, and behaviors. *Child Development, 67*, 267–282. doi:10.2307/1131813

Eisenberg, N., Cumberland, A., & Spinrad, T. L. (1998). Parental socialization of emotion. *Psychological Inquiry, 9*, 241–273. doi:10.1207/s15327965pli0904_1

Eisenberg, N., Fabes, R. A., & Spinrad, T. L. (2006). Prosocial behavior. In W. Damon, R. M. Lerner (Series Eds.), & N. Eisenberg (Vol. Ed.), *Handbook of child psychology: Vol. 3. Social, emotional, and personality development* (6th ed., pp. 646–718). Hoboken, NJ: Wiley.

Eisenberg, N., & Morris, A. S. (2003). Children's emotion-related regulation. In R. V. Kail (Ed.), *Advances in child development and behavior* (Vol. 30, pp. 189–229). San Diego, CA: Academic Press. doi:10.1016/S0065-2407(02)80042-8

Eisenberg, N., Valiente, C., & Eggum, N. (2010). Self-regulation and school readiness. *Early Education and Development, 21*, 681–698. doi:10.1080/10409289.2010.497451

Ellis, B. J., & Boyce, W. T. (2011). Differential susceptibility to the environment: Toward an understanding of sensitivity to developmental experiences and context. *Development and Psychopathology, 23*, 1–5. doi:10.1017/S095457941000060X

Ellis, B. J., & Essex, M. J. (2007). Family environments, adrenarche, and sexual maturation: A longitudinal test of a life history model. *Child Development, 78*, 1799–1817. doi:10.1111/j.1467-8624.2007.01092.x

Ellis, B. J., McFadyen-Ketchum, S., Dodge, K. A., Pettit, G. S., & Bates, J. E. (1999). Quality of early family relationships and individual differences in the timing of pubertal maturation in girls: A longitudinal test of an evolutionary model. *Journal of Personality and Social Psychology, 77*, 387–401. doi:10.1037/0022-3514.77.2.387

Erel, O., & Burman, B. (1995). Interrelatedness of marital relations and parent–child relations: A meta-analytic review. *Psychological Bulletin, 118*, 108–132. doi:10.1037/0033-2909.118.1.108

Fletcher, A. C., Steinberg, L., & Williams-Wheeler, M. (2004). Parental influences on adolescent problem behavior: Revisiting Stattin and Kerr. *Child Development, 75*, 781–796. doi:10.1111/j.1467-8624.2004.00706.x

Gershoff, E. T. (2002). Corporal punishment by parents and associated child behaviors and experiences: A meta-analytic and theoretical review. *Psychological Bulletin, 128*, 539–579. doi:10.1037/0033-2909.128.4.539

Gershoff, E. T., & Bitensky, S. H. (2007). The case against corporal punishment of children: Converging evidence from social science research and international human rights law and implications for U.S. public policy. *Psychology, Public Policy, and Law, 13*, 231–272. doi:10.1037/1076-8971.13.4.231

Gottman, J., & Declaire, J. (1998). *Raising an emotionally intelligent child.* New York, NY: Simon & Schuster.

Gottman, J. M., Katz, L. F., & Hooven, C. (1996). Parental meta-emotion philosophy and the emotional life of families: Theoretical models and preliminary data. *Journal of Family Psychology, 10*, 243–268. doi:10.1037/0893-3200.10.3.243

Gottman, J. M., Katz, L. F., & Hooven, C. (1997). *Meta-emotion: How families communicate emotionally.* Mahwah, NJ: Erlbaum.

Gray, M. R., & Steinberg, L. (1999). Unpacking authoritative parenting: Reassessing a multidimensional construct. *Journal of Marriage and the Family, 61*, 574–587. doi:10.2307/353561

Grusec, J. E., & Goodnow, J. J. (1994). Impact of parental discipline methods on the child's internalization of values: A reconceptualization of current points of view. *Developmental Psychology, 30*, 4–19. doi:10.1037/0012-1649.30.1.4

Haeffel, G. J., Getchell, M., Koposov, R. A., Yrigollen, C. M., DeYoung, C. G., af Klinteberg, B., . . . Grigorenko, E. L. (2008). Association between polymorphisms in the dopamine transporter gene and depression: Evidence for a gene–environment interaction in a sample of juvenile detainees. *Psychological Science, 19,* 62–69. doi:10.1111/j.1467-9280.2008.02047.x

Harold, G. T., & Conger, R. D. (1997). Marital conflict and adolescent distress: The role of adolescent awareness. *Child Development, 68,* 333–350.

Henry, C. S., Robinson, L. C., Neal, R. A., & Huey, E. L. (2006). Adolescent perceptions of overall family system functioning and parental behaviors. *Journal of Child and Family Studies, 15,* 319–329. doi:10.1007/s10826-006-9051-z

Hoffman, M. L. (2001). *Empathy and moral development.* Cambridge, England: Cambridge University Press.

Holden, G. W. (2002). Perspectives on the effects of corporal punishment: Comment on Gershoff (2002). *Psychological Bulletin, 128,* 590–595. doi:10.1037/0033-2909.128.4.590

Holden, G. W. (2010). Childrearing and developmental trajectories: Positive pathways, off-ramps, and dynamic processes. *Child Development Perspectives, 4,* 197–204. doi:10.1111/j.1750-8606.2010.00148.x

Houltberg, B. J., Henry, C. S., & Morris, A. S. (2012). Family interactions, exposure to violence, and emotion regulation: Perceptions of children and early adolescents at risk. *Family Relations, 61,* 283–296. doi:10.1111/j.1741-3729.2011.00699.x

Jodl, K. M., Bridges M., Kim J. E., Mitchell, A. S., & Chan R. W. (1999). Relations among relationships: A family systems perspective. *Monographs of the Society for Research in Child Development, 64,* 150–183.

Joussemet, M., Landry, R., & Koestner, R. (2008). A self-determination theory perspective on parenting. *Canadian Psychology, 49,* 194–200. doi:10.1037/a0012754

Kakihara, F., Tilton-Weaver, L., Kerr, M., & Stattin, H. (2010). The relationship of parental control to youth adjustment: Do youths' feelings about their parents play a role? *Journal of Youth and Adolescence, 39,* 1442–1456. doi:10.1007/s10964-009-9479-8

Kerr, M., & Stattin, H. (2000). What parents know, how they know it, and several forms of adolescent adjustment: Further support for a reinterpretation of monitoring. *Developmental Psychology, 36,* 366–380. doi:10.1037/0012-1649.36.3.366

Kerr, M., Stattin, H., & Burk, W. J. (2010). A reinterpretation of parental monitoring in longitudinal perspective. *Journal of Research on Adolescence, 20,* 39–64. doi:10.1111/j.1532-7795.2009.00623.x

Kochanska, G., Aksan, N., & Joy, M. E. (2007). Children's fearfulness as a moderator of parenting in early socialization. *Developmental Psychology, 43,* 222–237. doi:10.1037/0012-1649.43.1.222

Lahey, B. B., Rathouz, P. J., Lee, S. S., Chronis-Tuscano, A., Pelham, W. E., Waldman, I. D., & Cook, E. H. (2011). Interactions between early parenting and a polymorphism of the child's dopamine transporter gene in predicting future child conduct disorder symptoms. *Journal of Abnormal Psychology, 120,* 33–45. doi:10.1037/a0021133

Laird, R. D., Criss, M. M., Pettit, G. S., Dodge, K. A., & Bates, J. E. (2008). Parents' monitoring knowledge attenuates the link between antisocial friends and adolescent delinquent behavior. *Journal of Abnormal Child Psychology, 36*, 299–310. doi:10.1007/s10802-007-9178-4

Larzelere, R. E., & Kuhn, B. R. (2005). Comparing child outcomes of physical punishment and alternative disciplinary tactics: A meta-analysis. *Clinical Child and Family Psychology Review, 8*, 1–37. doi:10.1007/s10567-005-2340-z

Lewis, C. C. (1981). The effects of parental firm control: A reinterpretation of findings. *Psychological Bulletin, 90*, 547–563. doi:10.1037/0033-2909.90.3.547

Lunkenheimer, E. S., Shields, A. M., & Cortina, K. S. (2007). Parental emotion coaching and dismissing in family interaction. *Social Development, 16*, 232–248. doi:10.1111/j.1467-9507.2007.00382.x

Maccoby, E. E., & Martin, J. A. (1983). Socialization in the context of the family: Parent–child interaction. In P. H. Mussen (Series Ed.) & E. M. Hetherington (Vol. Ed.), *Handbook of child psychology: Vol. 4. Socialization, personality, and social development* (4th ed., pp. 1–101). New York, NY: Wiley.

Masten, A. S. (2007). Resilience in developing systems: Progress and promise as the fourth wave rises. *Development and Psychopathology, 19*, 921–930. doi:10.1017/S0954579407000442

McHale, J., Lauretti, A., Talbot, J., & Pouquette, C. (2002). Retrospect and prospect in the psychological study of coparenting and family group process. In J. P. McHale & W. S. Grolnick (Eds.), *Retrospect and prospect in the psychological study of families* (pp. 127–165). Mahwah, NJ: Erlbaum.

Morris, A. S., Silk, J. S., Morris, M. D. S., Steinberg, L., Aucoin, K. J., & Keyes, A. W. (2011). The influence of mother–child emotion regulation strategies on children's expression of anger and sadness. *Developmental Psychology, 47*, 213–225. doi:10.1037/a0021021

Morris, A. S., Silk, J. S., Steinberg, L., Myers, S. S., & Robinson, L. R. (2007). The role of the family context in the development of emotion regulation. *Social Development, 16*, 361–388. doi:10.1111/j.1467-9507.2007.00389.x

Morris, A. S., Steinberg, L., Sessa, F. M., Avenevoli, S., Silk, J. S., & Essex, M. J. (2002). Measuring children's perceptions of psychological control: Developmental and conceptual considerations. In B. K. Barber (Ed.), *Intrusive parenting: How psychological control affects children and adolescents* (pp. 125–159). Washington, DC: American Psychological Association. doi:10.1037/10422-005

Mupinga, E. E., Garrison, M., & Pierce, S. H. (2002). An exploratory study of the relationships between family functioning and parenting styles: The perceptions of mothers of young grade school children. *Family and Consumer Sciences Research Journal, 31*, 112–129. doi:10.1177/1077727X02031001005

Nix, R. L., Pinderhughes, E. E., Dodge, K. A., Bates, J. E., Pettit, G. S., & McFadyen-Ketchum, S. A. (1999). The relation between mothers' hostile attribution tendencies and children's externalizing behavior problems: The mediating role of mothers' harsh discipline practices. *Child Development, 70,* 896–909. doi:10.1111/1467-8624.00065

Noller, P. (2005). Sibling relationships in adolescence: Learning and growing together. *Personal Relationships, 12,* 1–22. doi:10.1111/j.1350-4126.2005.00099.x

Ogren, M. P., & Lombroso, P. J. (2008). Epigenetics: Behavioral influences on gene function: Part I. Maternal behavior permanently affects adult behavior in offspring. *Journal of the American Academy of Child & Adolescent Psychiatry, 47,* 240–244. doi:10.1097/CHI.0b013e3181635e13

Olsen, S. F., Yang, C., Hart, C. H., Robinson, C. C., Wu, P., Nelson, D. A., . . . Wo, J. (2002). Maternal psychological control and preschool children's behavioral outcomes in China, Russia, and the United States. In B. K. Barber (Ed.), *Intrusive parenting: How psychological control affects children and adolescents* (pp. 235–262). Washington, DC: American Psychological Association. doi:10.1037/10422-008

Olson, D. H., McCubbin, H. I., Barnes, H., Larsen, A., Muxem, A., & Wilson, M. (1992). *Family inventories* (2nd ed.). St. Paul, MN: University of Minnesota, Family Social Science.

Parke, R. D. (2002). Fathers and families. In M. Bornsetin (Ed.) *Handbook of Parenting: Vol. 3. Being and becoming a parent* (2nd ed., pp. 27–73). Mahwah, NJ: Erlbaum.

Parke, R. D., & Buriel, R. (2006). Socialization in the family: Ethnic and ecological perspectives. In W. Damon, R. M. Lerner (Series Eds.), & N. Eisenberg (Vol. Ed.), *Handbook of child psychology: Vol. 3. Social, emotional, and personality development* (6th ed., pp. 429–504). Hoboken, NJ: Wiley.

Peterson, G. W., & Hann, D. (1999). Socializing children and parents in families. In M. B. Sussman, S. K. Steinmetz, & G. W. Peterson (Eds.), *Handbook of marriage and family* (2nd ed., pp. 327–370). New York, NY: Plenum Press.

Pettit, G. S., & Mize, J. (1993). Substance and style: Understanding the ways in which parents teach children about social relationships. In S. Duck (Ed.), *Learning about relationships* (pp. 118–151). Thousand Oaks, CA: Sage.

Rothbart, M. K., & Ahadi, S. A. (1994). Temperament and the development of personality. *Journal of Abnormal Psychology, 103,* 55–66. doi:10.1037/0021-843X.103.1.55

Rothbart, M. K., & Bates, J. E. (2006). Temperament. In W. Damon, R. M. Lerner (Series Eds.), & N. Eisenberg (Vol. Ed.), *Handbook of child psychology: Vol. 3. Social, emotional, and personality development* (6th ed., pp. 99–166). Hoboken, NJ: Wiley.

Silk, J. S., Morris, A. S., Kanaya, T., & Steinberg, L. (2003). Psychological control and autonomy granting: Opposite ends of a continuum or distinct constructs? *Journal of Research on Adolescence, 13,* 113–128. doi:10.1111/1532-7795.1301004

Silk, J. S., Shaw, D. S., Prout, J. T., O'Rourke, F., Lane, T., & Kovacs, M. (2011). Socialization of emotion and offspring internalizing symptoms of mothers with childhood-onset depression. *Journal of Applied Developmental Psychology, 32,* 127–136. doi:10.1016/j.appdev.2011.02.001

Snyder, J., Bank, L., & Burraston, B. (2005). The consequences of antisocial behavior in older male siblings for younger brothers and sisters. *Journal of Family Psychology, 19*, 643–653. doi:10.1037/0893-3200.19.4.643

Stattin, H., & Kerr, M. (2000). Parental monitoring: A reinterpretation. *Child Development, 71*, 1072–1085. doi:10.1111/1467-8624.00210

Steinberg, L. (2001). We know some things: Parent–adolescent relationships in retrospect and prospect. *Journal of Research on Adolescence, 11*, 1–19. doi:10.1111/1532-7795.00001

Steinberg, L. (2005a). Psychological control: Style or substance? *New Directions for Child and Adolescent Development, 108*, 71–78. doi:10.1002/cd.129

Steinberg, L. (2005b). *The 10 basic principles of good parenting.* New York, NY: Simon & Schuster.

Steinberg, L. (2011). *You and your adolescent: The essential guide for ages 10–25.* New York, NY: Simon & Schuster.

Steinberg, L., Dahl, R., Keating, D., Kupfer, D. J., Masten, A. S., & Pine, D. S. (2006). The study of developmental psychopathology in adolescence: Integrating affective neuroscience with the study of context. In D. Cicchetti & D. J. Cohen (Eds.), *Developmental psychopathology: Vol. 2. Developmental neuroscience* (pp. 710–741). Hoboken, NJ: Wiley.

Steinberg, L., Elmen, J. D., & Mounts, N. S. (1989). Authoritative parenting, psychosocial maturity, and academic success among adolescents. *Child Development, 60*, 1424–1436. doi:10.2307/1130932

Steinberg, L., & Morris, A. S. (2001). Adolescent development. *Annual Review of Psychology, 52*, 83–110. doi:10.1146/annurev.psych.52.1.83

Susman, E. J., & Dorn, L. D. (2009). Puberty: Its role in development. In R. M. Lerner & L. Steinberg (Eds.), *Handbook of adolescent psychology* (3rd ed., pp. 116–151). New York, NY: Wiley. doi:10.1002/9780470479193.adlpsy001006

Thayer, E. S., & Zimmerman, J. (2001). *The co-parenting survival guide: Letting go of conflict after a difficult divorce.* Oakland, CA: New Harbinger.

II

AUTHORITATIVE INTEGRATION OF CONTROL AND NEGOTIATION

3

THE CENTRALITY OF CONTROL TO PARENTING AND ITS EFFECTS

BRIAN K. BARBER AND MINGZHU XIA

In authoring the authoritative parenting construct, Baumrind introduced an approach to the study of parenting and its effects that concentrates on patterns of parenting behaviors. The approach has sound ecological validity because discrete parental behaviors do not occur in isolation (Baumrind, Larzelere, & Owens, 2010). Baumrind has repeatedly demonstrated this at varying levels of abstraction from the early prototypic groupings of authoritative, authoritarian, and permissive parenting (Baumrind, 1971) on through to the most recent superordinate groupings of balance and commitment (Baumrind et al., 2010).

This typological approach to understanding parenting is often contrasted with what has been termed a *dimensional* or *variable* approach that prefers to give more explicit attention to certain parenting behaviors or dimensions of them, such as various measures of parental support and control (e.g., Darling & Steinberg, 1993; Rollins & Thomas, 1979). In contrast to

DOI: 10.1037/13948-004
Authoritative Parenting: Synthesizing Nurturance and Discipline for Optimal Child Development, Robert E. Larzelere, Amanda Sheffield Morris, and Amanda W. Harrist (Editors)

measuring patterns of interrelated variables as in the typological approach, the dimensional approach has sought to identify the unique contribution to child development of discrete parenting dimensions. In further contrast, although there is much observational or mixed-method research that uses a more dimensional than typological approach (e.g., extensive research by Rand Conger, Thomas Dishion, and Gregory Pettit, among others), much of the dimensional research uses methods that are quite different from Baumrind's: namely, self-reported, often cross-sectional surveys, typically of older children and adolescents.

These basic differences notwithstanding, the approaches are fundamentally compatible, making a review of dimensions of parenting appropriate to a volume on authoritative parenting such as this. Most important, although the degree of detail and nuance offered through the different approaches varies substantially, the essential conclusion of both approaches is that effective parenting consists of a small set of general, interrelated components: nurturance (e.g., support, acceptance, responsiveness), adequate and reasonable regulation of behavior, and an absence of intrusive behaviors that manipulate or demean the child's individuality. The basic reason for the commonality in findings is that both approaches are undergirded by the same legacies of research, particularly that of Schaefer (1965), who was one of the first to articulate and distinguish these three elements of effective parenting. To the point of this specific chapter, the approaches have shared a common purpose of illustrating and distinguishing the role of parental control in the effective socialization of children.

In the ensuing discussion, we refer interchangeably to *children, adolescents,* and *youth.* We do this because the basic dimensions of parenting that are discussed were conceived and have been found to be salient across age, gender, and culture. They are also salient across the gender of the parent, and thus the term *parent* is used to refer to both mothers and fathers. Finally, most of the research that is used to support the nature and relevance of these constructs has been conducted on normative samples.

The best testament to the centrality of parental control in understanding effective parenting is that now through more than a half century of continuous study by thousands of scholars around the world, the broadband construct is ever more prominent in discussions, research designs, and debates about parenting and its study. In the first instance, Baumrind's classic typological approach is essentially grounded on the belief, supported by decades of evidence, that although effective parenting certainly involves attention to and consideration of the value and role of children in the parent–child relationship (i.e., responsiveness), it also consists fundamentally of the appropriate exercise of parental authority (demandingness) through types and/or patterns of parental control.

In turn, the dimensional approach to parenting has for decades identified control as an essential realm of parenting (e.g., Rollins & Thomas, 1979). Importantly, however, it is unlike another central domain of parenting, namely, parental supportive or nurturant behavior, which, although multifaceted, is noncontroversial and widely endorsed philosophically, ethically, and scientifically. Further, it has been found to have a ubiquitous positive relationship with healthy child development (Rollins & Thomas, 1979). Instead, conceptualization and measurement of parental control has been acknowledged by virtually all as complex and challenging (e.g., Barber, Olsen, & Shagle, 1994; Grolnick & Pomerantz, 2009; Rollins & Thomas, 1979; Steinberg, 1990).

This chapter is structured by the distinction between parental psychological and behavioral control. Steinberg's (1990) admonition to differentiate between these types of parental control has stimulated a dramatic surge of research, particularly on psychological control. Moreover, in recent years that volume of empirical attention to psychological control has been accompanied by several theoretical attempts to enhance its understanding. Before proceeding to the treatments of psychological and behavioral control, we first ground the logic for making the distinction between the two forms of control–territory that both the typological and dimensional approaches share.

THE DUALITY OF FREEDOM AND CONTROL

The intricacy of parental control centers on one fundamental duality of human development, namely, that optimal functioning is undergirded by a basic tension between individual freedom (autonomy) and control (regulation, conformity). Baumrind (1978) identified these contradictions of social living, and they have otherwise been discussed across the decades by parenting researchers. Some examples are freedom and control (Baumrind, 1966), personal integrity and conformity to cultural demands (Baldwin, 1948), individual freedom and submission to the general will of society (Peterson, 1995), and the need for psychological autonomy and demandingness (Steinberg, 1990), firm control (Schaefer, 1965), or sufficient regulation (Barber et al., 1994). Moreover, ample theory has focused explicitly on control, as in sociological theories of social control (e.g., Hirschi, 1969; Reckless, 1967), and parenting researchers have often invoked compatible constructs, such as regulation (Barber, Stolz, & Olsen, 2005) or structure (Grolnick & Pomerantz, 2009; Lewin, 1935; Soenens & Vansteenkiste, 2010).

DISTINGUISHING PSYCHOLOGICAL CONTROL AND BEHAVIORAL CONTROL

The distinction that was made by Steinberg (1990, 2005) and Barber (Barber, 1996; Barber et al., 1994; Barber et al., 2005), among others, between behavioral and psychological control was intended to clarify how both elements of this fundamental duality can be honored and facilitated by parents when focusing on dimensions of parental control. The explicit distinction can be traced to Steinberg (1990):

> The two forms of control [psychological and behavioral] appear to have opposite effects on the adolescent . . . Adolescents appear to be adversely affected by psychological control—the absence of "psychological autonomy"—but positively influenced by behavioral control—the presence of "demandingness." (pp. 273–274)

Steinberg's (1990) commentary is instructive in several ways. First, it acknowledges the fundamental duality described previously by recommending sensitivity to a child's need for control and autonomy. Second, it articulates that operationalizing this duality is a matter of considering two distinct types of control (in part because of their differential effects). Third, regarding behavioral control, it focuses on the presence versus absence of control as opposed to identifying specific dimensions of behavioral control or by asserting a linear continuum of control. Fourth, it alerts one to the possibility that different realms of adolescent functioning are impacted by the two types of control.

Our own early attempt to reiterate the tension between autonomy and control and how it can be pursued in parenting reads as follows:

> The evolution of research on parental control has not included careful attention to the locus of parental control attempts, that is, whether the particular parental behavior tries to exercise control over the child's psychological world or is an attempt to regulate the child's behavior . . . Two fundamental presuppositions about human development justify the distinction between psychological control and behavioral control. They are that developing children require: (1) an adequate degree of psychological autonomy, that is, that they learn through their social interactions that they are effective, competent individuals with a clear sense of personal identity; and (2) sufficient regulation of behavior to enable them to learn that social interaction is governed by rules and structures that must be recognized and adhered to in order to be a competent member of society. (Barber et al., 1994, pp. 1120–21)

We excerpt at length in the preceding quote because in the course of work that has followed these early distinctions between control types there has been a tendency to cite selectively from them, which has led to incomplete or inaccurate characterizations about the nature and distinctiveness of parental control (See section on Behavioral Control beginning on p. 75).

PSYCHOLOGICAL CONTROL

In 2002, we published a comprehensive review of the scientific literature on parental psychological control and related constructs, including authoritarian parenting (Barber & Harmon, 2002). In that review, we noted a sharp rise in the study of the construct, with only five of the 71 studies published before 1990 (the year Steinberg reminded researchers about the distinction between psychological control and behavioral control). The post-1990 upsurge in attention to parental psychological control has continued, with approximately 110 further studies published since the 2002 review. With very few exceptions this literature has found significant associations between psychological control and problematic child functioning.

The majority of studies of psychological control have been conducted among European American families, but studies have also emerged in Asia, Europe, the Middle East, South Africa, and South America. The majority of studies are still cross-sectional. Most appear to use either the Child's Report of Parental Behavior Inventory (Schaefer, 1965) or the Psychological Control Scale (PCS; Barber 1996) as measures of the construct. As would be expected from the conceptualization of psychological control, the majority of the studies have correlated it with internalizing and externalizing problem behaviors.

Finally, as was evident in the 2002 reviews, the overall corpus of literature on psychological control reads more like a listing of a variety of outcome variables than an exploration of carefully specified models that would more precisely define the pathways of its effects. Important exceptions to this pattern are discussed in the sections that follow as we focus on several recent attempts to clarify the construct of psychological control.

Advances in Understanding the Construct of Psychological Control

In the past few years, several specific efforts have been made to more precisely define parent psychological control theoretically and empirically. These efforts include conceptualizing psychological control as control of the personal domain, strategic manipulation and pressure, conditional regard, coercion, and disrespect. These advances are briefly reviewed in the next sections.

Psychological Control as Control of the Personal Domain

Social domain theorists Larry Nucci and Judi Smetana and their colleagues have recently made a useful bridging between psychological control and the personal domain of a child's life (Nucci, Hasebe, & Lins-Dyer, 2005;

Smetana, Crean, & Compione-Barr, 2005; Smetana & Daddis, 2002). When reviewing the construct of psychological control, both concentrated on two of its fundamental principles: that it is domain specific (i.e., it is distinguished from other types or styles of control by centering on the personal psychological realm of a child's experience, i.e., the "psychological world"; Barber et al., 1994; Smetana & Daddis, 2002) and that the basic effect of an intrusion into the personal realm is interference with the development of self, identity, and psychological autonomy (and the associated symptoms of internalized problems).

In showing the compatibility of these principles with social domain theory, they noted that the personal domain of a young person's life (e.g., the private aspects such as diary contents, issues of preference and choice about friends, and state of one's body) is central to psychological development and likely so in order to establish boundaries between the self and others and to develop an individual identity (Nucci, 1996; Nucci et al., 2005; Smetana & Daddis, 2002). In turn, efforts by parents to manage issues or behaviors within that private realm would be viewed as intrusive, and thus children resist or reject such regulation, as opposed, for example, to more readily accepting parental authority over other domains, such as the moral, conventional, or prudential domains (Nucci, 1996; Nucci et al., 2005).

Both Nucci and Smetana have found and otherwise reviewed important evidence for the relevance of a personal domain in a variety of cultural and ethnic groups (e.g., Hasebe, Nucci, & Nucci, 2004; Lins-Dyer & Nucci, 2007; Nucci et al., 2005; Smetana et al., 2005). They concluded that across cultures and social classes parents and children differentiate between actions and activities that should be under parental authority from those in a private realm that should be at the discretion of children and that children as young as 4 to 7 distinguish a personal domain (from a moral domain) and link it to self and identity (Lagattuta, Nucci, & Bosacki, 2010).

Further, Smetana illustrated the association between parental control of that personal domain and parental psychological control in her study of African American adolescents: Those who believed that parents should have less control over ambiguously personal acts and who also judged their parents as actually exerting control over such acts rated their mothers higher on a general measure of psychological control (Smetana & Daddis, 2002). Also, the body of work mirrors that of parental psychological control more generally in demonstrating that such control of the personal domain is associated with internalizing problems in children (Hasebe et al., 2004).

On the basis of these fundamental conceptual and empirical parallels, Nucci and Smetana recommended that the conceptualization of psychological control be extended to explicitly articulate that parental attempts to control behaviors in the child's personal domain represent psychological control (Nucci et al., 2005; Smetana et al., 2005).

Psychological Control as Manipulation and Pressure

Much of the recent work on psychological control has been conducted by Bart Soenens and Maarten Vansteenkiste. Their work, which has typically studied Belgian adolescents, has addressed theoretical and measurement issues related to psychological control, explored its distinctiveness from other parenting constructs, studied determinants of parental psychological control, and specified pathways of the commonly found association between psychological control, and the problematic functioning of youths (see Soenens & Vansteenkiste, 2010, for details on these several studies).

The work of Soenens and colleagues has culminated in two particularly extensive pieces published in 2010. One is an ambitious attempt to view the full complexity of parental psychological control through the theoretical lens of self-determination theory (SDT; Soenens & Vansteenkiste, 2010). The other is a three-part study of a new measure of psychological control constructed by the authors (Soenens, Vansteenkiste, & Luyten, 2010).

According to SDT, psychological control—particularly manipulative forms such as love withdrawal, guilt induction, and conditional regard—is by definition controlling because its purpose is to coerce the child into feeling pressured to control or change him- or herself (i.e., his or her thoughts, feelings, and behaviors). In turn, theoretically this self-pressure to conform impedes or prevents the volitional functioning of the child, a cardinal principle of self-determined autonomous functioning in SDT (e.g., Deci & Ryan, 2000).

According to the theory, when confronted with such control attempts over time, the child internalizes the pressure to change self according to perceived parental demands and does so out of a desire to avoid anxiety, guilt, and shame. Soenens and Vansteenkiste (2010) noted that empirical evidence for these elements of the posited psychological process and their sequence is still needed. Of the evidence they reviewed in the 2010 piece, the most thorough appears to come from studies of parental conditional regard of Israeli youths conducted by Avi Assor and colleagues. Because that work also invokes a SDT framework and because the second significant work of Soenens and colleagues published in 2010 to be reviewed in the next section appears to be fundamentally informed by the work on conditional regard, brief explicit coverage of conditional regard is warranted at this point in this discussion.

Psychological Control as Conditional Regard

Assor and colleagues have produced a series of studies investigating how and why conditional regard from parents is effective in achieving the compliance that the control intends (e.g., Assor, Roth, & Deci, 2004; Assor & Tal, 2012). Consistent with the arguments provided in the previous section, parenting that makes affection or regard contingent on specific child behaviors is controlling according to SDT because it pressures children to perform or conform either to gain parental affection or out of fear of losing that affection. This leads, theoretically, to fluctuations in self-esteem, temporary satisfaction, and feelings of failure and unworthiness (Assor et al., 2004). Such a process is consistent with the essential principle of psychological control's impact on the psychological realm of children's experience that has been reviewed previously, in suggesting that children experiencing such control will learn not to value their independent worth but to consider themselves acceptable individuals only to the degree that they do/become what their parents demand (Assor et al., 2004).

In a set of studies, Assor and colleagues provided empirical evidence that parental conditional regard is indeed effective in eliciting children's behavioral enactment in various domains as well as fluctuations in their self-esteem, feelings of low self-worth, a sense of disapproval from parents, resentment toward parents, and more (Assor et al., 2004). In a further set of studies, the researchers distinguished between positive and negative conditional regard and found both to be related to maladaptive outcomes of shame following failure and challenge avoidance (e.g., Assor & Tal, 2012).

This last set of studies is especially pertinent to this discussion on psychological control because the researchers provided empirical comparisons between parental conditional regard and a commonly used general measure of psychological control, the PCS (Barber, 1996). Conditional regard was associated at bivariate and multivariate levels with the PCS (on the order of .60). In a model predicting multiple measures of academic coping, both the conditional regard and psychological control predicted the mediator of shame after failure, but conditional regard was uniquely related to the mediator of self-aggrandizement. Thus, there was evidence that conditional parental regard functioned similarly to psychological control and that it offered unique additional understanding, specifically of the pathways in which control might impact achievement-related coping.

The second piece published in 2010 by Soenens et al. was a set of three studies designed to present and test a new measure of psychological control. The essential purpose of the studies was to show that strategic psychological control can attempt to shape not just the child's behavioral performance but also the nature of his or her psychological bond with the parent. They characterized this latter form of control—*dependency-oriented psychological control*—as attempts to make the child psychologically and emotionally dependent on the parent. In contrast, *achievement-oriented psychological control* demands excessively high degrees of achievement by the children. In the set of studies of Belgian youths and parents, Soenens and colleagues found evidence for the distinctiveness of both forms of psychological control and for the uniqueness of their associations with parenting characteristics and mediators of the controls' effect on youths' depression. They confirmed these findings further when comparing samples of Belgian and South Korean youths (Soenens, Park, Vansteenkiste, & Mouratidis, 2012).

We review this work here under the section Psychological Control as Conditional Regard because the instrument that Soenens et al. (2010) wrote and have tested—the Dependency-Oriented and Achievement-Oriented Psychological Control Scales (DAPCS)—was grounded in the work on conditional regard (and its historical antecedent of love withdrawal in the psychological control literatures). Nineteen of the 20 DAPCS items explicitly articulate the contingency of parental regard (e.g., with *if* or *when* or *as long as*; e.g., "shows that s/he is disappointed with me if I do not rely on her/him for a problem").

Soenens and colleagues (2010) reported bivariate correlations between the DAPCS and the PCS of approximately .50 to .70 and partial correlations (when accounting for the alternate dimension) that ranged from approximately .30 to .55 (Soenens et al., 2010, 2012). They do not yet appear to have tested the DAPCS in conjunction with a general measure of psychological control when predicting youth outcomes, so it is not yet clear what the degree of overlap is between the versions of psychological control and, specifically, if and to what degree conditional regard (as measured by the DAPCS) is uniquely predictive of youth functioning beyond a general measure of the construct (as Assor and colleagues found).

Psychological Control as Coercion

As yet another lens on psychological control, the formal use of the construct of coercion in Baumrind's most recent analyses provides an immediate bridge between the dimensional and typological bodies of work, and it also assists in elevating to prominence the construct of coercion in the study of psychological control. She noted in her review (Baumrind et al., 2010) that coercive parental practices have long been studied and found to be associated with internalizing and externalizing adverse outcomes in children (for an early review, see Rollins & Thomas, 1979). In interpreting her recent longitudinal analyses, Baumrind and colleagues (2010) concluded that both authoritative and authoritarian parents use "confrontive discipline which is firm, direct, forceful, and consistent," but in addition, authoritarian parents use "coercive discipline, which is peremptory, domineering, arbitrary, and concerned with retaining hierarchical family relationships" (p. 158).

This distinction is useful for the present discussion of psychological control in several ways. First, it gives a different example of how parental control attempts can be invasive and interfere with the development of their children. Thus, although parents can psychologically control their children through the manipulative conditional regard discussed previously, it is also the case that they can psychologically control through excessive domineering interactions with their children (i.e., without necessarily making their affection contingent). This is consistent with early definitions of coercion as

> behavior of the parent in a contest of wills, which results in considerable external pressure on the child to behave according to parents' desires. Such a control attempt might be either an initiating control technique or a reaction to noncompliance. (Rollins & Thomas, 1979, p. 321)

In that review, Rollins and Thomas (1979) took the same position that coercion was distinct from love withdrawal, and foreshadowing the relevance of coercion to authoritarian parenting, they determined in a second-order factor analysis of Baumrind's early data that at a variable level her set of parenting practices essentially described coercion and induction.

Baumrind's conceptualization also facilitates the precise linkage of coercive parental behaviors to psychological control. She explicitly included psychological control (measured as a composite of *intrusive* and reverse-scored *encourages independence and individuation* parental practices) in the collection of behaviors that she expected to indicate coercive practices (along with unqualified power assertion, arbitrary discipline, severe physical punishment, and hostile verbal criticism). Moreover, in variable-level analyses, she found that of the set of coercive practices, psychological control emerged as uniquely detrimental. Consistent with the theorizing about the salience of psychological control to the internal psychological development of children and with the empirical evidence discussed previously, psychological control was especially predictive of internalizing problems and poor self-efficacy. That this replication was made in a study that varies so significantly in design from many of the available works on psychological control is meaningful validation of the salience and target of psychological control.

Psychological Control as Disrespect

Our own recent efforts to enhance the understanding of parental psychological control were targeted to address one of the key limitations of work on the construct: the failure to solicit the views of young people, the targets and perceivers of the control. This limitation is fundamental for at least two reasons. First, because psychological control so closely implicates the psychological world of young people (i.e., the personal, private, and self-related spheres of youths' experience, as this review has detailed), their perceptions are critical both to test the validity of investigators' treatments of the construct and to identify further items or types of psychological control.

Further, even though the cross-cultural salience of the construct as traditionally measured has been clearly demonstrated, that evidence speaks only to the degree to which the *investigator-defined* presentation of the construct is meaningful to diverse groups of young people. Thus, whatever it is that current measures of psychological control are tapping appears to be commonly experienced. Pointedly, however, the predefinition and measurement of the construct has not allowed for any potential diversity in the experience of psychological control to be reflected.

Accordingly, in partnership with the World Health Organization, we conducted a phased, multimethod project among adolescents in five distinct cultural or racial groups in Costa Rica, Thailand, and South Africa (Barber, Xia, Olsen, McNeely, & Bose, 2012). In the first phase, we asked 120 youths to give examples of psychological control that their parents engage in. Because the youths would not understand the term *psychological control*, they were asked to give examples of what their parents do that leads them to feel that their parents do not respect them as worthy individuals. This approach to understanding psychological control tested our earlier suggestions that the main function of psychological control might be to not respect the individuality of young people (Barber et al., 2005).

Analyses of these interview data determined eight main types of psychological control, which were labeled *ridiculing, embarrassing in public, invalidating, violation of privacy, guilting, excessive expectations, comparing to others,* and *ignoring.* Next, corresponding survey items were written for these types of psychological control, and they were included with the PCS and various other parenting scales and indexes of adolescent psychosocial functioning in a self-report survey administered in classrooms to 2,100 youths from the same cultural and racial groups.

In an assessment of both the interitem consistency of the newly created items and their correspondence with the PCS items, exploratory and confirmatory factor analyses indicated that model fit was best when considering the new set of items as separate from the PCS items; the new items were labeled the Psychological Control—Disrespect Scale (PCDS). Additional item-level analyses across culture and parent showed that seven of the eight items had full conceptual, functional, and configural equivalence and partial metric and scalar equivalence (Manzi, Barber, & Regalia, 2011).

Significant correlations between the PCS and the PCDS across all groups for both parents provided some convergent validity for the PCDS as a measure of psychological control. Interfactor correlations from confirmatory factor analyses ranged from .33 to .48 for reports of fathers and from .35 to .54 for reports of mothers. Ensuing structural equation testing reinforced this by indicating that the PCDS functioned precisely as does the PCS in predicting internalized and externalized problem behaviors. Moreover, the PCDS explained additional unique variance in both forms of functioning, whereas the PCS was no longer significantly associated with either form of problematic functioning.

In sum, similar to both the Assor and Soenens work described previously, the PCDS was significantly correlated with the same traditional measure of psychological control, the PCS. But beyond adding unique explanation, the PCDS fully displaced the effects of the PCS. Several things were learned in this project that bear directly on the ideas and findings that have been discussed thus far in this chapter.

Strategic Versus Nonstrategic Control. In both conducting the project and interpreting its results, we confronted more thoroughly than before a dualism in definitions of psychological control relating to whether the parental behaviors are intentional and tactical in trying to shape the child (e.g., intentionally manipulative and/or coercive). While invoking such tactical behaviors in his original definition of psychological control, for example, Schaefer (1965) was also clear in emphasizing that the effect on the child of psychological control was to impede the child's ability to develop as an individual apart from the parent.

Because it has not been clear in past work that many of the behaviors used to index parental psychological control are necessarily strategic control attempts, we have endeavored from the beginning to ensure that the conceptualization and measurement of the construct not be restricted purely to strategic control attempts. This is reflected in an early definition:

> Psychological control is a rather insidious type of control that potentially inhibits or intrudes upon psychological development through manipulation and exploitation of the parent–child bond (e.g., love-withdrawal and guilt induction), negative, affect-laden expressions and criticisms (e.g., disappointment and shame), and excessive personal control (e.g., possessiveness, protectiveness). (Barber, 1996, p. 3297)

In other words, although psychologically intrusive elements of the parent–child or parent–adolescent interaction can include the strategic manipulative tactics and the coercive control referred to previously, it is apparent that these and other parental behaviors associated with psychological control, such as invalidating feelings, constraint of expression, excessive criticism or personal attack, are not necessarily strategically invoked by the parent. Instead, they may actually reflect general parental styles of relating to others as much or more so than they describe strategic control attempts in discrete interactional moments (Barber, Bean, & Erickson, 2002). What they all have in common, however, is the potential intrusion into or exploitation of the psychological experience of the child, specifically as it relates to self and identity.

To this end, our prior work has concentrated not on specific manifestations of psychological control that make up scales used to measure the construct but on the potential psychological consequences of such aggregated representations of psychological control. Consistent with Schaefer's definition that psychological control impedes the ability of the child to develop individually apart from the parent, our efforts have conceptualized psychological control as violation, interference, or disrespect of a child's individuality, uniqueness, adequacy, self-expression, and more (Barber, 1996; Barber & Harmon, 2002; Barber et al., 1994, 2005).

The Broad Reach of Psychological Control. By leaving it up to the adolescents to identify the specific parental practices that they felt assault their individuality, it became apparent that such practices are broad and diverse. Some of the practices were consistent with historic conceptualizations of psychological control (i.e., guilting, invalidating), but others extended the reach of the conceptualization to parenting practices not typically well developed in the specific work on psychological control. In so doing, these practices support several of the recent extensions of the work discussed earlier.

First, to the degree that the personal domain can be extended past issues of decision-making authority to include the private space of an adolescent's life, the violation of privacy category that the youths nominated is consonant with Nucci's and Smetana's proposition that psychological control be extended to cover the personal domain. At the same time, the extension of psychological control to the private or personal realm of a young person recommends the relevance of the specific work on violation of privacy (e.g., Petronio, 2004). This is consonant with suggestions in early work (e.g., Barber, 1996; Barber et al., 2005) suggesting that psychological control is compatible with the work on family dyads and systems in which constructs such as enmeshment, intrusiveness, lack of acknowledgement, and boundary violation are central (e.g., Barber & Buehler, 1996; Kerig, 2005; Manzi, Vignoles, Regalia, & Scabini, 2006).

Second, the excessive expectations category parallels the essence of Soenens et al.'s (2010) specification of achievement-oriented psychological control. Third, the inclusion of parental behaviors such as ridiculing in the set of disrespectful behaviors is consistent with Baumrind's recent focus on coercive parental practices, which are defined in part by verbal hostility. In so doing, it also opens the door to much other work on harsh and hostile parental behaviors (e.g., Buehler, Benson, & Gerard, 2006; Conger, Ge, Elder, Lorenz, & Simons, 1994).

Further, ridiculing, embarrassing, and comparing to others are compatible with past work on shaming (e.g., Fung, 1999), which, along with disappointment, was suggested in early conceptualizations of psychological control (Barber, 1996) and of constraining family interactions (e.g., Hauser, 1991). Relevant also is the substantial evidence across many cultures of the damage to young people of parental rejection (e.g., Khaleque & Rohner, 2002), which includes direct analogues to some of the set of disrespectful behaviors defined in the interviews (e.g., being ridiculed, embarrassed, and ignored).

The Disrespecting Function of Psychological Control. Finally, the term *disrespect* has not been used commonly in past characterizations of psychological control, except for the recent suggestion that parental psychological control represents a failure to create the broader socialization condition of respect for individuality (Barber et al., 2005). Consistent with that suggestion, the work described previously shows that a variety of parental behaviors collectively communicated disrespect in the minds of diverse groups of adolescents. Importantly, the youths themselves equated such behaviors with disrespect. Together with the empirical evidence that items written to capture it explained all and more of the effect of a traditional measure of psychological control, this suggests that one effective way to generally characterize the injury of psychological control is the disrespect it shows to children and youth.

Summary: Psychological Control as a Violation of the Self

Virtually all conceptualizations of parental psychological control have viewed it as infringing particularly on the psychological development and autonomy of the child. The empirical work continues to provide evidence of this association; recently, substantial progress has been made in more carefully depicting that effect. As is evident in the preceding review, this intrusion into and violation of the self is manifested when parents control the personal domain of a child's life. It is evident also when parents intentionally manipulate and pressure a child to perform or conform to parental standards, when coercive disciplinary tactics are used to achieve conformity or respond to misbehavior, and when parents behave in a variety of disrespectful ways.

What is particularly compelling about the strong interest in the construct and the consistent and coherent findings relative to it is its compatibility with a range of well-established theoretical descriptions of the human condition. Whether that be philosophy's tension between freedom and control or basic theory in social psychology (e.g., Mead, 1934), developmental psychology (e.g., Harter, Waters, & Whitesell, 1998; Nucci, 1996), or motivational psychology (e.g., Deci & Ryan, 2000; Soenens & Vansteenkiste, 2010), it appears ever clearer that people, including young persons, are aware of a private, personal, psychological aspect of themselves and are sensitive to its violation. With specific respect to Baumrind's typologies of parenting, it is clear that psychological control is central, serving as it does as a key marker of the distinction between authoritative and authoritarian parenting (Baumrind, et al., 2010).

BEHAVIORAL CONTROL

The pace and clarity of the study of parental behavioral control do not match those of parental psychological control. As we have reviewed, the work on psychological control has had an escalating pace of explicit study, the empirical findings are uniform and largely consistent across cultures, and recent attempts to clarify the construct conceptually are converging to support and refine foundational definitions of the construct as a violation of the psychological world of the child.

In contrast, the study of parental behavioral control appears sporadic, unsystematic, and controversial. Conceptually, there is no consensus on labeling parental behavioral control at either the molar or dimensional level. This complexity was noted decades ago (e.g., Rollins & Thomas, 1979), and inspection of contemporary literatures reveals the same. Indeed, just examining work published in past 2 years (2008–2010), treatment of behavioral control includes at least the following diversity: permissiveness or strictness (e.g., Rohner, Parmar, & Ibrahim, 2010); rules, limits, and restrictions on freedoms (Kakihara & Tilton-Weaver, 2009); parental knowledge (Grundy, Gondoli, & Salafia, 2010); lax control (Putnick et al., 2008); inconsistent control (Edens, Skopp, & Cahill, 2008); solicitation (Laird, Marrero, & Sentse, 2010); control (Kerr, Stattin, & Burk, 2010); structure (Grolnick & Pomerantz, 2009); and regulation (Arim, Marshall, & Shapka, 2010).

There is not space here to provide a detailed review of this complexity. Such a review would require an in-depth examination of the theoretical and conceptual correspondence within the variety of renditions of control as well as the design and methods of studies. Instead, we focus here on a limited set of issues that have been raised in some of the recent work on behavioral control, the clarification of which might assist in moving the research more consistently forward.

Behavioral Control and Parental Monitoring and Knowledge

The two publications in 2000 by Margaret Kerr and Hakan Stattin (Kerr & Stattin, 2000; Stattin & Kerr, 2000) have had a substantial impact on the study of parental control. The essence of that work was to challenge the construct of behavioral control, at least as it might be measured through parental monitoring. Specifically, Kerr and Stattin called into question the propriety of a commonly used measure of parental monitoring, one that assesses the extent to which youth perceive their parents to *know* details of their lives (e.g., where they go, who their friends are). Using data on Swedish families, they showed that parental knowledge was more strongly correlated with youth disclosure to their parents than were the researchers' measures of monitoring (i.e., concrete parental behaviors to surveil or control adolescents; Stattin & Kerr, 2000). They showed further that the significant negative association between parental knowledge and a variety of indices of youth problem behaviors was not reduced when they added monitoring or control to the equation, but it was in most cases reduced when self-disclosure was added to the equation. On the basis of these findings they concluded that parental knowledge was primarily a function of youth self-disclosure and therefore was not a measure of behavioral control (i.e., monitoring, as defined by parents' active monitoring efforts).

This conclusion has received widespread acceptance, with researchers regularly dismissing parental knowledge as primarily a function of youth self-disclosure (e.g., Kakihara & Tilton-Weaver, 2009, among many). The dismissal is problematic in two ways. First, insisting strictly that parental monitoring is only achieved by active parental efforts to surveil or control is inconsistent with the long-standing theoretical work that conceptualizes parental monitoring as the psychological presence of the parent in the mind of the child (Hirschi, 1969). In that conceptualization, how much a child believes his or her parents know or are aware of him or her is central to the deviance-deterring effect of parental monitoring. This is especially true of adolescents who spend much time away from their parents (and thus away from active monitoring attempts).

Second, dismissing parental knowledge as little more than self-disclosure—and, in turn, not pursuing further study of parental knowledge—is actually not justified by the findings. Specifically, in the Swedish studies, after controlling for self-disclosure, parental knowledge uniformly retained significant associations with outcomes variables, including numerous assessments of problem behaviors. This was the case in findings from both the cross-sectional (Kerr & Stattin, 2000; Stattin & Kerr, 2000) and longitudinal data (Kerr et al., 2010). In essence, then, one is still left with the ubiquitous finding made over the decades that parental knowledge functions just as parental behavioral control does, namely, that it is significantly negatively associated with youth dysfunction and, in particular, externalized problem behaviors.

Thus, although the shift to the study of how, why, and when youth self-disclose to their parents that has followed Kerr and Stattin's conclusions has produced a rich and useful literature, it has not contributed directly to understanding the role of parental control in youth functioning. Rather than dismissing parental knowledge from further analyses of parental control (e.g., Kerr et al., 2010; Stattin & Kerr, 2000), researchers need to conduct a concentrated study of parental knowledge to determine how it is derived and how it reflects parental control. Such work should include more complex modeling of relevant variables, as Soenens, Vansteenkiste, Luyckx, and Goossens (2006) did in showing that parental (active) monitoring and control of Belgian adolescents predicted parental knowledge by way of disclosure. Vieno, Nation, Pastore, and Santinello (2009) made the same finding in a study of Italian adolescents but also found direct prediction of knowledge by parental behavioral control.

Their additional finding that parent–child closeness directly predicted parental knowledge (for girls) usefully extends the investigation of the sources of parental knowledge in another important way, namely, by acknowledging that parenting variables are not static, and many are reflections of an interactional history between the parent and child. This is especially true of constructs such as parental knowledge that are typically assessed as general reflections of how much parents know (i.e., the knowledge is tied neither to a content domain nor to a specific time period). Thus, how much parents generally know about their adolescent-aged children is ultimately a reflection of a complex history, part of which is an evolved and general parental style (e.g., Darling & Steinberg, 1993).

Vieno et al.'s (2009) finding that parental closeness predicts knowledge (directly and indirectly through self-disclosure) is actually consistent with Stattin and Kerr's treatment of parental knowledge (Kerr & Stattin, 2000; Stattin & Kerr, 2000) as a reflection of closeness. We suggest, in addition, that the parenting and interactional styles that evolve between parent and children are informed critically by elements of parental behavioral control (e.g., goals, expectations, monitoring, discipline, enforcement) such that parental knowledge in the end is in fact partially reflective of parental control. Indeed, the essential lesson learned from Baumrind's extensive work on parenting typologies is that effective parenting is a coalition between responsiveness and demandingness. Thus, efforts to document the salience of parental control to parental knowledge should extend past assessments of the degree to which parents currently exercise behavioral control to an attempt to capture the role of control in the evolved styles of parenting and parent–child interactions.

Characterizing the Effect of Behavioral Control

One of the reasons that parental behavioral control is more complicated to understand than parental psychological control has to do with complexities in the nature of the effect of behavioral control. These complexities have to do with higher order effects, such as linearity or contingency of effect (e.g., interaction with other parenting variables).

Nonlinearity

For psychological control, there is neither theoretical nor empirical evidence that suggests the impact of intrusive parenting is anything but linear (see Barber et al., 2005; Soenens et al., 2010, for empirical evidence of this linearity in multiple cultures). The same linear characterization has not been made in the literatures that have distinguished and developed the construct of behavioral control. Instead, the thinking has concentrated on the presence versus absence of some level of behavioral control, with an absence or inadequacy of control highlighted as the risk for problem behaviors.

Consistent with the tension between freedom and control introduced at the chapter's outset, most approaches refer to the presence of (nonpsychological) control as valuable (i.e., something other than complete behavioral freedom). Not surprisingly, therefore, some of the most consistent research on behavioral control addresses its absence or laxness. This notion of laxness is classic in early formulations of parenting from both a dimensional perspective (e.g., firm vs. lax control; Schaefer, 1965) and a typological perspective (e.g., permissiveness; Baumrind, 1966, 1971, 1991).

As for the work that explicitly invokes the construct of behavioral control, as noted at the beginning of this chapter, Steinberg, when admonishing to distinguish the two types of control, argued for the positive influence on young people of parental behavioral control by way of the presence of demandingness and because inadequate behavioral control may leave children without adequate guidance or supervision (Steinberg, 1990). Barber maintained that focus repeatedly, referring variously to behavioral undercontrol, the absence of sufficient behavioral control, and inadequate or unregulated family environments (e.g., Barber, 1996; Barber et al., 1994, 2005).

In other words, arguments for the effectiveness of parental behavioral control have concentrated on the lower portion of the effect (i.e., from an absence of control to an adequate or appropriate level of control) and have explicitly not contended that any level of behavioral control would be considered positive. Indeed, the nonlinear nature of the construct (i.e., risky to youths at both low and high levels) has been repeatedly acknowledged (e.g., Barber et al., 1994, 2005; Mason, Cauce, Gonzales, & Hiraga, 1996; Miller, McCoy, Olsen & Wallace, 1986; Olweus, 1980).

We recall this historical conceptualization of behavioral control in detail for several reasons. First, it is apparent that some recent work has misunderstood the essential characterization of the construct. For example, Kakihara and Tilton-Weaver's (2009) construal that the literature on behavioral control implies that the more behavioral control parents exercise the better off their children are is inaccurate, as should be evident from the previous discussion. And, accordingly, what they offer as an alternative proposition—that behavioral control would have a curvilinear effect on child outcomes—is actually a restatement of what has long been known.

Second, this misunderstanding of the fundamental characterization of parental behavioral control forces explicit attention to how behavioral control is measured and analyzed. Nonlinear relationships are difficult to capture using typical response scales that have a limited range of options and in which the high point does not necessarily capture excessive control. A good example of this is the parental monitoring/knowledge variable in which youths are asked to rate how much their parents know about their activities and more. Although a low score (e.g., parent does not know at all) can reasonably be considered an indication of an absence of control, it is not clear that a high score (e.g., parent knows a lot) would be considered excessive. The difference between knowing a little (a midrange response) and knowing a lot does not appear to span a threshold of knowledge that would distinguish between adequate and excessive parental monitoring/knowledge.

The same is true of scales of lax control, a construct that is not only consistent with grounding conceptualizations of behavioral control (e.g., Schaefer, 1965) but also not complicated with the monitoring/knowledge debate. Youths who indicate that a statement such as "lets me do anything I want" describes a parent well could be considered to be inadequately controlled, but a response that indicates that the statement does not describe the parent well gives no indication as to whether whatever control the parent exercises is excessive or not. Thus, response patterns that are typically used to assess certain types of behavioral control are only measuring (intentionally) the lower portion of the effect (i.e., absence vs. presence). As such, these types of indexes of parental control actually can be considered to be linear in the sense that they range from absence of control to presence of some level of control, but, crucially, they do not address control that might exceed a threshold of adequacy. Indeed, thorough explicit tests revealed the linear nature of the effect of parental knowledge in multiple cultures (Barber et al., 2005). In fact, rather than curvilinear, the more appropriate expected effect might be a connected piecewise linear effect (e.g., spline regression; Marsh & Cormier, 2001) wherein behavioral control is linear (positive) to some threshold, after which it is again linear (but negative).

One lesson from this particularity is that researchers need to carefully fit the measurement, conceptualization, and analysis of specific indexes of parental control. Given the widespread recognition of the nonlinear nature of behavioral control, any investigation of it would need to clarify that the measure of choice is intended only to capture one portion of the effect (as discussed previously). Or, if the elected measure is conceived to range across the entire effect (i.e., capturing both inadequate and excessive control), the research would need to assure that somehow that full range is covered in the measure and then make explicit empirical tests of linearity. Although there are certainly studies that have assessed the linearity of behavioral control, it is of concern that many of the recent studies that have intended explicitly to clarify the complexity of behavioral control have not tested it (e.g., Arim et al., 2010; Kakihara, Tilton-Weaver, Kerr, & Stattin, 2010; Wang, Pomerantz, & Chen, 2007).

The findings by Arim and colleagues (2010) support those reported in the preceding section of this chapter in which control over personal domains was experienced as inappropriate (i.e., psychological control). They also support the distinction between parental behavioral control and psychological control in their finding that behavioral control was not associated with internalized difficulties but that psychological control was.

Just these few recent studies illustrate the lack of clarity relative to the effects of control—with higher behavioral control associated directly (and linearly) with both positive and negative outcomes, depending on the study. Although some of the discrepancy of these findings is surely attributable to differences in measurement—and with the real complexity of control (i.e., appropriate in some domains and not others)—part of the inconsistency might also be due to the failure to test for nonlinear effects. It is possible, therefore, that the findings of significant linear effects may not have accurately captured the real effect of behavioral control in any particular study (i.e., depending on the measure and its response options, the found effects may only be speaking to the upper or lower portion of the effect). Adding explicit attention to nonlinear effects would be consistent with conceptualizations of behavioral control as nonlinear, and it would aid in better pinpointing just what levels (of which types) of behavioral control transverse the threshold from negative to positive.

Finally, with regard to authoritative parenting, it should be made clear that conceptualizing and assessing the linearity of the effect of parenting on children is a concern that is more particular to the dimensional approach to parenting. It is that approach's focus on discrete dimensions of parenting (i.e., rather than on an assembly of dimensions into a typology) with ordinal or continuous measures that justifies the test for linearity. More relevant to the typological approach is the following concern on the contingency of parenting effects.

Joint Effects

Another intricacy associated with efforts to understand behavioral control is the potential contingency of its effect on the presence, absence, or level of other parenting dimensions. Here it is the conjunction of different parenting behaviors or styles (not the level of any given behavior or style) that defines the effect. This characterization of joint effects underlies the typological approach. Thus, although the disciplinary practices of both authoritative and authoritarian parents include high behavioral control (i.e., demandingness), those of authoritarian parents also use psychological control (Baumrind et al., 2010).

In other words, the eventual impact on children of behavioral control is contingent on the presence or absence of psychological control (and responsiveness). Such joint effects can be understood in multiple ways, such as with additive models (i.e., in this case, the presence of psychological control subtracts from or suppresses the positive effects of behavioral control) or interactive models (e.g., the effects of behavioral control are only positive to the degree that psychological control is not present). The general point, however, is that efforts to understand the effectiveness of behavioral control need not exclusively assert nonlinear effects and define thresholds of effective control, as shown previously. Rather, it is possible to conceive of some forms of behavioral control as linear, but the strength of its effect on child outcomes depends on other elements of the parent–child relationship. Indeed, when using a variable approach to analyzing her most recent data, Baumrind et al. (2010) also found positive linear effects of demandingness on competence and lower problem behaviors, once controlling for psychological control.

In sum, the complex and sometimes competing characterizations of the effect of behavioral control requires researchers to be very explicit about their approach to its study. If a nonlinear effect is theorized, then it must be measured appropriately, and explicit tests of nonlinearity must be conducted to verify and illustrate the effect. If, on the other hand, studies treat behavioral control as linear, then the researchers must confront the theoretical challenges of such a rendering of behavioral control by explaining how the effect could be positive (e.g., the more behavioral control, the better adjustment of the child) or negative (the more control, the worse adjustment). Otherwise, if the essence of the theoretical position relative to behavioral control is that its linear effect is somehow contingent on other aspects of the parent–child relationship, then researchers should articulate and test whether the operation of that contingency is additive, interactive, or otherwise. Alternatively, given the possibility that the nonlinear nature of behavioral control might not be curvilinear but rather piecewise linear, researchers should explicitly acknowledge which portion of the effect of parental control they are measuring—whether it is the linear effect from absence of control to the presence of adequate or reasonable control or the linear effect from adequate control to excessive control.

CONCLUSION

Revisiting the central purposes of this chapter by way of this summary affords attention to one further issue that would benefit from some clarification. Essentially, we used the chapter to reiterate the grounding philosophical notions that have both supported the value of parental control in the lives of children and established the distinction between behavioral and psychological control. Specifically, the fundamental duality of social living—that is, the benefits of both freedom and control—is the basis for distinguishing between the two types of parental control. Acknowledging this foundation is critical to understanding why the terms *psychological* and *behavioral* have been used.

These are shorthand labels for complex phenomena, and thus there is risk that the fundamental concepts that the single terms represent are not fully understood or carried forward as the constructs are investigated further. One example of this risk is recent work that challenges the distinctiveness of psychological and behavioral control. Some scholars (e.g., Grolnick & Pomerantz, 2009; Soenens et al., 2010) have construed the distinction between the two types of control rather simply as control either over "thoughts and feelings" (i.e., psychological control) or "control over behavior" (behavioral control). (This illustrates the selective use of elements of broader conceptualizations raised at the beginning of this chapter.) They have challenged the distinction between the two types of parental control by noting that psychological control can be exercised over behavior and that behavioral control can be applied to thoughts and feelings. This would be an understandable challenge if those construals of the constructs were satisfactory.

As this chapter, we hope, indicates, however, the distinctiveness of the control constructs does not center on an artificial polarization of thoughts and feelings in contrast with behavior. Indeed, it is hard to imagine that thoughts, feelings, and behaviors are ever disconnected. Rather, the constructs have been meant to clarify that parental control is injurious when it intrudes on or disrespects the psychological development of the child (e.g., self-development, identity, individuality) and that it is beneficial when it facilitates conformity to social or cultural expectations, which typically find expression in behavioral standards. This distinctiveness continues to be evidenced by the impact these differing types of control appear to have on children and youth. Although effects will never be unique—because the types of control are to some degree correlated, as are the types of outcomes—it appears clear that the prime impact of psychological control is disturbance in self-development and psychological functioning and that a principal effect of an absence of appropriate control is heightened deviance. As noted at the outset, the two forms of control are fully compatible with Baumrind's conceptualization of parental authority and control. These general findings relative to the effects of each type of control are also consistent with her empirical work, as demonstrated particularly in her most recent wave of results discussed in Chapter 1 of this volume and elsewhere (Baumrind et al., 2010).

REFERENCES

Arim, R. G., Marshall, S. K., & Shapka, J. D. (2010). A domain-specific approach to adolescent reporting of parental control. *Journal of Adolescence, 33*, 355–366. doi:10.1016/j.adolescence.2009.10.001

Assor, A., Roth, G., & Deci, E. L. (2004). The emotional costs of perceived parents' conditional regard: A self-determination theory analysis. *Journal of Personality, 72*, 47–88. doi:10.1111/j.0022-3506.2004.00256.x

Assor, A., & Tal, K. (2012). When parents' affection depends on child's achievement: Parental conditional positive regard, self-aggrandizement, shame and coping in adolescents. *Journal of Adolescence, 35*, 249–260. doi:10.1016/j.adolescence.2011.10.004

Baldwin, A. L. (1948). Socialization and the parent–child relationship. *Child Development, 19*, 127–136.

Barber, B. K. (1996). Parental psychological control: Revisiting a neglected construct. *Child Development, 67*, 3296–3319. doi:10.2307/1131780

Barber, B. K., Bean, R. L., & Erickson, L. D. (2002). Expanding the study and understanding of psychological control. In B. K. Barber (Ed.), *Intrusive parenting: How psychological control affects children and adolescents* (pp. 263–289). Washington, DC: American Psychological Association. doi:10.1037/10422-009

Barber, B. K., & Buehler, C. (1996). Family cohesion and enmeshment: Different constructs, different effects. *Journal of Marriage and the Family, 58*, 433–441.

Barber, B. K., & Harmon, E. (2002). Violating the self: Parental psychological control of children and adolescents. In B. K. Barber (Ed.), *Intrusive parenting: How psychological control affects children and adolescents* (pp. 15–52). Washington, DC: American Psychological Association. doi:10.1037/10422-002

Barber, B. K., Olsen, J. E., & Shagle, S. C. (1994). Associations between parental psychological and behavioral control and youth internalized and externalized behaviors. *Child Development, 65*, 1120–1136. doi:10.2307/1131309

Barber, B. K., Stolz, H. E., & Olsen, J. A. (2005). Parental support, psychological control, and behavioral control: Assessing relevance across time, culture and method. *Monographs of the Society for Research in Child Development, 70*(4), 1–137.

Barber, B. K., Xia, M., Olsen, J. A., McNeely, C., & Bose, K. (2012). Feeling disrespected by parents: Refining the measurement and understanding of psychological control. *Journal of Adolescence, 35*, 273–287. doi:10.1016/j.adolescence.2011.10.010

Baumrind, D. (1966). Effects of authoritative parental control on child behavior. *Child Development, 37*, 887–907. doi:10.2307/1126611

Baumrind, D. (1971). Current patterns of parental authority. *Developmental Psychology Monographs, 4*(1, Pt. 2), 1–103. doi:10.1037/h0030372

Baumrind, D. (1978). Parental disciplinary practices and social competence in children. *Youth & Society, 9*, 239–276.

Baumrind, D. (1991). The influence of parenting style on adolescent competence and substance use. *The Journal of Early Adolescence, 11*, 56–95. doi:10.1177/0272431691111004

Baumrind, D., Larzelere, R. E., & Owens, E. B. (2010). Effects of preschool parents' power assertive patterns and practices on adolescent development. *Parenting: Science and Practice, 10*, 157–201. doi:10.1080/15295190903290790

Buehler, C., Benson, M. J., & Gerard, J. M. (2006). Interparental hostility and early adolescent problem behavior: The mediating role of specific aspects of parenting. *Journal of Research on Adolescence, 16*, 265–292. doi:10.1111/j.1532-7795.2006.00132.x

Conger, R. D., Ge, X., Elder, G. H., Lorenz, F. O., & Simons, R. L. (1994). Economic stress, coercive family process, and developmental problems of adolescents. *Child Development, 65*, 541–561. doi:10.2307/1131401

Darling, N., & Steinberg, L. (1993). Parenting style as a context: An integrative model. *Psychological Bulletin, 113*, 487–496. doi:10.1037/0033-2909.113.3.487

Deci, E. L., & Ryan, R. M. (2000). The "What" and "Why" of goal pursuits: Human needs and the self determination of behavior. *Psychological Inquiry, 11*, 227–268. doi:10.1207/S15327965PLI1104_01

Edens, J. F., Skopp, N. A., & Cahill, M. A. (2008). Psychopathic features moderate the relationship between harsh and inconsistent parental discipline and adolescent antisocial behavior. *Journal of Clinic Child and Adolescent Psychology, 37*, 472–476. doi:10.1080/15374410801955938

Fung, H. (1999). Becoming a moral child: The socialization of shame among young Chinese children. *Ethos, 27*, 180–209. doi:10.1525/eth.1999.27.2.180

Grolnick, W. S., & Pomerantz, E. M. (2009). Issues and challenges in studying parental control: Toward a new conceptualization. *Child Development Perspectives, 3*, 165–170. doi:10.1111/j.1750-8606.2009.00099.x

Grundy, A. M., Gondoli, D. M., & Salafia, E. H. B. (2010). Maternal knowledge and maternal behavior control as predictors of preadolescent behavioral competence. *The Journal of Early Adolescence, 30*, 410–431. doi:10.1177/0272431609333302

Harter, S., Waters, P., & Whitesell, N. R. (1998). Relational self-worth: Differences in perceived worth as a person across interpersonal contexts among adolescents. *Child Development, 69*, 756–766.

Hasebe, Y., Nucci, L., & Nucci, M. S. (2004). Parental control of the personal domain and adolescent symptoms of psychopathology: A cross-national study in the United States and Japan. *Child Development, 75*, 815–828. doi:10.1111/j.1467-8624.2004.00708.x

Hauser, S. (1991). *Families and their adolescents*. New York, NY: Free Press.

Hirschi, T. (1969). *Causes of delinquency*. Berkeley: University of California Press.

Kakihara, F., & Tilton-Weaver, L. (2009). Adolescents' interpretations of parental control: Differentiated by domain and types of control. *Child Development, 80*, 1722–1738. doi:10.1111/j.1467-8624.2009.01364.x

Kakihara, F., Tilton-Weaver, L., Kerr, M., & Stattin, H. (2010). The relationship of parental control to youth adjustment: Do youths' feeling about their parents play a role? *Journal of Youth and Adolescence, 39*, 1442–1456. doi:10.1007/s10964-009-9479-8

Kerig, P. K. (2005). Introduction: Contributions of the investigation of boundary dissolution to the understanding of developmental psychopathology and family process. *Journal of Emotional Abuse, 5*(2-3), 1–4. doi:10.1300/J135v05n02_01

Kerr, M., & Stattin, H. (2000). What parents know, how they know it, and several forms of adolescent adjustment: Further support for a reinterpretation of monitoring. *Developmental Psychology, 36*, 366–380. doi:10.1037/0012-1649.36.3.366

Kerr, M., Stattin, H., & Burk, W. J. (2010). A reinterpretation of parental monitoring in longitudinal perspective. *Journal of Research on Adolescence, 20*(1), 39–64. doi:10.1111/j.1532-7795.2009.00623.x

Khaleque, A., & Rohner, R. P. (2002). Reliability of measures assessing the pancultural association between perceived parental acceptance–rejection and psychological adjustment: A meta-analysis of cross-cultural and intracultural studies. *Journal of Cross-Cultural Psychology, 33*, 87–99. doi:10.1177/0022022102033001006

Lagattuta, K. H., Nucci, L., & Bosacki, S. L. (2010). Bridging theory of mind and the personal domain: Children's reasoning about resistance to parental control. *Child Development, 81*, 616–635. doi:10.1111/j.1467-8624.2009.01419.x

Laird, R. D., Marrero, M. D., & Sentse, M. (2010). Revisiting parental monitoring: Evidence that parental solicitation can be effective when needed most. *Journal of Youth and Adolescence, 39*, 1431–1441. doi:10.1007/s10964-009-9453-5

Lewin, K. (1935). *A dynamic theory of personality.* New York, NY: McGraw-Hill.

Lins-Dyer, M. T., & Nucci, L. (2007). The impact of social class and social cognitive domain on northeastern Brazilian mothers' and daughters' conceptions of parental control. *International Journal of Behavioral Development, 31*, 105–114. doi:10.1177/0165025407073577

Manzi, C., Barber, B. K., & Regalia, C. (2011). *Disrespect is disrespect: The cross-cultural equivalency of a new measure of perceived parental psychological control.* Manuscript submitted for publication.

Manzi, C., Vignoles, V., Regalia, C., & Scabini, E. (2006). Cohesion and enmeshment revisited: Differentiation, identity, and well-being in two European cultures. *Journal of Marriage and the Family, 68*, 673–689. doi:10.1111/j.1741-3737.2006.00282.x

Marsh, L. C., & Cormier, D. R. (2001). *Spline regression models.* Thousand Oaks, CA: Sage.

Mason, C. A., Cauce, A., Gonzales, N., & Hiraga, Y. (1996). Neither too sweet nor too sour: Problem peers, maternal control, and problem behavior in African American adolescents. *Child Development, 67*, 2115–2130. doi:10.2307/1131613

Mead, G. H. (1934). *Mind, self and society.* Chicago, IL: University of Chicago Press.

Miller, B. C., McCoy, J. K., Olson, T. D., & Wallace C. M. (1986). Parental discipline and control attempts in relation to adolescent sexual attitudes and behavior. *Journal of Marriage and the Family, 48*, 503–512.

Nucci, L. P. (1996). Morality and personal freedom. In E. S. Reed, E. Turiel, & T. Brown (Eds.), *Values and knowledge* (pp. 41–60). Mahwah, NJ: Erlbaum.

Nucci, L. P., Hasebe, Y., & Lins-Dyer, M. T. (2005). Adolescent psychological well-being and parental control of the personal. In W. Damon & J. Smetana (Eds.), *New directions for child and adolescent development* (Vol. 108, pp. 17–30). New York, NY: Wiley.

Olweus, D. (1980). Familial and temperamental determinants of aggression behavior in adolescents—A causal analysis. *Developmental Psychology, 16*, 644–660.

Peterson, G. W. (1995). Autonomy and connectedness in families: Toward a family science perspective. In R. D. Day, K. R. Giblert, B. H. Settles, & W. R. Burr (Eds.), *Research and theory in family science* (pp. 20–41). Pacific Grove, CA: Brooks/Cole.

Petronio, S. (2004). Road to developing communication privacy management theory: Narrative in progress, please stand by. *Journal of Family Communication, 4*, 193–207.

Putnick, D. L., Bornstein, M. H., Hendricks, C., Painter, K. M., Suwalsky, J. T., & Collins, W. A. (2008). Parenting stress, perceived parenting behaviors, and adolescent self-concept in European American families. *Journal of Family Psychology, 22*, 752–762. doi:10.1037/a0013177

Reckless, W. C. (1967). *Crime problems* (4th ed.). New York, NY: Russell Sage Foundation.

Rohner, R. P., Parmar, P., & Ibrahim, M. (2010). Perceived teachers' acceptance, parental acceptance, behavioral control, school conduct, and psychological adjustment among school-age children in Kuwait. *Cross-Cultural Research, 44*, 269–282. doi:10.1177/1069397110366935

Rollins, B. C., & Thomas, D. L. (1979). Parental support, power, and control techniques in the socialization of children. In W. R. Burr, R. Hill, F. I. Nye, & I. I. Reiss (Eds.), *Contemporary theories about the family: Vol. 1. Research based theories* (pp. 317–364). New York, NY: Free Press.

Schaefer, E. S. (1965). Children's reports of parental behavior: An inventory. *Child Development, 36*, 413–424. doi:10.2307/1126465

Smetana, J., Crean, H. F., & Compione-Barr, N. (2005). Adolescents' and parents' changing conceptions of parental authority. In W. Damon & J. Smetana (Eds.), *New directions for child and adolescent development* (Vol. 108, pp. 31–46). New York, NY: Wiley.

Smetana, J. G., & Daddis, C. (2002). Domain-specific antecedents of psychological control and parental monitoring: The role of parenting beliefs and practices. *Child Development, 73*, 563–580. doi:10.1111/1467-8624.00424

Soenens, B., Park, S., Vansteenkiste, M., & Mouratidis, A. (2012). Perceived parental psychological control and adolescent depressive experiences: A cross-cultural study with Belgian and South-Korean adolescents. *Journal of Adolescence, 35*, 261–272.

Soenens, B., & Vansteenkiste, M. (2010). A theoretical upgrade of the concept of parental psychological control: Proposing new insights on the basis of self-determination theory. *Developmental Review, 30*, 74–99. doi:10.1016/j.dr.2009.11.001

Soenens, B., Vansteenkiste, M., Luyckx, K., & Goossens, L. (2006). Parenting and adolescent problem behavior: An integrated model with adolescent self-disclosure and perceived parental knowledge as intervening variables. *Developmental Psychology, 42*, 305–318. doi:10.1037/0012-1649.42.2.305

Soenens, B., Vansteenkiste, M., & Luyten, P. (2010). Toward a domain-specific approach to the study of parental psychological control: Distinguishing between dependency-oriented and achievement-oriented psychological control. *Journal of Personality, 78*, 217–256. doi:10.1111/j.1467-6494.2009.00614.x

Stattin, H., & Kerr, M. (2000). Parental monitoring: A reinterpretation. *Child Development, 71*, 1072–1085. doi:10.1111/1467-8624.00210

Steinberg, L. (1990). Autonomy, conflict, and harmony in the family relationship. In S. S. Feldman & G. R. Elliot (Eds.), *At the threshold: The developing adolescent* (pp. 255–276). Cambridge, MA: Harvard University Press.

Steinberg, L. (2005). Psychological control: Style or substance? In changing boundaries of parental authority during adolescence. In W. Damon & J. Smetana (Eds.), *New directions for child and adolescent development* (Vol. 108, pp. 71–78). New York, NY: Wiley.

Vieno, A., Nation, M., Pastore, M., & Santinello, M. (2009). Parenting and antisocial behavior: A model of the relationship between adolescent self-disclosure, parental closeness, parental control, and adolescent antisocial behavior. *Developmental Psychology, 45*, 1509–1519. doi:10.1037/a0016929

Wang, Q., Pomerantz, E. M., & Chen, H. (2007). The role of parents' control in early adolescents' psychological functioning: A longitudinal investigation in the United States and China. *Child Development, 78*, 1592–1610. doi:10.1111/j.1467-8624.2007.01085.x

4

RESPONDING TO MISBEHAVIOR IN YOUNG CHILDREN: HOW AUTHORITATIVE PARENTS ENHANCE REASONING WITH FIRM CONTROL

ROBERT E. LARZELERE, RONALD B. COX JR., AND JELANI MANDARA

In the latest *Handbook of Child Psychology*, Parke and Buriel (2006) considered Baumrind's parenting styles to be the most influential typological approach for understanding parental socialization of children but noted three concerns. The first concern, whether the findings are due to child effects, has been addressed by longitudinal evidence that parenting styles predict 1-year changes in adolescence (Steinberg, Lamborn, Darling, Mounts, & Dornbusch, 1994) and 10-year changes from preschool to adolescence after controlling for initial differences (Baumrind, Larzelere, & Owens, 2010). The latter study showed large 10-year effect sizes favoring authoritative parenting over authoritarian and permissive parenting (mean $ds = 1.22$ and 0.85, respectively), whereas neglectful parenting predicted the most adverse changes in adolescence (Steinberg et al., 1994). The second concern, cultural generalizability, is addressed by Sorkhabi and Mandara in this book (see Chapter 5). The third concern was the limited evidence on the "processes that account

DOI: 10.1037/13948-005
Authoritative Parenting: Synthesizing Nurturance and Discipline for Optimal Child Development, Robert E. Larzelere, Amanda Sheffield Morris, and Amanda W. Harrist (Editors)

for the effects of different styles on children's development" (Parke & Buriel, 2006, p. 437).

In this chapter, we focus on specific processes consistent with authoritative parental responses to misbehavior, especially in 2- to 8-year-old children, whether clinically referred or not. *Misbehavior* refers to behavior considered inappropriate by parents, whether considered intentional or not. The chapter applies to both mothers and fathers.

AUTHORITATIVE RESPONSES TO MISBEHAVIOR

Two of Baumrind's studies indicate specific kinds of reasoning and power assertion that authoritative parents use to respond to misbehavior. An early study documented how her three prototypical parenting styles varied in specific parenting practices (Baumrind, 1967). Her most recent longitudinal analyses differentiated the kinds of power assertion used by authoritative parents from the harmful kinds used by authoritarian parents (Baumrind et al., 2010).

Overall, Baumrind's authoritative parents used reasoning and negotiating but also insisted on cooperation within the limits they deemed appropriate. They were willing to use (and did use) negative sanctions, although they preferred respectful communication to achieve a mutually acceptable solution. Clarifying how authoritative responses to misbehavior differ from those by authoritarian and permissive parents requires distinguishing effective from counterproductive kinds of power assertion. Research also needs to clarify how power assertion, reasoning, and nurturance can best work together for optimal child development.

In Baumrind's (1967) first study, authoritative parents scored higher on all parent–child communication measures than permissive or authoritarian parents. They used reasoning to get cooperation, encouraged verbal give-and-take, and respected the child's decisions. Note that authoritative parents were more open to mutually agreeable compromises than other parents. Authoritative parents want children not only to cooperate but also to understand and apply principles for appropriate behavior. Verbal give-and-take supports active cognitive processing and learning to coordinate one's own interests with the interests of others. It also helps parents choose a response to fit each unique disciplinary situation (see Davidov & Grusec, 2006).

As for power assertion, authoritative parents were more likely than permissive parents to obtain positive outcomes by persistence and less likely to give in to whining or to evade issues (Baumrind, 1967). Authoritative parents were also less likely to frighten the child than authoritarian parents and less likely to use love withdrawal or ridicule than permissive parents. Authoritative parents used corporal punishment an average amount, slightly less than authoritarian parents and slightly more than permissive parents. Only authoritarian and permissive parents differed significantly from each other on their use of corporal punishment.

Baumrind et al.'s (2010) longitudinal study distinguished the kinds of power assertion used by authoritative parents from those used by authoritarian parents. Confrontive discipline was the only power-assertive factor that was typical in authoritative families and predicted successful long-term child outcomes in the full sample. The confrontive discipline construct can best be understood from its factor loadings, in order from the highest ones: "confronts when child disobeys, cannot be coerced by the child, successfully exerts force or influence, enforces after initial noncompliance, exercises power unambivalently, uses negative sanctions freely, and discourages defiant stance" (Baumrind et al., 2010, p. 199). Authoritative parents also avoided four kinds of power assertion that contributed to the adverse outcomes of authoritarian parenting. In order, these adverse kinds of power assertion were verbal hostility, psychological control, severe physical punishment, and arbitrary discipline. Psychological control was a combination of being overly intrusive and not permitting age-appropriate independence and autonomy. Authoritative parents were average in using physical punishment, which failed to predict either better or worse 10-year outcomes in the full sample, except for the adverse effects of severe physical punishment, which authoritative parents never used (Baumrind et al., 2010).

Thus, Baumrind's authoritative parents used more extensive reasoning and negotiation than did less effective parenting styles. They also used power assertion when needed to enforce a satisfactory resolution to noncompliance. This included some forceful negative sanctions, including an average use of physical punishment. How do these components work together, and which of them are essential for the long-term effectiveness of authoritative parenting? In the next section, we address these questions by gleaning relevant information from other parenting research.

TWO RESEARCH LITERATURES: TOWARD AN INTEGRATIVE MODEL

There is substantial support for the authoritative combination of reasoning with power assertion. For example, Grusec, Goodnow, and Kuczynski (2000) provided the following "general prescription for effective childrearing": "Parents who have positive relationships with their children, who are firm but not overly controlling, and who rely more on reasoning and persuasion than on the use of power are seen to be most effective" (p. 205). Similarly, in Hoffman's (2000) theory of moral internalization, the verbal content of disciplinary responses has the most direct influence on moral internalization, whereas the power assertion component needs to be just enough to maximize the child's attention and cognitive processing. Another leading expert advocates disciplinary reasoning but acknowledges that some children may need some form of punishment or reward to accompany the reasoning (Steinberg, 2004, p. 163).

Consistent with this authoritative synthesis, a combination of reasoning and power-assertive consequences is more effective than either one alone. Studies have consistently found that reasoning is more effective when used more intensely for most children. Greater intensity has been manifested both by affective intensity (Kuczynski, 1982; Zahn-Waxler, Radke-Yarrow, & King, 1979) and by combining reasoning with negative consequences or intentional ignoring (Chapman & Zahn-Waxler, 1982; Cheyne, 1972; Crockenberg & Litman, 1990; Davies, McMahon, Flessati, & Tiedemann, 1984; Larzelere, Schneider, Larson, & Pike, 1996).

The combination of reasoning and punishment is also more effective than punishment alone (Cheyne & Walters, 1969; Larzelere et al., 1996; Parke, 1969). Adding reasoning to punishment overcomes some problematic requirements for maximizing the effectiveness of punishment. For example, punishment's effectiveness increases with its level of aversiveness and the precision of its timing (Van Houten, 1983). Combining reasoning with punishment makes it possible to maximize effectiveness at lower levels of aversiveness (Larzelere & Merenda, 1994; Parke, 1969), consistent with Hoffman's (2000) theory. The addition of reasoning also relaxes the requirement for the punishment to be precisely timed (Cheyne & Walters, 1969; Parke, 1969) and cushions the coercive characteristic of unqualified power assertion (Hoffman, 2000, p. 147). Reasoning by parents makes it more likely that children will use their own reasoning to generalize their parents' expectations appropriately. So, the addition of reasoning to punishment can enhance its effectiveness with less aversiveness and facilitates appropriate generalization in understanding, making moral internalization more likely.

Despite this support for the authoritative synthesis of reasoning and power assertion, much parenting research emphasizes one to the near exclusion of the other. After summarizing Hoffman's theory, for example, Grusec (1997) concluded that his "message has lost its subtlety [and the] emphasis has been on the superiority of reasoning over power assertion" (p. 9). Other leading parenting experts in child development seem to take an unqualified position against power assertion (e.g., Grolnick, 2003; Holden, 1997, pp. 122–123; Kochanska, Aksan, & Joy, 2007, p. 233). For example, Kochanska et al. (2007) opposed all power assertion even though their observational measures of it are dominated by verbal prohibitions (e.g., "No!") and included such mild examples as "any sense of a clash of will, however subtle" (p. 225). This seems to implicate even the mildest kinds of power assertion, defined as the "use of superior power to control the child's behavior (including techniques such as forceful commands, physical restraint, spanking, and withdrawal of privileges)" (Shaffer & Kipp, 2007, p. 585). Note that *punishment* is a subset of power assertion, defined as an aversive consequence of misbehavior, broadly defined herein to include nonpreferred experiences such as time out (Van Houten, 1983).

The contribution of power assertion or punishment to the optimal outcomes of authoritative parenting remains controversial, at least from a reasoning-focused perspective. Is the effectiveness of authoritative parenting due only to its nurturance and communication components and not to its power-assertive components? If some power-assertive characteristics are an inherent part of authoritative parenting (Baumrind et al., 2010), then how is effective power assertion distinguished from ineffective or counterproductive power assertion?

To find examples of effective use of power-assertive tactics, we need look no further than the consequence-focused research that dominates behavior management research to treat oppositional defiance and conduct disorders in 2- to 8-year-olds. Five of the six most effective clinical treatments for these disorders teach parents to use power-assertive tactics systematically, including clear commands, single warnings, time out, and enforcements for time out (Eyberg, Nelson, & Boggs, 2008). Currently, enforcements for time out vary from a brief forced isolation (Hembree-Kigin & McNeil, 1995; Roberts & Powers, 1990), chores or privilege removal (Forgatch & Patterson, 2010), and a gentle restraint (M. Sanders, personal communication, May 2, 2011). In contrast to a reasoning-focused perspective, the only kind of disciplinary reasoning permitted in behavior management's responses to misbehavior is a concise description of the disciplinary consequences (e.g., Hembree-Kigin & McNeil, 1995, pp. 78–79) or, in one variation, brief statements showing empathy or addressing fairness (M. Sanders, personal communication, May 2, 2011). Parental rationales and negotiations are not considered permissible responses to misbehavior.

To summarize, some prominent parenting researchers support an authoritative combination of disciplinary reasoning and power assertion. In contrast, some conclusions from child developmental research seem to oppose all power assertion, whereas the best-supported parent management treatments for disruptive behavior disorders train parents in some power-assertive tactics while limiting the use of reasoning mostly to clarifying consequences. How can these contrasting perspectives help clarify the authoritative integration of disciplinary reasoning and power assertion? Bell's control system model suggests a synthesis that accounts for the contrasting evidence while showing how reasoning, power assertion, and other aspects of discipline can best work together in authoritative parenting.

Bell's control system model explains how parents and children regulate each other's behavior (Bell & Chapman, 1986; Bell & Harper, 1977). The model is derived from general control systems theory and from Bell's (1968) classic article incorporating child effects into an understanding of parental influences on children. Figure 4.1 illustrates how this model applies to children with competent or oppositional behavior, to the different emphases found in reasoning-focused and consequence-focused research, and for comparative purposes, to a central heating and air-conditioning system. Bell's model posits that parents have hierarchically organized disciplinary responses, which are elicited in a predictable way by the child's behavior. Parents select corrective actions from their repertoire when child behavior exceeds upper or lower limits of tolerance for the intensity and appropriateness of the child's behavior.

Children elicit upper limit controls from parents as a result of excessive or inappropriate behavior (e.g., out-of-control behavior, impulsivity), and this process is thus relevant for understanding disciplinary responses to misbehavior. Common upper limit controls, according to Bell, include prohibitions, verbal corrections (questioning, rule statements, rationales), distractions, reinforcement of appropriate behavior, redirections, restraints, and disciplinary punishments. The intended function of upper limit controls is to restore child behavior to the range of acceptable behavior, analogous to the role of furnaces in restoring home temperatures into the desired range. Bell and Harper (1977) showed that parents use verbal corrections and reasoning in their initial responses to misbehavior and switch to power assertion only in later stages or to address an extreme infraction (see also Hoffman, 2000; Ritchie, 1999). What is not as clear is what determines the long-term effectiveness of switching from verbal correction to power assertion.

Bell stimulated an extensive series of studies showing that the usual parent–child disciplinary correlations could be explained by child effects (Bell & Chapman, 1986; Bell & Harper, 1977). For example, Brunk and Henggeler (1984) trained child confederates to role play either conduct disorder or anxious and withdrawn behavior. The children were then paired with adults whom they had not met before. Consistent with Bell's model, conduct disorder elicited more commands, discipline, and ignoring from the adults, whereas acting anxious and withdrawn elicited more verbal helping and rewards. Bell and Chapman (1986) summarized 13 other studies that used innovative methods to document child effects as explanations of the associations between parental disciplinary actions and child outcomes.

Bell was not saying that parents have no influence. Instead, his point was that an accurate understanding of parental effects must fully account for ongo-

Discipline as Control System (Bell)

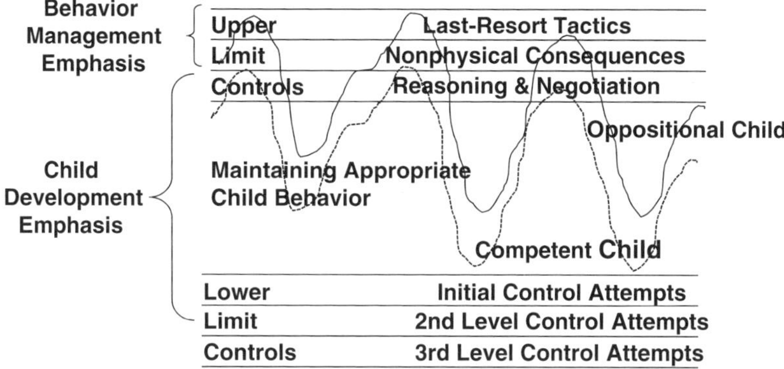

Central Air and Heating System

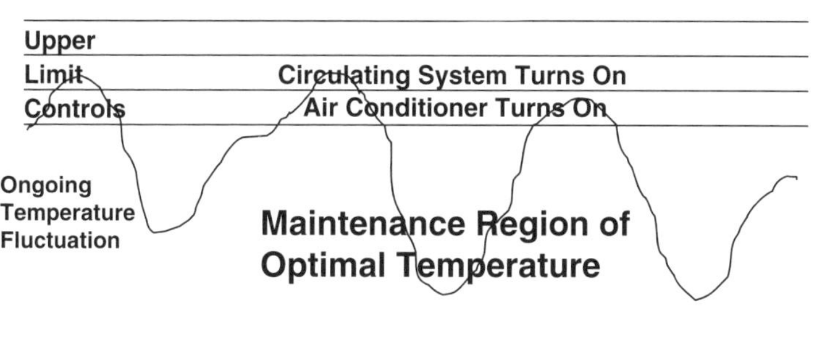

Figure 4.1. Two applications of Bell's control system model.

ing child effects in a control system. Correlations between parental disciplinary responses and child outcomes are based on the equilibrium that has been achieved between a parent and a child and, as such, tell little about the causal mechanisms that produced that equilibrium (Bell & Harper, 1977). Other models of bidirectionality are also important for moving beyond unidirectional socialization models (Kuczynski, 2003), but Bell's model is especially relevant for elucidating parental influences within a bidirectional system.

To the extent that parental discipline operates as a control system, effective actions to restore behavior into an acceptable range will look harmful according to correlations, thus accounting for the bias against power assertion in cross-sectional and longitudinal designs. After making that case in the next section, we summarize causal evidence supporting one particular conditional sequencing of disciplinary tactics that is consistent with authoritative parenting. Thus, Bell's model can account for both the correlational evidence against power assertion and its role in effective parental management for oppositional children. We conclude by summarizing other implications of Bell's model, first that the relative effectiveness of reasoning and power assertion varies by child temperament and that the sequence of disciplinary actions provides a basis for reducing the need for parents to use power assertion.

Correlational Analyses of a Control System

To understand the implications of Bell's model, it is helpful to consider using correlations to study a familiar control system such as a central heating and air-conditioning system. Because furnaces are activated by cold temperatures, cross-sectional correlations would indicate that furnace operation is associated with colder home temperatures (e.g., 68° F) than air-conditioner operation (77° F), and typical longitudinal data would strengthen such conclusions further. For example, imagine a longitudinal study of home furnaces in Canada and Hawaii. More furnace activity during one winter (in Canada) would be associated with colder home temperatures the following winter (compared with Hawaii). The standard interpretation of these correlations would be that furnaces are making homes colder, both short-term and long-term. The recommendation would follow that Canadians should start heating their homes like Hawaiians to enjoy Hawaii-like warmth in the winter. Of course, the cross-sectional and longitudinal associations are due to the contrasting challenges the control systems are facing in Canada and Hawaii, not the causal effect of corrective actions to restore temperatures to the desirable range (i.e., furnace operation).

It is informative to consider how heating-system advocates could respond to this kind of challenge. Longitudinal methodologists would recommend controlling for initial differences in home temperatures to get stronger causal evidence. Statistical controls could produce unbiased causal evidence if all relevant confounds were controlled for perfectly (Steiner, Cook, Shadish, & Clark, 2010), but that ideal is usually achieved only partially. Even if that could be done, we are skeptical that the actual causal effect of furnace operation during one winter could be detected as increases in home temperatures 12 months later. Similarly, the typical interval in longitudinal studies may be poorly matched with a reasonable causal lag for studying parental influences on children (Gershoff, Aber, & Clements, 2009). A simpler response to the longitudinal evidence would be to demonstrate short-term effects: When furnaces operate, homes get warmer; otherwise, they get colder when challenged by wintry conditions. This suggests that dismissing similar short-term causal effects from parents (e.g., to enhance compliance) on the basis of long-term correlations can lead to faulty causal conclusions. (Note that oppositional defiance is a key step in the development of delinquency [Timmermans, van Lier, & Koot, 2009].) Short-term influences from parents are also less likely than longitudinal correlations to be accounted for by shared genetic influences. The substantial genetic component in parent–child correlations may be due to the influence of the child on the equilibria on which those correlations are based via evocative genotype–environment correlations (Burt, 2009). Short-term parental influences may be less confounded with genetic influences.

Implications for Disciplinary Responses

This analogy fits corrective disciplinary actions well. Just as central heating systems operate to keep home temperatures in a desirable range, so parents use corrective actions to restore their children's behaviors into a desirable range when its boundaries are exceeded. The system equilibrium is determined by the combination of three influences: the behavioral challenge from the child, the parent's disciplinary effectiveness, and the acceptable range of child behavior. Bell insisted that correct conclusions about any of those three interrelated causes of the observed equilibrium required taking the other two causes into account. Parenting research needs to address the "most basic and fundamental defect of past correlational studies, [which] is that they do not provide a sensible basis for sorting out the direction of effects" (Bell & Harper, 1977, p. 120). Those correlations do show, however, that the most desirable outcome is an optimally developing child with parents who rarely need to use any power assertion but negotiate mutually acceptable conflict resolutions when needed. This ideal equilibrium is consistent with the correlational evidence from cross-sectional and longitudinal studies.

Admittedly, a human system is more complex than a mechanical central heating system. For one thing, human control systems come with memories, as Bell and Chapman (1986) recognized. Child developmental experts, such as Hoffman (2000), have emphasized cognitive influences on moral internalization, whereas parent management experts, such as Patterson (1982), have emphasized memories of contingent consequences. According to Hoffman, the verbal portion of disciplinary responses has the most direct influence on moral internalization, whereas the power assertion component needs to be just enough to maximize the child's attention and cognitive processing. The optimal level can often be achieved by background power assertion, which is the memory of previous use of power assertion by parents (Hoffman, 2000, pp. 146–147). Whereas Hoffman's theory focuses on disciplinary characteristics thought to maximize moral learning in a given discipline episode, Patterson's focus was on how the successes or failures of actions in previous disciplinary episodes influence the probability that those actions will be tried later by the child or the parent. Putting the two together, Patterson's contingencies from previous episodes can provide the background power assertion that is ideal for maximizing moral internalization according to Hoffman. To Patterson (1982, p. 111), the most important skill to teach parents of defiant children is how to use punishment effectively, referring to time out or privilege removal. Effective use of time out to enforce compliance improves cooperation with parental requests because the child's defiance no longer succeeds in getting the parents to drop their demands. Oppositional children learn to cooperate with a milder verbal discipline tactic to the extent it has been enforced effectively with time out or similar negative consequences in prior episodes. Whereas mild verbal discipline is limited to commands and warnings in behavior management, the same contingencies can also enforce the kinds of disciplinary explanations emphasized in the reasoning-focused perspective (Larzelere, Sather, Schneider, Larson, & Pike, 1998). This illustrates the potential of integrating processes involving both reasoning and consequences into a single model consistent with authoritative parenting. This systematic sequence of disciplinary tactics not only accounts for the effectiveness of behavior management but also explains why correlations are biased against all power-assertive tactics.

Correlational Bias Against Corrective Actions

Bell's model implies that most cross-sectional and longitudinal analyses are biased against all disciplinary responses to misbehavior, especially power-assertive tactics. Accordingly, recent research has opposed a rapidly increasing number of corrective actions by parents, including corrective disciplinary tactics. For example, Gershoff et al. (2010) investigated 11 disciplinary tactics, nine of which are used mostly to correct misbehavior. Out of 88 hypothesis tests, not one tactic was ever associated with lower externalizing or internalizing behavior problems in children. Five of the nine corrective disciplinary tactics were associated with more aggressive behavior or anxiety symptoms in children, including time out and expressing disappointment to children as well as physical punishment, yelling or scolding, and shaming (Gershoff et al., 2010). Other studies have found that sending children to their room, grounding, privilege removal, and nonphysical punishment in general were associated with more antisocial behavior or hyperactivity later (Larzelere, Cox, & Smith, 2010; Larzelere, Ferrer, Kuhn, & Danelia, 2010). This correlational bias also makes nondisciplinary corrective actions appear harmful, including helping children with homework (Hill & Tyson, 2009), certain racial socialization practices (Hughes et al., 2006; Quintana et al., 2006), and warning adolescents about the dangers of smoking and of unprotected sex (de Leeuw, Scholte, Sargent, Vermulst, & Engels, 2010; Deptula, Henry, & Schoeny, 2010). Some of these studies have gone beyond unqualified conclusions against these corrective actions to discriminate among more versus less effective ways of implementing them (Deptula et al., 2010; Hughes et al., 2006). Similar discriminations need to be made about corrective disciplinary actions to clarify how authoritative parents use them to respond effectively to misbehavior.

The associations of corrective actions with negative child outcomes are due to an inherent selection bias caused by child effects (Larzelere, Kuhn, & Johnson, 2004). Parents are less likely to use corrective actions when children are cooperative, respond well to reasoning, do well in school, do not experience racial discrimination, and are unlikely to smoke or be sexually precocious. Quite simply, the correlational evidence underlying these conclusions occurs because parents need no corrective actions when children are doing well and not facing risky environments. Many parent–child associations in the literature may therefore reflect statistical artifacts due to child effects rather than true causal effects.

This type of artifact explains why corrective actions shown to be effective in randomized trials appear harmful according to longitudinal correlations. For example, longitudinal analyses show that psychotherapy and Ritalin appear to be as harmful as spanking and nonphysical punishment, even after controlling for preexisting differences on child outcomes (Larzelere, Cox, et al., 2010; Larzelere, Ferrer, et al., 2010).

Correlations cannot discriminate between effective versus harmful corrective actions if those actions are activated by a control system process like Bell's model. Indeed, a perfect corrective action would produce a correlation of $r = .00$ with subsequent measures of the problem being corrected because it would make recipients indistinguishable from those who never had the problem. Relevant causal evidence about corrective disciplinary actions must overcome this bias to clarify how disciplinary tactics can best be sequenced in a manner that is consistent with authoritative parenting.

Sequencing Disciplinary Tactics

Consequence-focused research has documented causal evidence to support one way that power-assertive tactics can be sequenced to support verbal corrections. Several principles about how authoritative parents might use power assertion to support appropriate verbal discipline can be illustrated from this research. Cooperation by the child with time out is essential for the effectiveness of behavior management, but this is difficult to obtain for many clinically referred children (Roberts & Powers, 1988). In four studies, Roberts contrasted four ways to enforce cooperation with time out on a chair. Restraint and a child-determined release were the least effective enforcements for time out, whereas the traditional two-swat spank backup and a brief room isolation were the two most effective enforcements (e.g., Bean & Roberts, 1981; Roberts & Powers, 1990). The first principle herein is that research needs to compare alternative tactics for the same disciplinary situation, such as enforcing cooperation with time out. A second principle is that multiple options help parents find the best alternative for each child and each disciplinary situation. Roberts and Powers (1990) found that the two best enforcements each worked when the other one failed to achieve compliance with time out after several attempts. The availability of multiple alternatives is desirable at any stage of a sequence of tactics to prevent unnecessary increases in forcefulness. A third principle is illustrated by the fact that the mildest enforcement for time out worked for some children even though it was the least effective overall. That is, the child-determined release worked for children who sat on the time out chair for more than a few seconds.

A fourth principle was illustrated by Roberts's (1982) research on a single warning preceding time out. Compliance improved just as rapidly as in no-warning sequence, but the number of time outs needed to achieve compliance was reduced by an average of 74%. This step in the sequence of tactics thus reduced forcefulness (e.g., number of time outs) without compromising effectiveness.

This conditional sequence of disciplinary tactics helps clinically defiant children learn to cooperate with verbal discipline in the form of commands and warnings and enables parents to phase out the most forceful tactics in the sequence, starting with the time-out enforcement and then decreasing the frequency of time out itself (McNeil & Hembree-Kigin, 2010). Children thus learn to cooperate with the milder verbal tactics that developmental scholars have found to be correlated with more appropriate child behavior (Roberts & Powers, 1990). Thus, consequence-focused and reasoning-focused perspectives share the goal of maintaining appropriate cooperation with mild verbal discipline tactics. Behavior management research, however, has produced causal evidence showing how power-assertive tactics can be sequenced to achieve this goal, even for the most oppositional young children (Eyberg et al., 2008; Pelham & Fabiano, 2008; Roberts & Powers, 1990).

Disciplinary reasoning cannot influence moral internalization unless children pay attention to it. Consistent with authoritative parenting, the effectiveness of disciplinary reasoning depends on it being backed up with

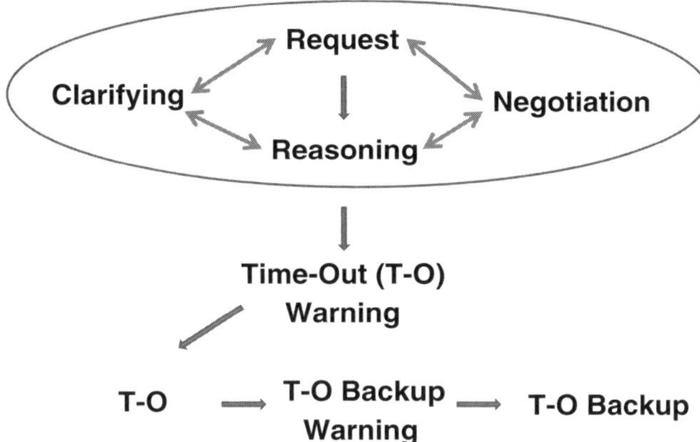

Figure 4.2. Example of a conditional sequence model for authoritative parenting.

nonphysical punishment when needed, thereby extending the conditional sequence of tactics to disciplinary reasoning (see Figure 4.2). Larzelere et al. (1998) found that the effectiveness of disciplinary reasoning alone for delaying the next misbehavior recurrence in 2- and 3-year-olds depended on how recently it had been enforced by nonphysical punishment (time out or privilege removal). The greatest reduction in oppositional and aggressive behavior during the next 20 months occurred when mothers reasoned frequently but enforced reasoning with nonphysical punishment at least 10% of the time. In contrast, the greatest increase in these disruptive behaviors occurred when mothers reasoned frequently but rarely enforced it with nonphysical punishment. The role of nonphysical punishment in enforcing disciplinary reasoning and thereby reducing subsequent disruptive behavior was shown in nine of 10 analyses (including three of the four with stronger causal evidence) compared with only four of 10 for physical punishment and one of 10 for forced compliance or distraction in enforcing reasoning. The advantage of nonphysical punishment may be that punishment emphasizes the child's responsibility for listening to verbal correction (in contrast to forced compliance or distraction) but does so with milder consequences than physical punishment (although mean child distress was identical for physical and nonphysical punishment; Larzelere, Silver, & Polite, 1997). Thus, Figure 4.2 shows one example of nonphysical punishment as the preferred enforcement for reasoning, with stronger tactics reserved for enforcing nonphysical punishment.

In sum, there is strong causal evidence for the conditional sequence of power-assertive tactics used in the consequence-focused perspective, which has been extended to incorporate disciplinary reasoning. The principles from this extended conditional sequence show a plausible way that authoritative parents use power-assertive tactics to support disciplinary reasoning.

Bell's model predicts that the ideal combination of reasoning and power assertion will favor reasoning more for easily managed children than for difficult children. In an important overview article, Grusec and Goodnow (1994) noted that the greater effectiveness of reasoning compared with power assertion held "for middle-class but not for lower-class families" and also varied by "age, sex, and temperament" (p. 6). The common denominator is that child outcomes of reasoning are better than those of power assertion primarily in samples with low rates of oppositional behavior. Consistent with this, Kochanska (1997; Kochanska et al., 2007) has shown repeatedly that observed power assertion is correlated with lower subsequent moral behavior for temperamentally fearful preschoolers but not for fearless preschoolers. This follows from Bell's model in that power-assertive tactics will be needed more often for children with difficult temperaments (compare the competent and oppositional children in Figure 4.1). Oppositional children need a balance of appropriate verbal corrections and power assertion, whereas power assertion is less necessary with easily managed children and may even hinder their moral internalization (Morris & Gibson, 2011). Accordingly, authoritative parents use minimally sufficient power for cooperation, whereas authoritarian parents use too much forcefulness, and permissive parents use too little (Baumrind et al., 2010, p. 185). Power assertion can be minimized more readily in Kochanska's fearful children for two reasons. First, milder verbal corrections are more likely to be effective without power assertion for fearful children than for fearless children. Second, parents can rely on background power assertion more quickly for fearful children than for fearless children. In either case, a combination of moderate power assertion and reasoning would be more effective for fearless children (Hoffman, 2000, p. 154). The role of moderate power assertion in defiant situations outside the laboratory would have been missed by correlational analyses of the mild power assertion observed in Kochanska's lab.

The other side of the continuum predicts that the greater effectiveness of power assertion over exclusively positive tactics will be most evident among clinically referred children. Patterson (1982) initially tried to help parents manage their disruptive children by emphasizing reinforcement of appropriate behaviors. By 1982, he concluded, "If I were allowed to select only one concept to use in training parents of antisocial children, I would teach them how to punish more effectively" (p. 111), referring to time out as his punishment of choice. This does not mean that positive parenting skills are unimportant with oppositional children: Showing enthusiasm about what the child is interested in was shown to be a common component of more effective behavior management interventions in a meta-analysis (Kaminski, Valle, Filene, & Boyle, 2008). The effectiveness of positive parenting actions such as reinforcement (Wahler, 1969) or reasoning (Larzelere et al., 1998) can also be enhanced by time out.

A Preventative Sequence

Bell's model also suggests the possibility of applying the conditional sequence in a preventative manner. Whereas power-assertive tactics can be used to enforce cooperation with verbal tactics, the conditional sequence model suggests that verbal tactics can also be used to reduce the need for power-assertive tactics. This was especially true of Baumrind's (1971) harmonious parents, 5% of her sample in which the parents "*had control* but did not *exercise control* . . . [but] they focused . . . upon developing principles for resolving differences and for right living" (p. 99, italics in original). Although authoritative parents were more likely to use negative sanctions when necessary to achieve a desirable conclusion to a discipline episode, they preferred using appropriate verbal disciplinary responses, which reduces the need for power-assertive tactics. Similarly, maternal cooperation with 6- to 9-year-olds' desires predicted child cooperation in a cleanup task, but only for non-resistant children (Davidov & Grusec, 2006). Mothers' accuracy in predicting children's evaluations of disciplinary responses predicted greater cooperation in initially resistant children. This contrast fits well with Bell's model in that the most crucial parenting skills vary by stage in the control system process.

AN AUTHORITATIVE-PARENTING SYNTHESIS FOR RESPONDING TO MISBEHAVIOR

In this chapter, we have used four sources to clarify the specific ways that authoritative parents respond to misbehavior in young children: informative studies by Baumrind, reasoning-focused research, consequence-focused research, and research combining reasoning with consequences. Whereas authoritative parents respond with reasoning but combine it with some power assertion when warranted, the two major areas of scientific parenting research often emphasize either reasoning or power assertion with little attention to an authoritative synthesis of the two. Clarifying the specific ways that authoritative parents respond to misbehavior requires combining the strengths of both perspectives.

Bell's control system model explains why the two perspectives emphasize distinct responses to misbehavior and how reasoning and power-assertive tactics can support each other in a complementary fashion consistent with authoritative parenting. Although it incorporates a sequence of power-assertive consequences such as the ones used in behavior management, it shows that parents can reduce the need for power assertion tactics by skillful use of the mild verbal disciplinary responses emphasized in the reasoning-focused perspective.

Baumrind's authoritative parents were skilled at using mild verbal tactics to keep from using power-assertive tactics whenever possible. They not only preferred reasoning over power assertion but also engaged children in give-and-take discussions about their misbehavior and about appropriate ways to cooperate. They showed more respect and negotiated more than other parents. They wanted their children to learn why they should cooperate in appropriate ways and not to merely force their cooperation, but they were willing to do so when warranted. Their communication is useful for clarifying the child's perspective, which has been associated with positive child outcomes (Grusec & Davidov, 2007; Grusec et al., 2000). Such clarification would help them fit their disciplinary responses to the situation, another characteristic of authoritative parenting (Smetana, 1995).

Authoritative parents also use power assertion more effectively than other parents, but the crucial distinctions have not been clarified as well. Bell's model accounts for the difficulty of finding any correlational research to support power assertion, although there are some exceptions consistent with authoritative parenting. For example, two studies overcame the bias against corrective actions and found that power-assertive tactics predicted self-regulation in rural Black 6- to 9-year-olds and competency in preschoolers but only when combined with parental nurturance (Brody & Flor, 1998; Towe-Goodman & Teti, 2008, respectively). The correlational bias against corrective actions explains why child outcomes are similar for nonphysical punishments, physical punishment, and professional interventions, raising doubts about differentiating effective from counterproductive power assertion on the basis of the tactic used. How and when disciplinary tactics are implemented seems to be a more important distinction between effective and counterproductive kinds of power assertion.

Baumrind et al. (2010) investigated power-assertive distinctions directly and found that verbal hostility, psychological control, severe physical punishment, and arbitrary discipline were the most harmful kinds of power assertion and represent four distinct ways that power assertion can be misused. Authoritative parents used confrontive discipline without resorting to those harmful kinds of power assertion. Based on its factor loadings, the confrontive discipline used by authoritative parents involved dealing directly with misbehavior and insisting on compliance in response to child coercion or defiance. Although authoritative parents preferred achieving those goals with appropriate verbal tactics, they were willing to apply negative sanctions unambivalently when warranted. Although Baumrind (1967) did not specify the negative sanctions used, her authoritative parents probably varied their sanctions to fit the situation. Consistent with the conditional sequence, they reduced their spanking frequency by the time children were 8 years old to a level slightly lower than most other parents, including those who had been permissive parents during the preschool years.

Authoritative parenting can probably be implemented without spanking in many cases. Baumrind's authoritative parents, however, all used spanking sometimes, indicating that authoritative parenting can be compatible with nonsevere spanking. As Morris et al. point out in Chapter 2 of this volume, more research is needed to distinguish overly harsh punishment from appropriate negative sanctions. They summarize an increasingly common viewpoint that even mild spanking harms children, but they note the causal ambiguity of the predominantly correlational evidence. To reduce the correlational bias against corrective disciplinary actions, Larzelere and Kuhn's (2005) meta-analysis included all studies that investigated physical punishment and alternative disciplinary responses using the same research methods on the same samples. Child outcomes were more adverse for physical punishment than for alternative tactics only when it was overly severe or the primary disciplinary method, as would be typical of authoritarian parenting. On the other hand, nonabusive spanking led to more compliance or less aggression in 2- to 6-year-old children than 10 of 13 alternative tactics when used for defiant responses to milder disciplinary tactics, such as time out or reasoning. This type of spanking is more compatible with authoritative parenting. Behavior management research indicates that authoritative parenting often requires a backup for time out as effective as the traditional two-swat spank, at least with young defiant children (Roberts & Powers, 1990).

Principles from the conditional sequence of tactics used in behavior management suggest ways to minimize the use of physical punishment in authoritative parenting. First, skillful use of the intermediate steps in the sequence enables authoritative parents to achieve a satisfactory conclusion while reducing their use of any last step enforcement. Examples in the consequence-focused sequence included a single warning and time out. Consistent use of that kind of sequence achieves cooperation with the minimum level of power assertion necessary to accomplish that goal. Second, multiple options at each step can help parents find the best alternative for each child in each situation. Behavior management has expanded its range of last step enforcement tactics that can be used to find the best option for each case even from options shown to be less effective on average such as the child-determined release from time out. The more options that parents have, the better they can vary disciplinary responses to fit the situation, a skill typical of authoritative parenting.

Future research can discriminate more precisely between more versus less effective disciplinary responses by overcoming correlational biases in longitudinal research and expanding the options investigated in consequence-focused research to include more verbal options. Regardless of the enforcement used for milder negative consequences, consistent use of the type of sequence used in behavior management enables parents to phase out power-assertive tactics, starting with the last step enforcement, followed by milder kinds of power assertion such as time out. Then background power assertion is sufficient for children to attend to and cooperate with optimal verbal disciplinary corrections. Overgeneralized prohibitions against power-assertive tactics can undermine parents' ability to get defiant children to cooperate with time out and reasoning, increasing the risk of escalations toward abuse and of an extreme type of permissive parenting that cannot set any limits on a child's behavior because of the child's coercion (Patterson & Fisher, 2002, p. 74).

The hallmark of authoritative parenting, however, is that power-assertive tactics are used to support parents' preference for using appropriate verbal disciplinary responses for misbehavior. Skillful use of a systematic sequence of disciplinary consequences can be extended to support the broader range of verbal disciplinary responses used by authoritative parents. It could be that authoritative parents use a clear signal to distinguish give-and-take verbal conflict resolutions from occasions when the parent is insisting on an acceptable conclusion to the misbehavior episode. The single warning could serve as this signal. Their ability to then use a version of the conditional sequence to obtain an acceptable conclusion when desired would enhance their confidence about getting appropriate cooperation when needed. As Bugental (2009) showed, such parental confidence reduces the extent to which parents resort to power-assertive tactics, which would free authoritative parents to explore a wider range of verbal resolutions that fit the situation. Background power assertion would cause the child to pay more attention to verbal resolution attempts by the parent, further enhancing the parent's effectiveness (Hoffman, 2000).

CONCLUSION

An authoritative parenting style that incorporates nurturance and demandingness has been shown to lead to optimal child development. The specific processes used by authoritative parents to respond to misbehavior are not sufficiently understood, however. In this chapter, we have integrated findings from both reasoning- and consequence-focused perspectives using Bell's control system model to help clarify how authoritative parents use power assertion when warranted to support their preference for verbal resolutions to discipline episodes. To further clarify how authoritative parents respond effectively to misbehavior, a healthy cross-fertilization of these two fields and improved methods for making finer discriminations and valid causal inferences are needed. This cross-fertilization should focus also on ways to encourage appropriate behavior and prevent misbehavior in addition to this chapter's focus on responding to misbehavior. Bell's model suggests that parental influences can be accurately understood only when accounting fully for child effects in an ongoing control system of bidirectional influences. The substantive and methodological strengths of both perspectives are needed to clarify how authoritative parenting skillfully matches the most appropriate kinds of verbal correction and power assertion to each disciplinary situation.

REFERENCES

Baumrind, D. (1967). Child care practices anteceding three patterns of preschool behavior. *Genetic Psychology Monographs, 75,* 43–88.

Baumrind, D. (1971). Harmonious parents and their preschool children. *Developmental Psychology, 4,* 99–102. doi:10.1037/h0030373

Baumrind, D., Larzelere, R. E., & Owens, E. B. (2010). Effects of preschool parents' power assertive patterns and practices on adolescent development. *Parenting: Science and Practice, 10,* 157–201. doi:10.1080/15295190903290790

Bean, A. W., & Roberts, M. W. (1981). The effect of time-out release contingencies on changes in child noncompliance. *Journal of Abnormal Child Psychology, 9,* 95–105. doi:10.1007/BF00917860

Bell, R. Q. (1968). A reinterpretation of the direction of effects in studies of socialization. *Psychological Review, 75,* 81–95. doi:10.1037/h0025583

Bell, R. Q., & Chapman, M. (1986). Child effects in studies using experimental or brief longitudinal approaches to socialization. *Developmental Psychology, 22,* 595–603. doi:10.1037/0012-1649.22.5.595

Bell, R. Q., & Harper, L. V. (1977). *Child effects on adults.* Hillsdale, NJ: Erlbaum.

Brody, G. H., & Flor, D. L. (1998). Maternal resources, parenting practices, and child competence in rural, single-parent African American families. *Child Development, 69,* 803–816. doi:10.2307/1132205

Brunk, M. A., & Henggeler, S. W. (1984). Child influences on adult controls: An experimental investigation. *Developmental Psychology, 20,* 1074–1081. doi:10.1037/0012-1649.20.6.1074

Bugental, D. (2009). Predicting and preventing child maltreatment: A biocognitive transactional approach. In A. Sameroff (Ed.), *The transactional model of development: How children and contexts shape each other* (pp. 97–115). Washington, DC: American Psychological Association. doi:10.1037/11877-006

Burt, S. A. (2009). Rethinking environmental contributions to child and adolescent psychopathology: A meta-analysis of shared environmental influences. *Psychological Bulletin, 135,* 608–637. doi:10.1037/a0015702

Chapman, M., & Zahn-Waxler, C. (1982). Young children's compliance and noncompliance to parental discipline in a natural setting. *International Journal of Behavioral Development, 5,* 81–94.

Cheyne, J. A. (1972). Punishment and "reasoning" in the development of self-control. In R. E. Parke (Ed.), *Recent trends in social learning theory* (pp. 77–91). New York, NY: Academic Press.

Cheyne, J. A., & Walters, R. H. (1969). Intensity of punishment, timing of punishment, and cognitive structure as determinants of response inhibition. *Journal of Experimental Child Psychology, 7,* 231–244.

Crockenberg, S., & Litman, C. (1990). Autonomy as competence in two-year-olds: Maternal correlates of child defiance, compliance, and self-assertion. *Developmental Psychology, 26,* 961–971. doi:10.1037/0012-1649.26.6.961

Davidov, M., & Grusec, J. E. (2006). Multiple pathways to compliance: Mothers' willingness to cooperate and knowledge of their children's reactions to discipline. *Journal of Family Psychology, 20,* 705–708. doi:10.1037/0893-3200.20.4.705

Davies, G. R., McMahon, R. J., Flessati, E. W., & Tiedemann, G. L. (1984). Verbal rationales and modeling as adjuncts to a parenting technique for child compliance. *Child Development, 55,* 1290–1298. doi:10.2307/1129998

de Leeuw, R. N. H., Scholte, R. H. J., Sargent, J. D., Vermulst, A. A., & Engels, R. C. M. E. (2010). Do interactions between personality and social-environmental factors explain smoking development in adolescence? *Journal of Family Psychology, 24,* 68–77. doi:10.1037/a0018182

Deptula, D. P., Henry, D. B., & Schoeny, M. E. (2010). How can parents make a difference? Longitudinal associations with adolescent sexual behavior. *Journal of Family Psychology, 24,* 731–739. doi:10.1037/a0021760

Eyberg, S. M., Nelson, M. M., & Boggs, S. R. (2008). Evidence-based psychosocial treatments for children and adolescents with disruptive behavior. *Journal of Clinical Child and Adolescent Psychology, 37,* 215–237. doi:10.1080/15374410701820117

Forgatch, M. S., & Patterson, G. R. (2010). Parent Management Training—Oregon Model: An intervention for antisocial behavior in children and adolescents. In J. R. Weisz & A. E. Kazdin (Eds.), *Evidence-based psychotherapies for children and adolescents* (2nd ed., pp. 159–177). New York, NY: Guilford Press.

Gershoff, E. T., Aber, J. L., & Clements, M. (2009). Parent learning support and child reading ability: A cross-lagged panel analysis for developmental transactions. In A. Sameroff (Ed.), *The transactional model of development: How children and contexts shape each other* (pp. 203–220). Washington, DC: American Psychological Association. doi:10.1037/11877-011

Gershoff, E. T., Grogan-Kaylor, A., Lansford, J. E., Chang, L., Zelli, A., Deater-Deckard, K., & Dodge, K. A. (2010). Parent discipline practices in an international sample: Associations with child behaviors and moderation by perceived normativeness. *Child Development, 81,* 487–502. doi:10.1111/j.1467-8624.2009.01409.x

Grolnick, W. S. (2003). *The psychology of parental control: How well-meaning parenting backfires.* Mahwah, NJ: Erlbaum.

Grusec, J. E. (1997). A history of research on parenting strategies and children's internalization of values. In J. E. Grusec & L. Kuczynski (Eds.), *Parenting and children's internalization of values* (pp. 3–22). New York, NY: Wiley.

Grusec, J. E., & Davidov, M. (2007). Socialization in the family: The role of parents. In J. E. Grusec & P. D. Hastings (Eds.), *Handbook of socialization: Theory and research* (pp. 284–308). New York, NY: Guilford Press.

Grusec, J. E., & Goodnow, J. J. (1994). Impact of parental discipline methods on the child's internalization of values: A reconceptualization of current points of view. *Developmental Psychology, 30,* 4–19. doi:10.1037/0012-1649.30.1.4

Grusec, J. E., Goodnow, J. J., & Kuczynski, L. (2000). New directions in analyses of parenting contributions to children's acquisition of values. *Child Development, 71,* 205–211. doi:10.1111/1467-8624.00135

Hembree-Kigin, T. L., & McNeil, C. B. (1995). *Parent–child interaction therapy.* New York, NY: Plenum Press.

Hill, N. E., & Tyson, D. F. (2009). Parental involvement in middle school: A meta-analytic assessment of the strategies that promote achievement. *Developmental Psychology, 45,* 740–763. doi:10.1037/a0015362

Hoffman, M. L. (2000). *Empathy and moral development.* Cambridge, England: Cambridge University Press.

Holden, G. W. (1997). *Parents and the dynamics of child rearing.* Boulder, CO: Westview Press.

Hughes, D., Rodriguez, J., Smith, E. P., Johnson, D. J., Stevenson, H. C., & Spicer, P. (2006). Parents' ethnic-racial socialization practices: A review of research and directions for future study. *Developmental Psychology, 42,* 747–770. doi:10.1037/0012-1649.42.5.747

Kaminski, J. W., Valle, L. A., Filene, J. H., & Boyle, C. L. (2008). A meta-analytic review of components associated with parent training program effectiveness. *Journal of Abnormal Child Psychology, 36,* 567–589. doi:10.1007/s10802-007-9201-9

Kochanska, G. (1997). Multiple pathways to conscience for children with different temperaments: From toddlerhood to age 5. *Developmental Psychology, 33,* 228–240. doi:10.1037/0012-1649.33.2.228

Kochanska, G., Aksan, N., & Joy, M. E. (2007). Children's fearfulness as a moderator of parenting in early socialization: Two longitudinal studies. *Developmental Psychology, 43,* 222–237. doi:10.1037/0012-1649.43.1.222

Kuczynski, L. (1982). Intensity and orientation of reasoning: Motivational determinants of children's compliance to verbal rationales. *Journal of Experimental Child Psychology, 34,* 357–370. doi:10.1016/0022-0965(82)90066-2

Kuczynski, L. (2003). Beyond bidirectionality: Bilateral conceptual frameworks for understanding dynamics in parent–child relations. In L. Kuczynski (Ed.), *Handbook of dynamics in parent–child relations* (pp. 3–24). Thousand Oaks, CA: Sage.

Larzelere, R. E., Cox, R. B., Jr., & Smith, G. L. (2010). Do nonphysical punishments reduce antisocial behavior more than spanking? A comparison using the strongest previous causal evidence against spanking. *BMC Pediatrics, 10*(10). doi:10.1186/1471-2431-10-10

Larzelere, R.E., Ferrer, E., Kuhn, B.R., & Danelia, K. (2010). Differences in causal estimates from longitudinal analyses of residualized versus simple gain scores: Contrasting controls for selection and regression artifacts. *International Journal of Behavioral Development, 34*, 180–189. doi:10.1177/0165025409351386

Larzelere, R.E., & Kuhn, B.R. (2005). Comparing child outcomes of physical punishment and alternative disciplinary tactics: A meta-analysis. *Clinical Child and Family Psychology Review, 8*, 1–37. doi:10.1007/s10567-005-2340-z

Larzelere, R.E., Kuhn, B.R., & Johnson, B. (2004). The intervention selection bias: An underrecognized confound in intervention research. *Psychological Bulletin, 130*, 289–303. doi:10.1037/0033-2909.130.2.289

Larzelere, R.E., & Merenda, J.A. (1994). The effectiveness of parental discipline for toddler misbehavior at different levels of child distress. *Family Relations, 43*, 480–488. doi:10.2307/585381

Larzelere, R.E., Sather, P.R., Schneider, W.N., Larson, D.B., & Pike, P.L. (1998). Punishment enhances reasoning's effectiveness as a disciplinary response to toddlers. *Journal of Marriage and the Family, 60*, 388–403. doi:10.2307/353856

Larzelere, R.E., Schneider, W.N., Larson, D.B., & Pike, P.L. (1996). The effects of discipline responses in delaying toddler misbehavior recurrences. *Child & Family Behavior Therapy, 18*(3), 35–57. doi:10.1300/J019v18n03_03

Larzelere, R.E., Silver, C., & Polite, K. (1997). Nonabusive spanking: Parental liberty or child abuse? *Children's Legal Rights Journal, 17*(4), 7–17.

McNeil, C.B., & Hembree-Kigin, T.L. (2010). *Parent–child interaction therapy* (2nd ed.). New York, NY: Springer.

Morris, S.Z., & Gibson, C.L. (2011). Corporal punishment's influence on children's aggressive and delinquent behavior. *Criminal Justice and Behavior, 38*, 818–839. doi:10.1177/0093854811406070

Parke, R.D. (1969). Effectiveness of punishment as an interaction of intensity, timing, agent nurturance, and cognitive structuring. *Child Development, 40*, 213–235. doi:10.2307/1127169

Parke, R.D., & Buriel, R. (2006). Socialization in the family: Ethnic and ecological perspectives. In W. Damon, R.M. Lerner (Series Eds.), & N. Eisenberg (Vol. Ed.), *Handbook of child psychology. Vol. 3: Social, emotional, and personality development* (6th ed., pp. 429–504). Hoboken, NJ: Wiley.

Patterson, G.R. (1982). *Coercive family process*. Eugene, OR: Castalia Press.

Patterson, G.R., & Fisher, P.A. (2002). Recent developments in our understanding of parenting: Bidirectional effects, causal models, and the search for parsimony. In M.H. Bornstein (Ed.), *Handbook of parenting: Vol. 5. Practical issues in parenting* (2nd ed., pp. 59–88). Mahwah, NJ: Erlbaum.

Pelham, W.E., Jr., & Fabiano, G.A. (2008). Evidence-based psychosocial treatments for attention-deficit/hyperactivity disorder. *Journal of Clinical Child and Adolescent Psychology, 37*, 184–214. doi:10.1080/15374410701818681

Quintana, S.M., Aboud, F.E., Chao, R.K., Contreras-Grau, J., Cross, W.E., Jr., Hudley, C., . . . Vietze, D.L. (2006). Race, ethnicity, and culture in child development: Contemporary research and future. *Child Development, 77*, 1129–1141. doi:10.1111/j.1467-8624.2006.00951.x

Ritchie, K. L. (1999). Maternal behaviors and cognitions during discipline episodes: A comparison of power bouts and single acts of noncompliance. *Developmental Psychology, 35*, 580–589. doi:10.1037/0012-1649.35.2.580

Roberts, M. W. (1982). The effects of warned versus unwarned time-out procedures on child noncompliance. *Child & Family Behavior Therapy, 4*, 37–53. doi:10.1300/J019v04n01_04

Roberts, M. W., & Powers, S. W. (1988). The compliance test. *Behavioral Assessment, 10*, 375–398.

Roberts, M. W., & Powers, S. W. (1990). Adjusting chair timeout enforcement procedures for oppositional children. *Behavior Therapy, 21*, 257–271. doi:10.1016/S0005-7894(05)80329-6

Shaffer, D. R., & Kipp, K. (2007). *Developmental psychology: Childhood & adolescence* (7th ed.). Belmont, CA: Thomson Advantage Books.

Smetana, J. G. (1995). Parenting styles and conceptions of parental authority during adolescence. *Child Development, 66*, 299–316. doi:10.2307/1131579

Steinberg, L. (2004). *The 10 basic principles of good parenting.* New York, NY: Simon & Schuster.

Steinberg, L., Lamborn, S. D., Darling, N., Mounts, N. S., & Dornbusch, S. M. (1994). Over-time changes in adjustment and competence among adolescents from authoritative, authoritarian, indulgent, and neglectful families. *Child Development, 65*, 754–770. doi:10.2307/1131416

Steiner, P. M., Cook, T. D., Shadish, W. R., & Clark, M. H. (2010). The importance of covariate selection in controlling for selection bias in observational studies. *Psychological Methods, 15*, 250–267. doi:10.1037/a0018719

Timmermans, M., van Lier, P. A. C., & Koot, H. M. (2009). Pathways of behavior problems from childhood to late adolescence leading to delinquency and underachievement. *Journal of Clinical Child and Adolescent Psychology, 38*, 630–638. doi:10.1080/15374410903103502

Towe-Goodman, N. R., & Teti, D. M. (2008). Power assertive discipline, maternal emotional involvement, and child adjustment. *Journal of Family Psychology, 22*, 648–651. doi:10.1037/a0012661

Van Houten, R. (1983). Punishment: From the animal laboratory to the applied setting. In S. Axelrod & J. Apsche (Eds.), *The effects of punishment on human behavior* (pp. 13–44). New York, NY: Academic Press.

Wahler, R. G. (1969). Oppositional children: A quest for parental reinforcement control. *Journal of Applied Behavior Analysis, 2*, 159–170. doi:10.1901/jaba.1969.2-159

Zahn-Waxler, C., Radke-Yarrow, M., & King, R. (1979). Child rearing and children's prosocial initiations toward victims of distress. *Child Development, 50*, 319–330. doi:10.2307/1129406

5

ARE THE EFFECTS OF BAUMRIND'S PARENTING STYLES CULTURALLY SPECIFIC OR CULTURALLY EQUIVALENT?

NADIA SORKHABI AND JELANI MANDARA

Baumrind's authoritative model has had a profound impact on the direction of parenting research. Research has found that European American children with authoritative parents are more competent, better adjusted emotionally, higher achieving, and less likely to use illicit drugs or engage in other risky behaviors compared with those with nonauthoritative parents (Baumrind, 1991b; Weiss & Schwarz, 1996). However, whether the typology accurately describes non–European American styles of parenting is not clear. Baumrind's primary sample was almost exclusively high-functioning two-parent middle-class European American families, which leaves open the possibility that the authoritative model is applicable only to such families. Furthermore, the earliest studies of parenting styles that included diverse samples found inconsistent results for non–European Americans (e.g., Baumrind, 1972; Dornbusch, Ritter, Leiderman, Roberts, & Fraleigh, 1987). This led some researchers to argue that the effects of parenting depend on

DOI: 10.1037/13948-006
Authoritative Parenting: Synthesizing Nurturance and Discipline for Optimal Child Development, Robert E. Larzelere, Amanda Sheffield Morris, and Amanda W. Harrist (Editors)

the cultural and social contexts in which it occurs (Chao, 2001; Mandara &
Murray, 2002). Other researchers however, maintained that the authoritative
model is essentially a universally optimal style of parenting that is applicable
across cultural and social contexts (Lamborn & Felbab, 2003). The purpose
of this chapter is to review the research and theories on the cultural differences in the nature and effects of parenting styles in order to draw empirically
supported conclusions about the applicability of the authoritative model for
non–European American youths.

CULTURAL DIFFERENCES IN EARLY PARENTING STYLES RESEARCH

In an early study, Baumrind (1972) found that African American parents were higher on firm enforcement and did not encourage individuality in
their preschool-age girls to the same degree as European American parents.
They also expected their girls to be more mature. In fact, about 50% of the
African American parents and only 13% of the European American parents
were classified as authoritarian. The main finding was that these authoritarian practices affected the groups differently. In spite of their relatively authoritarian parents, the African American girls were rated as more assertive and
independent than the European American girls. Baumrind (1972) argued
that the girls may have perceived their parents as nurturing, not rejecting,
and sufficiently identified with their strong mothers to emulate them.

Dornbusch et al. (1987) were the first to test the applicability of Baumrind's
parenting styles model in a large culturally diverse sample of youths. They
used self-report surveys and found that European Americans were lower on
the authoritarian and higher on the authoritative measures than Asian,
Latino, or African Americans. They also found that their measures of parenting were differentially related to each group's self-reported grade-point average (GPA). In general, for all the ethnic groups, the higher adolescents rated
their parents on authoritarian parenting, the lower their GPA. However, the
size of the authoritarian effect on self-reported GPA was largest for European
Americans and smallest for African Americans. They also found that the
authoritative measure was not significantly related to GPA for any group but
European Americans.

Building on these findings, Steinberg, Mounts, Lamborn, and Dornbusch
(1991) specifically tested the possibility that the authoritative model may not be
effective for youths in different social contexts. They assessed 10,000 ethnically
and economically diverse high school students from California and Wisconsin
on self-report measures of parental warmth, monitoring, and psychological
autonomy. They then classified the parents as authoritative if they scored

above the sample median on all three parenting measures. The remaining parents were considered nonauthoritative. They divided the sample according to ethnicity (Asian, African, Latino, and European Americans), whether the family was working class or middle class, and whether the adolescents lived in single- or two-parent homes. The researchers compared adolescents with authoritative and nonauthoritative parents within each of the 16 groups on indicators of adolescent adjustment. As with the Dornbusch et al. (1987) study, two-parent middle-class European American families were most likely to be authoritative, whereas working class African, Hispanic, and especially Asian American parents were least likely.

When Dornbusch et al. (1991) assessed the effects of authoritative parenting on the outcomes, they found that children with authoritative parents tended to have higher GPAs, were more self-reliant, and were lower in psychological distress and delinquency than those with nonauthoritative parents. Although the effect sizes varied across the 16 ecological niches, the pattern was generally the same for each subgroup. The main differences were that authoritativeness did not predict any outcomes for two-parent working-class African Americans and failed to predict GPA differences for single-parent working-class Asian Americans. However, the reliability of those specific findings is questionable because there were only 11 authoritative African American and four authoritative Asian American parents available for those comparisons. Thus, the authors concluded from their most reliable findings that adolescents with authoritative parents were overall better adjusted, regardless of their ethnic group.

In a follow-up study (Lamborn, Mounts, Steinberg, & Dornbusch, 1991), the same team examined the effects of parenting styles in more detail. Instead of simply comparing authoritative versus nonauthoritative, they classified the parents from the Steinberg et al. (1991) study into one of the four parenting style categories (authoritarian, authoritative, indulgent, and neglectful). To do so, they assessed each adolescent on the degree to which their parents were accepting/involved and strict/supervisory. They then classified parents into one of the four categories on the basis of their scoring in the upper or lower tertile of the acceptance or strictness measures, which left slightly more than 4,000 adolescents for the study. Adolescents with authoritative parents were found to be most adjusted across measures of school competence, psychosocial development, and problem behaviors. Furthermore, the effects of parenting style did not differ statistically by ethnic group, parental education, or adolescent gender.

The researchers assessed the youths 1 year later with the same instruments and classification methods (Steinberg, Lamborn, Darling, Mounts, & Dornbusch, 1994). After attrition and application of their classification method, the sample comprised 2,300 adolescents. They found that the advantages of the adolescents with authoritative parents either maintained or increased over the year. The authors concluded again that the authoritative model is the optimal form of parenting for most measures of adolescent outcomes.

One of the major findings in the prior studies was the interesting difference that Asian American youths were much less likely to have authoritative parents than European American youths, even though the Asian American adolescents' academic achievement was equal to or higher than all other groups. The effects of parenting style on academic achievement were less robust for African American adolescents overall. To better understand this difference, the research team assessed the degree to which peer networks influence the parenting style effects (reviewed in Steinberg, Dornbusch, & Brown, 1992). They found that the relative influence of parenting styles was much stronger for European American adolescents than for other youths, and peers had a greater influence on achievement for Asian American and African American adolescents. They further concluded that the high peer support for achievement helps Asian American youths overcome high levels of authoritarianism among their parents. For African American youths, the negative effects of low peer support for achievement seemed to counteract the potentially positive effects of authoritative parenting. Thus, the researchers concluded their work with these data sets by arguing that when it comes to behavior and mental health outcomes, authoritative parenting is optimal for all youths, but when it comes to academic achievement, the effects of parenting styles seem to depend on the social context in which youths must navigate.

CULTURAL SPECIFICITY PERSPECTIVE

The cultural specificity perspective in socialization was first introduced by Baumrind (1972; also see Baumrind et al., 2010), who argued that the parenting styles she identified with her sample of European American families cannot be extended to explain the parenting styles and associated outcomes of other ethnic groups. Baumrind (1972) reported exploratory data with a small sample of African American families to further illustrate the potential differences that might exist in parenting patterns and associated outcomes in different ethnic groups. Thus, an objective of the cultural specificity perspective was to understand different cultural groups on their own terms, which is an important part of countering the potential ethnocentric assumption that the norms and standards observed among middle-class European American families represent the ideal for other ethnic and social groups (Chao, 1994, 2001). The following four interrelated propositions define the cultural specificity perspective: (a) The values and socialization goals of parents in individualist and collectivist cultures differ, and therefore parents in different cultures engage in qualitatively different parenting; (b) the same parenting style (i.e., authoritarian parenting) has different effects on youths in different cultures; (c) children and adolescents in different cultures interpret the same parenting style in different ways; and (d) the emotional and cognitive characteristics of authoritarian parents differ in collectivist and individualist cultures.

Values and Socialization Goals of Parents Differ

The most influential framework for understanding cultural differences in parenting styles is based on the notion that there are cultural differences in child-rearing values and goals (Rudy & Grusec, 2006). In the broadest sense, the distinction has been made between *collectivist* and *individualist* groups. Collectivists are said to value obedience, deference to authority, and duty or obligation to the group (Markus, 2008). Individualists are said to value independence, self-expression, and self-interest. Researchers have largely classified those of African, Asian, and Latin descent as more collectivist in orientation and those of European descent as more individualist in orientation (Triandis, 1995).

Several researchers have argued that variations in parenting styles and practices are due to variations in value systems. Chao (1994, 2001) has been a prominent proponent of this view, proposing that considering parents of Asian descent as authoritarian or restrictive is misleading. She argued that European American cultural philosophy cannot be used to understand parenting and child outcomes for children and adolescents of Asian descent. Chao (1994) proposed that Asian parenting grows out of the Confucian philosophy of role relationships. In particular, she argued that to understand Asian parenting, one must understand the concept of *training*, defined as *chiao shun* (i.e., parental investment and involvement) and *guan* (i.e., organizational control). Chao (1994) indicated that chiao shun and guan are qualitatively different from notions of control and responsiveness common in the West. For instance, she argued that unlike European American parents, most Asian parents do not explicitly display affection by hugging and kissing their children. Rather, they show their responsiveness implicitly by engaging in self-sacrifice. Chao also indicated that Asian parents apply organizational control, emphasize family honor, and demand hard work, self-discipline, and achievement. Thus, she argued that training explains Asian American students' academic performance in a way that the authoritative model does not.

To test this idea, Chao (1994) compared 50 highly educated and English-speaking Chinese immigrant mothers with 50 equally educated European American mothers on standard measures of responsiveness and control as well as on the concepts of guan and chiao shun. The Chinese mothers were significantly higher on measures of authoritarian parenting that focused on unilateral control, supervision, and control by anxiety. As she predicted, the Chinese mothers were much higher on traditional Asian beliefs about child rearing. An interesting aspect of this finding is that these differences remained after she controlled for the mothers' scores on traditional measures of authoritarian parenting. Thus, she concluded that guan and chiao shun are qualitatively distinct from the responsiveness and demandingness dimensions used to describe parenting in individualist cultures.

In a follow-up study with a sample of 95 immigrant Chinese mothers and 52 European American mothers with the same demographics as in her first study, Chao (2000) assessed mothers on measures of parenting style, socialization goals, chiao shun, and school involvement. She essentially confirmed the results of her prior study and found that Chinese mothers were more likely to endorse authoritarian and training styles. She also found that European American mothers were more likely to focus on developing high self-esteem and self-expression in their children, whereas the Chinese mothers were more likely to focus on filial piety, family honor, and achievement.

Comparisons between Latino and European American parents have also found that Latino parents are more likely to value politeness and obedience (Smith & Krohn, 1995) and to focus on loyalty to family and respect for elders' authority (Valdes, 1996). Latino mothers also use more frequent discipline and physical guidance than European American mothers (Carlson & Harwood, 2003; Ispa et al., 2004). Some researchers have also suggested that achievement is less significant in Hispanic families than the quality of family and extended kin relationships (Forehand & Kotchick, 1996; Garcia Coll & Vasquez Garcia, 1995). However, it is important to note that Hispanic cultures are diverse, and variables such as country of origin, socioeconomic status, and parental education affect the emphasis that different Hispanic parents place on education relative to family and extended kin relationships (Garcia Coll & Pachter, 2002).

Similarly, Mandara and Murray (2002) argued that the different cultural values and social contexts in which African American parents live compared with European American parents have led to qualitatively different norms and standards for optimal parenting. They argued that one of the main differences is that most parents of color feel the need to preserve their cultural heritage and actively instill a sense of cultural pride in their children. To test this idea, Mandara and Murray assessed a sample of African American adolescents and their parents on a variety of parenting and family functioning variables. They then used various cluster-analytic and cross-validation procedures and uncovered three types of African American parents. Although the groups were similar to Baumrind's authoritative, authoritarian, and neglectful styles, they were also qualitatively different. The most unique group was called *cohesive-authoritative* because members displayed traditional authoritative parenting similar to Baumrind's notion and good quality family functioning. They were high in warmth, cohesion, achievement orientation, and autonomy granting. They were much higher on measures of behavioral control and structure than authoritative parents but similar to the directive parents Baumrind (1971) identified. They were quite different from European American parents in their focus on instilling in their children a sense of cultural pride and a belief that they could overcome obstacles through self-reliance.

The Same Parenting Style Has Different Effects in Different Cultures

A second point from the cultural specificity perspective is that the prevalence of a practice in a cultural group reflects its adaptive value in that specific ecological niche. Proponents of this hypothesis argue that because culture is defined as an adaptive system of rules and practices that are shared by a collective (Le Vine, 2009; Matsumoto & Juang, 2003), the prevalence of specific parenting practices or styles implies that it has become prevalent because of its value or functionality. Therefore, the implicit assumption is that authoritarian parenting style and practices will have more positive effects among those from collectivist than individualist cultures.

Several studies have directly or indirectly tested this hypothesis. In one of the more cited examples, Chao (2001) classified over 500 Chinese and European American parents of adolescents into either authoritative or authoritarian styles using the same measure and median split method from the earlier Steinberg et al. (1991) study. She further divided the Chinese Americans into first or second generation. The results showed that both groups of Chinese adolescents had higher GPAs and exhibited more school effort than the European American adolescents. Both Chinese groups were also more likely to have authoritarian parents but not less likely to have authoritative parents than the European American students. Most important, she found that the European American youths with authoritative parents had higher grades and school effort than their counterparts with authoritarian parents. There were no differences for first-generation Chinese American students from authoritative or authoritarian homes. The second-generation students were slightly higher in school effort when they had authoritative parents. She concluded that the authoritative versus authoritarian dichotomy may not have as much relevance for people from different cultures. However, as the Chinese American adolescents became more integrated into American society (as measured by generational status), the effects of authoritative parenting became similar to the effects for European Americans. Unlike in her previous study (Chao, 1994), authoritarian parenting included below-average involvement/acceptance, but authoritarian parenting was correlated with lower parent–child closeness only in European Americans, not in Chinese Americans (Chao, 2001, p. 1838).

A few studies have also found that controlling parental behavior may operate differently in Latino and European American families. A study with preadolescent European and Hispanic American children found that controlling and hierarchical parenting predicted more externalizing behaviors among the European American children only (Lindahl & Malik, 1999). Ispa et al. (2004) studied cultural differences in the effects of maternal intrusiveness during young children's free play. They observed over 1,200 lower socioeconomic status infants interacting with their mothers at 15 months and again at 25 months. They found that European American mothers were less intrusive and warmer than African or Mexican American mothers. European American infants were also rated as having less negativity but similar task engagement at 15 months. They also found that maternal intrusiveness at 15 months was negatively related to child engagement and dyadic mutuality at 25 months for European American mothers only. Ispa et al. argued that intrusiveness likely has a different cultural meaning for African Americans and members of collectivist cultures than for individualistic cultures.

Undoubtedly, much of the evidence used to support the cultural specificity model has been based on findings suggesting that behavioral control, harsh discipline, and even physical punishment have differential effects for European American and African American youths. The main argument, proposed by several researchers (Baumrind, 1972; Mason, Cauce, Gonzales, & Hiraga, 1996; Ogbu, 1981) is that because many African American youths are reared in dangerous urban environments, they require higher levels of behavioral control and strictness to keep them from being victimized or engaging in risky activities. However, to fully assess the benefits of harsh discipline and "strict" parenting for different ethnic and socioeconomic groups, further research is needed to compare outcomes for African American children living in safe environments and European American children living in dangerous environments.

The evidence for cultural differences on the effect of parental control and supervision on youth delinquency is equivocal. For instance, Cernkovich and Giordano (1987) assessed 824 adolescents on various measures of parenting and delinquency involvement and found that although parental control and supervision was an important predictor of less delinquency for both White and non-White youths (who were primarily Black), instrumental communication (i.e., whether parents discuss adolescents' future plans or problems at school with friends and teachers) was the best predictor of lower delinquency for White youths, whereas control and supervision was the best predictor of lower delinquency for non-Whites.

Another group of researchers assessed the unique and longitudinal effects of supportive parenting and harsh discipline on various outcomes (Pettit, Bates, & Dodge, 1997) for 585 children and their parents with a battery of instruments before the start of kindergarten and once every year thereafter through the sixth grade. After they controlled for kindergarten adjustment measures, they found that harsh discipline was associated with poorer sixth-grade academic performance for European American youths

($r = -.24$), but the association was in the opposite direction, although nonsignificant for African American youths ($r = .11$).

Probably the most controversial topic in parenting research is the use and value of physical discipline as a form of punishment. Those rightly concerned with child abuse and infringements on the human rights of children argue that physical discipline is not only detrimental but also a form of child abuse (Straus, 2000). There are also some major researchers who argue that ordinary nonabusive spanking can be effective at preventing unwanted behaviors when used in a consistent and rational manner (Baumrind et al., 2002). Most studies with European American youths tended to support the antispanking perspective because physical discipline was associated with higher rates of aggressive behavior at home and school (Straus, 2000). The definition of harsh and corporal punishment varied, but it usually allowed overly severe physical punishment to be grouped with what most would consider ordinary spankings for misbehavior (Baumrind et al., 2002). Therefore, most of these studies did not assess the effects of ordinary nonabusive spanking.

Studies that also examined the effects among African Americans have often found results counter to those with European American youths. An early study by Deater-Deckard, Dodge, Bates, and Petit (1996) followed an economically diverse sample of African American and European American children from kindergarten to the third grade. As in the prior studies, physical discipline was positively associated with peer and teacher ratings of peer aggression, teacher–child conflict, and other disruptive behavior for the European American students. However, no significant association was found for the African American students. In a similar longitudinal study with a sample of 4- to 11-year-old African and European American children, spanking was associated with fewer fights at school and lowered general aggression for African American children (Gunnoe & Mariner, 1997). Likewise, McLoyd and Smith (2002) found that African American children who received high levels of maternal emotional support had fewer behavior problems across 6 years of assessments, whether or not they were spanked. Others have found similar results (Polaha, Larzelere, Shapiro, & Pettit, 2004). The researchers of each study concluded that like parenting styles in general, physical discipline may have a different meaning in African American families because of the prevalence of spanking in their communities.

In what is likely the largest study on the topic, Simons et al. (2002) used a sample of 841 families of 10- to 12-year-old African Americans to directly test the hypothesis that the effects of behavioral control and spanking depend on community characteristics. Behavioral control (e.g., monitoring, reasoning) was associated with fewer conduct problems in most neighborhoods but especially in those with higher deviancy rates. Conduct problems included shoplifting, fighting, lying, setting fires, and burglary. Spanking was associated with more conduct problems only in neighborhoods where it was used rarely. The authors concluded that widespread acceptance of spanking in African American communities explains its differential effects on their children relative to European American children.

Children's Interpretations of the Same Parenting Style Differ in Different Cultures

A third point from the cultural specificity perspective is that children in individualist and collectivist cultures interpret authoritarian parenting differently. Several researchers (Chao, 1994; Fung, 1999; McLoyd & Smith, 2002) have argued that children in collectivist cultures do not interpret authoritarian parenting as a sign of hostility and dominance, as do most children in individualistic cultures. In fact, such behaviors, especially when accompanied by beliefs of parental sacrifice or warmth, are more likely to be interpreted as a sign of parental care, concern, and involvement (Chao, 1994, 2001; McLoyd & Smith, 2002).

Only a few studies have directly tested this hypothesis. In probably the most cited study on the issue thus far, Mason et al. (2004) sampled 288 predominately urban high school students. The students rated four prototypical parental control items with 15 questions that asked them how they felt when their primary caregiver acts in this manner. Students also rated the actual levels of parental warmth and control they received. A factor analysis of each set of the 15 affective response items uncovered three factors for each. The authors found that after controlling for perceptions of actual warmth and parental control, African Americans were more likely than others to report that controlling through guilt ("Says if I really cared for her, I would not do things that cause her to worry") and general control ("Insists that I must do exactly as I'm told") were signs of love and concern. They were also less likely to say they were hurt or angered by such parental behaviors. However, no ethnic differences were found for students' affective responses to the enforcement item ("Is very strict with me"), which they viewed positively, not as feeling controlled and manipulated, or the intrusiveness item ("Wants to know exactly where I am and what I am doing"), which they viewed negatively as feeling controlled and manipulated.

Emotional and Cognitive Characteristics of Authoritarian Parents Differ by Culture

Rudy and Grusec (2006) proposed that in individualist cultures, parents who hold collectivist values and practice authoritarian parenting are functioning in a way that is not considered appropriate or normative within their culture. Therefore, authoritarian parenting in individualist, but not in collectivist, cultures is likely to represent negative parent characteristics. Some evidence supports Rudy and Grusec's (2006) proposition for those from individualist cultures. Carlson and Harwood (2003) found that parental control of infants was related to secure attachment among a small sample of Puerto Rican mothers but to avoidant attachment among European American mothers. Rudy and Grusec (2006) compared Anglo Canadians with Canadians of Egyptian, Pakistani, Indian, and Iranian origin. Consistent with their hypothesis, a significant negative association was found between authoritarian parenting and warmth for Anglo Canadians, but a nonsignificant association was found for the other groups. Therefore, evidence does suggest that some forms of parental control are less indicative of low nurturance and thus are interpreted differently by children and adolescents from collectivist versus individualist cultures.

CULTURAL EQUIVALENCE PERSPECTIVE

Counter to the cultural specificity perspective, several other researchers have argued that the general features and premise of the authoritative model are consistent across cultural groups (Sorkhabi, 2005; Steinberg, 2001). According to this cultural equivalence perspective, for children to develop the universally important traits of self-control, concern for others, and a sense of agency, they all share the same fundamental needs for feeling loved, protected, and respected (Lamborn & Felbab, 2003). They also require guidance and structure until they are cognitively and emotionally mature enough to handle the demands of adulthood in their society. Thus, proponents of this perspective argue that the specific practices suggested by the authoritative model are important for all youths because they address these universal needs (Lamborn & Felbab, 2003). This basic premise and several studies led to the following four arguments counter to the cultural specificity perspective: (a) Values and socialization goals of parents in individualist and collectivist cultures are similar, and directive parenting as opposed to authoritarian parenting may better explain differences in prevalence of strict parenting in collectivist versus individualist cultures; (b) the same parenting style (i.e., authoritarian parenting) has the same effects on youths in different cultures; (c) children and adolescents in different cultures interpret the same parenting style in the same way; and (d) the emotional and cognitive characteristics of authoritarian parents in different cultures are the same.

Directive Parenting and Cultural Similarities in Parenting Styles, Values, and Goals

Baumrind's *directive* style could explain most of the inconsistencies in the research on non–European Americans. The directive style is exemplified by a group of parents found in Baumrind's (1991a, 1991b) research who are similar to the authoritative style in amount and type of control but only moderate in nurturance and autonomy support. Their 10-year child outcomes are nearly equivalent to those of authoritative parents in Baumrind's own data (Baumrind, Larzelere, & Owens, 2010). Baumrind et al. (2010) elaborated on the dimensions that distinguish the directive parents and found that they are less likely to use unqualified power assertion, psychological control, verbal hostility, or arbitrary discipline than the authoritarian parents. In contrast to authoritative parents, directive parents were only average on responsiveness. They also had the same socialization goals of obedience and conformity as the authoritarian parents. Thus, the positive type of parenting observed in non-Europeans resembles the directive parenting style and not the authoritarian style, which we argue is universally harmful to children.

For instance, Chao's (1994, 2001) description of Asian parenting as highly demanding; moderately warm and nurturing; and holding strong values of obedience, politeness, family honor, and respect for authority is very similar to the directive style. This is also evident in the fact that although Chao (2000) found that Chinese Americans were higher on measures of training, a sizable portion of European American parents endorsed these principles, and both Chinese and European American parents who endorsed training did not differ significantly from one another in endorsing the socialization goals of filial piety and academic achievement.

Other studies also have tested the assumption that the parenting styles typology is universal. Several studies using cluster-analytic and other multivariate procedures to empirically classify families on the basis of their naturally occurring patterns found that the same basic styles emerge in different ethnic groups. For instance, Brenner and Fox (1999) assessed over 1,000 mothers of young children on three parenting factors and then subjected the scores to cluster-analytic procedures. They derived a four-group typology similar to Baumrind's parenting styles that was represented across different ethnic groups. They also found that authoritative parents were the most educated and least likely to report behavioral problems with their child. A more methodologically sophisticated study of inner city African and Mexican American adolescents used cluster analysis and found four parenting types similar to Baumrind's styles in both groups (Gorman-Smith, Tolan, Henry, & Florsheim, 2000). They labeled the four groups exceptionally functioning, task oriented, struggling, and moderately functioning. The exceptionally functioning parents were like those using Baumrind's directive style in that they were similar to the authoritative prototype, but they were less responsive (emotion focused) and more focused on discipline than the prototypical authoritative parents. Similarly, in the Mandara and Murray (2002) study, the cohesive-authoritative parents were also essentially using the directive style because they exhibited all of the same traits as the prototypical authoritative style parents but were more discipline oriented and less responsive (acquiescent to child demands).

The Effects of Parenting Styles Are Similar in Collectivist and Individualist Cultures

The cultural equivalence perspective proposes that the positive effects of authoritative parenting are similar across different cultural and ethnic groups. One concept that influences this perspective is that the balance between communion and agency in child behavior and reciprocity in parent–child interactions may be important and relevant in both individualist and collectivist cultures (Sorkhabi & Baumrind, 2009). As Sorkhabi and Baumrind (2009) indicated, agentic and independent behavior is necessary not only for child and adolescent initiative but also for compliance with parental directives and conformity to societal requirements. A certain level of self-reliance and independence is necessary for a child to do what is said to be valued in collectivist cultures, which is to serve the interests of other group members and to be a productive member of society. Therefore, it appears that children in both individualist and collectivist cultures may benefit from authoritative and directive parenting that does not undermine agency and promotes communion. However, permissive and authoritarian parents undermine both agency and communion because both kinds of parents do not engage in reciprocal interactions with the child that would encourage the child to think about the purpose of societal rules or requirements for adult conduct and to critically assess and differentiate between situations in which compliance and conformity are adaptive and in which dissent and disobedience are adaptive.

If one extrapolates the principle of reciprocity to explain the negative effects of authoritarian and permissive parenting and the positive effects of authoritative and directive parenting, it becomes evident that authoritarian and permissive parents violate that principle by failing to understand and accommodate their child's needs, abilities, and individuality. For example, authoritarian parents violate the principle of reciprocity by failing to reciprocate a child's bids for closeness (i.e., low warmth) and by discouraging verbal give-and-take. The child's viewpoint is certainly not solicited by the authoritarian parent and is actively discouraged by various means, including verbal hostility and excessive punishment. Similarly, permissive parents do not engage in sustained verbal give-and-take, and instead of punishing or becoming verbally hostile as authoritarian parents do, they simply disengage and accept the child's viewpoint but without appropriately accommodating or taking the child's viewpoint seriously, especially when the child disagrees or is being critical of the parent (Caughlin & Malis, 2004; Lichtwarck-Aschoff,

Kunnen, & van Geert, 2009). Authoritative and directive parents, although also confrontive when necessary, do not violate the principle of reciprocity because they use a set of practices that includes verbal give-and-take, demanding compliance in concert with reason and explanation, attending to the child's perspective, and in turn requiring the child to attend to the parents' perspective. Authoritative and directive styles should be optimal in both individualistic and collectivistic cultural contexts because the possibility of conflict and misunderstanding is minimized and informed action is maximized when both parties attend to and care about one another's perspective.

In support of this contention, in the parenting style studies by Dornbusch et al. (1987) and Steinberg et al. (1991, 1994), authoritative parenting was associated with the best mental health and fewest behavioral problems for youths of all ethnic backgrounds. Those studies simply did not find differences in GPAs between authoritative and authoritarian parents for some subgroups of African and Asian Americans. Evidence from several other studies pointed also to the beneficial effects of authoritative parenting for Asian children (Ang, 2006; Florsheim, 1997; Garg, Levin, Urajnik, & Kauppi, 2005; Kim & Gim Chung, 2003; Radziszewska, Richardson, Dent, & Flay, 1996). One of the more recent studies of 85 Chinese immigrant mothers found that endorsement of authoritative practices was positively associated with their children's self-regulation skills and better behavioral ratings from teachers (Cheah, Leung, Tahseen, & Schultz, 2009).

Other studies with African American youths have found similar positive effects of authoritative parenting on responsible conduct and mental health. A study with 108 African American mothers of young children found that authoritative parenting was a stronger predictor of good child behavior compared with authoritarian or permissive parenting, even after several socioeconomic factors were controlled (Querido, Warner, & Eyberg, 2002). Similarly, Mandara and Murray (2002) found that adolescents with authoritative-cohesive (directive) type of parents were significantly higher than their counterparts with authoritarian or neglectful parents on measures of mental health, self-esteem, and positive ethnic identity. These findings persisted after measures of socioeconomic and parental marital status were controlled. Gorman-Smith et al. (2000) found similar results for internalizing and externalizing behavior. Thus, consistent with the earlier parenting styles studies, virtually every study to date has shown that African and Asian American youths with authoritative or directive parents have significantly better behavior and mental health than youths without such parents.

Even in areas of achievement, some studies have found similar effects. Taylor, Hinton, and Wilson (1995) used a large national sample of 5- to 18-year-old African Americans and found that those whose parents used an authoritative style had higher grades than those with authoritarian or permissive parents. Attaway and Bry (2004) found that African American mothers' beliefs in authoritarian control were negatively correlated with adolescent GPA. Gorman-Smith et al. (2000) found that African and Mexican American adolescents with exceptionally well functioning (i.e., directive) parents were higher over four waves on measures of educational aspirations and positive attitudes toward school compared with the others within their ethnic group. Thus, the existing evidence indicates that Baumrind's parenting model is applicable to youth outcomes in the domains of mental health, behavior, and achievement.

Authoritarian Parenting Is Interpreted Similarly in Collectivist and Individualist Cultures

Another tenet of the cultural equivalence perspective is that authoritarian parenting is interpreted in similar ways by children in collectivist and individualist cultures. Proponents suggest that children in collectivist cultures interpret and evaluate the authoritarian parenting style negatively (Sorkhabi, 2005). The extant literature on children's evaluations and interpretations of authoritarian parenting and dimensions such as shaming, social comparisons, derogatory attributions, emphasis on family honor, and arbitrary curtailment of child autonomy reveals that children in collectivist cultures equate authoritarian parental control with parental rejection, hostility, and disconnection, not parental care, concern, and involvement. Furthermore, children's perception of authoritarian control is also positively related to familial and parent–child conflict and negatively related to harmony and cohesion, which are said to be central values in collectivist cultures. For example, Rohner and Pettengill (1985) found that Korean adolescents view authoritarian control as a sign of parental hostility and rejection and authoritative control as a sign of parental warmth and involvement. Similarly, Lau and Cheung (1987) found that high school students in Hong Kong who reported restrictive parental control that did not serve a rational purpose to structure and organize adolescent activities, consistent with authoritarian parenting, also reported more familial conflict.

Such authoritarian control is also negatively related to family harmony and cohesion. An interesting study by McNeely and Barber (2010) examined the spontaneous views of adolescents in many cultures (India, Bangladesh, China, Bosnia, Palestine, Germany, United States, Colombia, South Africa, and Australia) about parenting behaviors they thought constituted supportive, loving parenting. Adolescents provided 25 different behaviors that parents should and should not engage in to make them feel loved. The 25 behaviors were classified into emotional and companionate support, instrumental support, moral guidance and advice, allowing freedoms, and showing respect or trust for the adolescent. McNeely and Barber found that 46% of adolescents in individualist and collectivist cultures reported that parental love and concern is evident in parental emotional and companionate support, including overt displays of physical affection, such as hugging and kissing. Adolescents also believed that parental control is a sign of parental love and support. However, adolescents distinguished between parental control that is punitive, such as parents yelling, hitting, straining, taxing, and stressing the adolescent either mentally or physically, versus control that is necessary and beneficial, such as parents giving the adolescent responsibilities or duties, disciplining or correcting the adolescent, providing guidance and advice, monitoring and setting limits, and worrying or being concerned about the adolescent's whereabouts and future. Therefore, there is some evidence that adolescents from a variety of cultures distinguish between punitive parental control and lack of responsiveness and affection that is consistent with the authoritarian parenting style and rational parental control and sufficient responsiveness and warmth consistent with authoritative and directive parenting styles.

Authoritarian Parenting in Both Individualist and Collectivist Cultures Is Associated With Negative Parental Emotional and Cognitive Characteristics

Contrary to the cultural specificity perspective that authoritarian parenting in collectivist cultures is associated with positive parental emotional and cognitive characteristics, there is evidence that authoritarian parenting is associated with parental psychological distress and negative affect and negative family dynamics and interactions in individualist and collectivist cultures. Rudy and Grusec (2001) compared Egyptian Canadian and Anglo Canadian authoritarian parents on the dimensions of parental warmth, cognitive attributions regarding child misbehavior, and parental anger. They found, contrary to their hypotheses, that authoritarian parenting in both types of cultures was associated with anger and low warmth. Chang, Lansford, Schwartz, and Farver (2004) found that in Hong Kong authoritarian parenting was related to maternal psychological distress and depression and frequent marital conflict. Cheah et al. (2009) also found that Chinese immigrant mothers with greater psychological well-being, lower parenting stress, and high social support were more likely to be authoritative. Among Asian Indian mothers, Sharma, Sharma, and Yadava (2010) found that authoritarian parenting was significantly and positively related to maternal depression. Thus, several studies have shown that authoritarian parenting and its associated practices are related to negative emotional and economic situations for parents from most cultures.

CONCLUSION

The bulk of the evidence indicates that Baumrind's four parenting styles typology of authoritarian, authoritative, permissive, and disengaged are represented in every cultural group assessed thus far. Once the directive style is included, the typology is an even better description of the diversity of styles among individualist and collectivist cultures. In fact, the evidence strongly suggests that the inclusion of the directive style will help clarify many of the inconsistencies in the parenting styles research on non-European Americans. The field may need to move beyond the four parenting styles typology and begin incorporating the directive and possibly other styles. The incorporation of the entire range of parenting styles including the directive style would be useful to identify the diverse forms of parenting within cultures so as to more effectively explain within-culture differences in child outcomes and to make more accurate and delineated comparisons between cultures. It would also be fruitful to examine parental goals and values in relation to the range of parenting styles, especially the authoritarian and directive styles, in different cultures.

After reviewing the evidence, it is abundantly clear that the positive effects of authoritative and directive parenting are strong and robust for every cultural group studied thus far. Youths with authoritative or directive parents, regardless of ethnic background, are better off in virtually every domain researchers have measured, even after family demographic factors are accounted for. However, another finding is that certain non–European American groups, particularly African and Asian Americans, are not as negatively impacted by strict parenting as are European American youths. This finding was apparently wrongly interpreted by many researchers to mean that authoritarian parenting is optimal for certain groups. Furthermore, the methodology used by the cultural equivalence view appears to be sounder than the cultural specificity perspective in that researchers who emphasize cultural equivalence have used more objective outcome measures (e.g., official school grades, sociometric peer and teacher reports) as well as more reliable and valid measures of parenting styles that match Baumrind's operationalization of the parenting styles. Also, shared source variance (i.e., data for the independent and dependent variables being obtained from the same source) is less of a problem for the cultural equivalence than the cultural specificity perspective.

Future research is needed to assess whether the optimal style for most collectivist groups is the pure authoritative style Baumrind originally described or alternatively the directive style, which emerged from her research with a European American sample as well as from analyses of different samples by other researchers. Future research should examine variability in parenting styles within cultures in relation to developmental outcomes so that different cultures are not homogenized by a focus on between-group comparisons that may inaccurately draw conclusions about the prevalence of a particular parenting style from study samples.

On the basis of this review, we conclude that children from collectivist cultures, like those from individualist cultures, distinguish between authoritarian control that is punitive, arbitrary, and intrusive versus directive and authoritative control that is nonpunitive, rational, and accommodative of child individuality. Emotional closeness or responsiveness, however, may have culturally specific components. Displays of physical affection are not the only way for parents to express love or develop close emotional bonds with their children. More research is needed to examine how adolescents in different cultures evaluate and interpret the differences among authoritarian, directive, authoritative, and permissive parenting styles and the effects that variations in interpretation have on developmental outcomes. However, regardless of how specific cultural groups define and express responsiveness, the fundamental premise of the authoritative model that children need to feel loved, respected, and firmly guided while they are maturing into adults seems to be true for all children.

REFERENCES

Ang, R. P. (2006). Effects of parenting style on personal and social variables for Asian adolescents. *American Journal of Orthopsychiatry, 76,* 503–511. doi:10.1037/0002-9432.76.4.503

Attaway, N. M., & Bry, B. H. (2004). Parenting styles and black adolescents' achievement. *Journal of Black Psychology, 30,* 229–247. doi:10.1177/0095798403260720

Baumrind, D. (1967). Child care practices anteceding three patterns of preschool behavior. *Genetic Psychology Monographs, 75,* 43–88.

Baumrind, D. (1971). Current patterns of parental authority. *Developmental Psychology Monographs, 4* (1, Pt. 2), 1–103.

Baumrind, D. (1972). An exploratory study of socialization effects on black children: Some Black–White comparisons. *Child Development, 43,* 261–267. doi:10.2307/1127891

Baumrind, D. (1991a). Effective parenting during the early adolescent transition. In P. E. Cowan & E. M. Hetherington (Eds.), *Advances in family research* (Vol. 2, pp. 111–163). Hillsdale, NJ: Erlbaum.

Baumrind, D. (1991b). The influence of parenting style on adolescent competence and substance use. *The Journal of Early Adolescence, 11,* 56–95. doi:10.1177/0272431691111004

Baumrind, D., Larzelere, R. A., & Cowan, P. (2002). Ordinary physical punishment—Is it harmful? *Psychological Bulletin, 128,* 580–589.

Baumrind, D., Larzelere, R. E., & Owens, E. B. (2010). Effects of preschool parents' power assertive patterns and practices on adolescent development. *Parenting: Science and Practice, 10*, 157–201. doi:10.1080/15295190903290790

Brenner, V., & Fox, R. A. (1999). An empirically-derived classification of parenting practices. *The Journal of Genetic Psychology: Research and Theory on Human Development, 160*, 343–356. doi:10.1080/00221329909595404

Carlson, V. J., & Harwood, R. L. (2003). Attachment, culture, and the caregiving system: The cultural patterning of everyday experiences among Anglo and Puerto Rican mother–infant pairs. *Infant Mental Health Journal, 24*(1), 53–73. doi:10.1002/imhj.10043

Caughlin, J. P., & Malis, R. S. (2004). Demand/withdraw communication between parents and adolescents: Connections with self-esteem and substance use. *Journal of Social and Personal Relationships, 21*(1), 125–148. doi:10.1177/0265407504039843

Cernkovich, S. A., & Giordano, P. C. (1987). Family relationships and delinquency. *Criminology, 25*, 295–319. doi:10.1111/j.1745-9125.1987.tb00799.x

Chang, L., Lansford, J. E., Schwartz, D., & Farver, J. M. (2004). Marital quality, maternal depressed affect, harsh parenting, and child externalizing in Hong Kong Chinese families. *International Journal of Behavioral Development, 28*, 311–318. doi:10.1080/01650250344000523

Chao, R. K. (1994). Beyond parental control and authoritarian parenting style: Understanding Chinese parenting through the cultural notion of training. *Child Development, 65*, 1111–1119. doi:10.2307/1131308

Chao, R. K. (2000). The parenting of immigrant Chinese and European American mothers: Relations between parenting styles, socialization goals, and parental practices. *Journal of Applied Developmental Psychology, 21*, 233–248. doi:10.1016/S0193-3973(99)00037-4

Chao, R. K. (2001). Extending research on the consequences of parenting style for Chinese Americans and European Americans. *Child Development, 72*, 1832–1843. doi:10.1111/1467-8624.00381

Cheah, C. S. L., Leung, C. Y. Y., Tahseen, M., & Schultz, D. (2009). Authoritative parenting among immigrant Chinese mothers of preschoolers. *Journal of Family Psychology, 23*, 311–320. doi:10.1037/a0015076

Deater-Deckard, K., Dodge, K. A., Bates, J. E., & Pettit, G. S. (1996). Physical discipline among African American and European American mothers: Links to children's externalizing behaviors. *Developmental Psychology, 32*, 1065–1072. doi:10.1037/0012-1649.32.6.1065

Dornbusch, S. M., Ritter, P. L., Leiderman, P. H., Roberts, D. F., & Fraleigh, M. J. (1987). The relation of parenting style to adolescent school performance. *Child Development, 58*, 1244–1257. doi:10.2307/1130618

Florsheim, P. (1997). Chinese adolescent immigrants: Factors related to psychosocial adjustment. *Journal of Youth and Adolescence, 26*, 143–163. doi:10.1023/A:1024548430764

Forehand, R., & Kotchick, B. A. (1996). Cultural diversity: A wakeup call for parent training. *Behavior Therapy, 27*, 187–206. doi:10.1016/S0005-7894(96)80014-1

Fung, H. (1999). Becoming a moral child: The socialization of shame among young Chinese children. *Ethos, 27*, 180–209. doi:10.1525/eth.1999.27.2.180

Garcia Coll, C., & Vasquez Garcia, H. A. (1995). Hispanic children and their families: On a different track from the very beginning. In H. E. Fitzgerald, B. M. Lester, & B. S. Zuckerman (Eds.), *Children of poverty: Research, health, and policy issues* (Vol. 23, pp. 57–83). New York, NY: Garland.

Garcia Coll, C., & Pachter, L. M. (2002). Ethnic minority parenting. In M. H. Bornstein (Ed.), *Handbook of parenting. Vol. 4: Social conditions and applied parenting* (pp. 1–46). Mahwah, NJ: Erlbaum.

Garg, R., Levin, E., Urajnik, D., & Kauppi, C. (2005). Parenting style and academic achievement in East Indian and Canadian adolescents. *Journal of Comparative Family Studies, 36*, 653–661.

Gorman-Smith, D., Tolan, P. H., Henry, D. B., & Florsheim, P. (2000). Patterns of family functioning and adolescent outcomes among urban African American and Mexican American families. *Journal of Family Psychology, 14*, 436–457. doi:10.1037/0893-3200.14.3.436

Gunnoe, M. L., & Mariner, C. L. (1997). Toward a developmental-contextual model of the effects of parental spanking on children's aggression. *Archives of Pediatrics & Adolescent Medicine, 151*, 768–775. doi:10.1001/archpedi.1997.02170450018003

Ispa, J. M., Fine, M. A., Halgunseth, L. C., Harper, S., Robinson, J., Boyce, L., . . . Brady-Smith, C. (2004). Maternal intrusiveness, maternal warmth, and mother–toddler relationship outcomes: Variations across low-income ethnic and acculturation groups. *Child Development, 75*, 1613–1631. doi:10.1111/j.1467-8624.2004.00806.x

Kim, H., & Gim Chung, R. H. (2003). Relationship of recalled parenting style to self-perception in Korean American college students. *The Journal of Genetic Psychology: Research and Theory on Human Development, 164*, 481–492. doi:10.1080/00221320309597891

Lamborn, S. D., & Felbab, A. J. (2003). Applying ethnic equivalence and cultural values models to African-American teens' perceptions of parents. *Journal of Adolescence, 26*, 601–618. doi:10.1016/S0140-1971(03)00059-9

Lamborn, S. D., Mounts, N. S., Steinberg, L., & Dornbusch, S. M. (1991). Patterns of competence and adjustment among adolescents from authoritative, authoritarian, indulgent and neglectful families. *Child Development, 62*, 1049–1065. doi:10.2307/1131151

Lau, S., & Cheung, P. C. (1987). Relation between Chinese adolescents' perception of parental control and organization and their perception of parental warmth. *Developmental Psychology, 23*, 726–729. doi:10.1037/0012-1649.23.5.726

Le Vine, R. A. (2009). Socialization of the child. In R. A. Shweder (Ed.), *The child: An encyclopedic companion* (pp. 929–933). Chicago, IL: University of Chicago Press.

Lichtwarck-Aschoff, A., Kunnen, S. E., & van Geert, P. L. C. (2009). Here we go again: A dynamic systems perspective on emotional rigidity across parent–adolescent conflicts. *Developmental Psychology, 45*, 1364–1375. doi:10.1037/a0016713

Lindahl, K. M., & Malik, N. M. (1999). Marital conflicts, family processes, and boys' externalizing behavior in Hispanic American and European American Families. *Journal of Clinical Child Psychology, 28*(1), 12–24. doi:10.1207/s15374424jccp2801_2

Mandara, J., & Murray, C. B. (2002). The development of an empirical typology of African American family functioning. *Journal of Family Psychology, 16*, 318–337. doi:10.1037/0893-3200.16.3.318

Markus, H. R. (2008). Pride, prejudice, and ambivalence: Toward a unified theory of race and ethnicity. *American Psychologist, 63*, 651–670. doi:10.1037/0003-066X.63.8.651

Mason, C. A., Cauce, A. M., Gonzales, N. A., & Hiraga, Y. (1996). Neither too sweet nor too sour: Problem peers, maternal control and problem behaviors in African American adolescents. *Child Development, 67*, 2115–2130. doi:10.2307/1131613

Mason, C. A., Walker-Barnes, C. J., Tu, S., Simons, J., & Martinez-Arrue, R. (2004). Ethnic differences in the affective meaning of parental control behaviors. *The Journal of Primary Prevention, 25*, 59–79. doi:10.1023/B:JOPP.0000039939.83804.37

Matsumoto, D., & Juang, L. (2003). *Culture and psychology* (3rd ed.). Belmont, CA: Wadsworth/Thomson Learning.

McLoyd, V. C., & Smith, J. (2002). Physical discipline and behavior problems in African American, European American, and Hispanic children: Emotional support as a moderator. *Journal of Marriage and Family, 64*, 40–53. doi:10.1111/j.1741-3737.2002.00040.x

McNeely, C. A., & Barber, B. K. (2010). How do parents make adolescents feel loved? Perspectives on supportive parenting from adolescents in 12 cultures. *Journal of Adolescent Research, 25*, 601–631. doi:10.1177/0743558409357235

Ogbu, J. U. (1981). Origins of human competence: A cultural-ecological perspective. *Child Development, 52*, 413–429. doi:10.2307/1129158

Pettit, G. S., Bates, J. E., & Dodge, K. A. (1997). Supportive parenting, ecological context, and children's adjustment: A seven-year longitudinal study. *Child Development, 68*, 908–923.

Polaha, J., Larzelere, R. E., Shapiro, S. K., & Pettit, G. S. (2004). Physical discipline and child behavior problems: A study of ethnic group differences. *Parenting: Science and Practice, 4*, 339–360. doi:10.1207/s15327922par0404_6

Querido, J. G., Warner, T. D., & Eyberg, S. M. (2002). Parenting styles and child behavior in African American families of preschool children. *Journal of Clinical Child and Adolescent Child Psychology, 31*, 272–277. doi:10.1207/153744202753604548

Radziszewska, B., Richardson, J. L., Dent, C. W., & Flay, B. R. (1996). Parenting style and adolescent depressive symptoms, smoking, and academic achievement:

Ethnic, gender, and SES differences. *Journal of Behavioral Medicine*, *19*, 289–305. doi:10.1007/BF01857770

Rohner, R. P., & Pettengill, S. M. (1985). Perceived parental acceptance–rejection and parental control among Korean adolescents. *Child Development*, *56*, 524–528. doi:10.2307/1129739

Rudy, D., & Grusec, J. E. (2001). Correlates of authoritarian parenting in individualist and collectivist cultures and implications for understanding the transmission of values. *Journal of Cross-Cultural Psychology*, *32*, 202–212. doi:10.1177/0022022101032002007

Rudy, D., & Grusec, J. E. (2006). Authoritarian parenting in individualist and collectivist group: Associations with maternal emotion and cognition and children's self-esteem. *Journal of Family Psychology*, *20*, 68–78. doi:10.1037/0893-3200.20.1.68

Sharma, M., Sharma, N., & Yadava, A. (2010). Depression in relation to parenting style and self-efficacy among female adolescents. *Indian Journal of Community Psychology*, *6*, 208–220.

Simons, R. L., Kuei-Hsiu, L., Gordon, L. C., Brody, G. H., Velma, M., & Conger, R. D. (2002). Community differences in the association between parenting practices and child conduct problems. *Journal of Marriage and Family*, *64*, 331–345. doi:10.1111/j.1741-3737.2002.00331.x

Smith, C., & Krohn, M. D. (1995). Delinquency and family life among male adolescents: The role of ethnicity. *Journal of Youth and Adolescence*, *24*, 63–93. doi:10.1007/BF01537561

Sorkhabi, N. (2005). Applicability of Baumrind's parent typology to collective cultures: Analysis of cultural explanations of parent socialization effects. *International Journal of Behavioral Development*, *29*, 552–563. doi:10.1080/01650250500172640

Sorkhabi, N., & Baumrind, D. (2009). Authority and obedience. In R. A. Shweder (Ed.), *The child: An encyclopedic companion* (pp. 81–86). Chicago, IL: University of Chicago Press.

Steinberg, L. (2001). We know some things: Parent–adolescent relationships in retrospect and prospect. *Journal of Research on Adolescence*, *11*, 1–19. doi:10.1111/1532-7795.00001

Steinberg, L., Dornbusch, S. M., & Brown, B. B. (1992). Ethnic differences in adolescent achievement: An ecological perspective. *American Psychologist*, *47*, 723–729. doi:10.1037/0003-066X.47.6.723

Steinberg, L., Lamborn, S. D., Darling, N., Mounts, N. S., & Dornbusch, S. M. (1994). Over-time changes in adjustment and competence among adolescents from authoritative, authoritarian, indulgent, and neglectful families. *Child Development*, *65*, 754–770. doi:10.2307/1131416

Steinberg, L., Mounts, N. S., Lamborn, S. D., & Dornbusch, S. M. (1991). Authoritative parenting and adolescent adjustment across varied ecological niches. *Journal of Research on Adolescence*, *1*, 19–36.

Straus, M. A. (2000). Corporal punishment and primary prevention of physical abuse. *Child Abuse & Neglect*, *24*, 1109–1114. doi:10.1016/S0145-2134(00)00180-0

Taylor, L. C., Hinton, I. D., & Wilson, M. N. (1995). Parental influences on academic performance in African American students. *Journal of Child and Family Studies, 4*, 293–302. doi:10.1007/BF02233964

Triandis, H. C. (1995). The self and social behavior in differing cultural contexts. In N. R. Goldberger & J. B. Veroff (Eds.), *The culture and psychology reader* (pp. 326–365). New York, NY: New York University Press.

Valdes, G. (1996). *Con respeto: Bridging the distances between culturally diverse families and schools: An ethnographic portrait.* New York, NY: Teachers College Press.

Weiss, L. H., & Schwarz, J. C. (1996). The relationship between parenting types and older adolescents' personality, academic achievement, adjustment, and substance use. *Child Development, 67*, 2101–2114. doi:10.2307/1131612

6

CONFLICT EMERGENCE AND ADAPTIVENESS OF NORMATIVE PARENT–ADOLESCENT CONFLICTS: BAUMRIND'S SOCIALIZATION THEORY AND COGNITIVE SOCIAL DOMAIN THEORY

NADIA SORKHABI

Surprisingly little research has directly examined the links among Baumrind's parenting styles and the emergence of parent–adolescent conflicts and the adaptiveness of parent–adolescent conflicts. In this chapter, I use Baumrind's socialization theory and research to analyze the ways in which conflicts emerge between parents and adolescents, examine whether and when normative everyday parent–adolescent conflicts are adaptive, and suggest future directions for research in this understudied area. With respect to the ways conflicts emerge, my conclusions are that the emphasis of much theory and research on adolescence, including cognitive social domain theory (e.g., Smetana, 2002), on the incompatibility of parents' goal to retain authority and adolescents' goal to attain autonomy represents one way in which conflicts may emerge. When Baumrind's parenting styles are taken into account, a wider range of reasons surfaces for the emergence of parent–adolescent conflicts because it becomes evident that not all parents aim to

DOI: 10.1037/13948-007
Authoritative Parenting: Synthesizing Nurturance and Discipline for Optimal Child Development, Robert E. Larzelere, Amanda Sheffield Morris, and Amanda W. Harrist (Editors)

137

maintain their authority; not all parents apply control in coercive ways or, conversely, are able to exercise and assert the authority they have as parents; and not all adolescents have to resist parental authority to gain autonomy from their parents. With respect to the adaptiveness of conflicts, my conclusions are that adolescent resistance to parental authority, which is proposed by some socialization theory and research, including cognitive social domain theory (e.g., Smetana, 1995a), to result in parental autonomy granting and relinquishment of control, needs to be examined in light of Baumrind's parenting styles. Such an examination reveals that parents with different parenting styles have different ways of interpreting and responding to adolescent resistance and ongoing daily conflicts. A second conclusion I draw regarding the adaptiveness of conflicts is that the patterned ways in which parents with different parenting styles assert control across domains or areas of adolescent activity are as important as the domains or the content they regulate (emphasized by cognitive social domain theorists such as Smetana, 1997, and others such as Grusec & Davidov, 2010).

With respect to the emergence of conflicts, cognitive social domain theorists (e.g., Nucci, 2008; Smetana, 2005) draw from Piaget (1932). Piaget theorized that the natural power differential between parents and children poses a significant impediment to children's ability to sufficiently overcome their egocentric tendencies and to understand the principle of equality, which is necessary for autonomous moral reasoning. Piaget further emphasized the centrality of equal social relationships (i.e., with peers), which were said to provide children the experiential basis to decenter, abstract the principle of equality, and surmount the impeding force of parental authority. Similarly, domain theorists (e.g., Smetana, 1995a, 1997, 2002) have posited equal relationships as a significant factor in adolescent development and depicted parent–adolescent conflicts as reflecting adolescents' need to construct a symmetrical relationship with parents who are either unable or unwilling to relinquish control and authority. Therefore, tension between parents' and adolescents' desires is purported to be a major source of conflict.

Also, consistent with Piaget's emphasis on the constructive role of conflicts in decentration and expansion of individual perspective, social domain theorists view normative conflicts as adaptive processes that force parents to decenter and accommodate adolescents' opposing viewpoints and claims to autonomy by reinterpreting the parameters of their authority (e.g., Smetana, 1995a). Domain theorists also propose that parent–adolescent conflicts and adolescent psychological adjustment are related primarily to parental regulation of the personal domain (i.e., actions and choices that involve individual taste or preference, such as selection of attire or music) and multifaceted issues (i.e., issues that share features of two or more domains, such as a boy wearing an earring or the cleanliness of an adolescent's room) and not to parental regulation of the socially regulated domains. The socially regulated domains include moral (i.e., issues that entail harm to others, such as hitting, fighting, stealing, inequity), conventional (i.e., issues that involve social order and predictability, such as doing chores), and prudential (i.e., actions that harm the individual actor but not others, such as alcohol use).

Baumrind's longitudinal program of research provides convincing evidence that to comprehensively analyze the developmental outcomes associated with normative parent–child interactions, normative variations in parenting styles and the history of the parent–adolescent relationship must be examined (Baumrind, Larzelere, & Owens, 2010). Domain theorists' cognitive focus does not capture variations in normative relationship contexts that contribute to the emergence and adaptive nature of parent–adolescent conflicts.

Domain theorists may not have intended to capture variations in normative parent–adolescent conflicts. However, to fully establish that conflicts emerge for the reasons that domain theorists propose, or to accept that everyday conflicts are adaptive as domain theorists suggest (Smetana, 1997, 2002), it is important to take into account the potential variations in the quality of normative parent–adolescent relationships. Examination of such variation enables researchers to identify the different ways conflicts potentially emerge and to verify whether everyday conflicts in varying relationship contexts are indeed adaptive.

Domain theorists have highlighted important factors, such as the content or domains of interaction, that affect parent–adolescent relationships and have offered a unique view of the factors that engender conflict and render conflicts adaptive. To expand on domain theory, Baumrind's authoritarian, authoritative, and permissive parenting styles are used herein to analyze the five propositions domain theorists (e.g., Nucci, Hasebe, & Lins-Dyer, 2005; Smetana, 1989, 1994, 1995a, 1995b, 1997, 2002, 2005) offer to explain the emergence of conflicts and the adaptiveness of conflicts. Three of the five propositions that pertain to conflict emergence are (a) a major parental goal is to maintain authority; (b) adolescents' goal is to attain freedom and separation from parents; and (c) parent–adolescent relationships are viewed by adolescents as hierarchical. With respect to these three propositions, I argue that when variations in parenting styles are taken into account, it becomes clear that conflicts are not inevitable and that conflicts may emerge for multiple reasons because not all parents wish to maintain authority; not all adolescents have the goal of freedom and separation from parents; and not all adolescents view their relationship with their parent as hierarchical. The remaining two of the five propositions of domain theory pertain to the proposed adaptiveness of everyday normative parent–adolescent conflicts: (d) Conflicts and adolescent resistance to parental authority force parents to relinquish control and grant autonomy to adolescents, and (e) parental regulation of the personal domain and not the socially regulated domains affects the adaptive nature of conflicts. With respect to these two propositions, I argue that by taking parenting styles into account, researchers can see that not all parents will be forced to relinquish control in response to adolescent resistance and that parents vary in their interpretation of and response to adolescent resistance, which can affect the adaptiveness of parent–adolescent conflicts. Furthermore, the ways parents regulate adolescents' activities within any domain can significantly impact the adaptiveness of conflicts.

VARIATIONS AMONG AUTHORITARIAN, AUTHORITATIVE, AND PERMISSIVE PARENTS' SOCIALIZATION GOALS OF CONTROL AND AUTONOMY AND WILLINGNESS TO ASSERT CONTROL

The incompatibility of parents' and adolescents' goals has been proposed by domain theorists to lead to parent–adolescent conflicts (e.g., Nucci et al., 2005; Smetana, 1989, 2005). Parents are said to have the primary goals of retaining their authority and enforcing social conventions, and adolescents are said to have the primary goal of attaining autonomy by creating a personal domain that is outside of parental control. For example, Smetana (2005) stated,

> The findings from these studies indicate that . . . whereas parents were concerned with social conventions, social regulation, and parental authority, these concerns were rarely voiced by adolescents. In contrast, attaining personal freedoms and maximizing personal choices were much on the minds of adolescents. (pp. 73–74)

The lack of common goals between parents and adolescents is also evident in Smetana's (1989) conclusion based on empirical evidence that "conflict emerges when adolescents' attempts to assert autonomy over such issues [physical appearance, chores, interpersonal relationships, behavioral style] compete with parents' conventional goals of regulating the household, maintaining authority, and upholding conventional standards" (p. 1064). Smetana and Asquith (1994) also echoed the conclusion involving the divergence of parent and adolescent goals by indicating that "these generational differences most likely reflect the hierarchical structure of the family. Parents have a greater investment in maintaining the familial moral and social order, whereas adolescents desire greater autonomy within it" (p. 1159).

Smetana (1997) indicated that in hypothetical scenarios parents recognize not just their own authority but also the autonomy needs of adolescents and even of young children. However, Smetana also indicated that although parents may recognize children's autonomy needs in hypothetical scenarios, in practice they do not grant autonomy in areas in which they judge in hypothetical scenarios children should have autonomy. In practice, maintaining authority is said to be more important or salient to parents than child or adolescent autonomy, which creates conflicts. For example, according to Smetana (1997), "the same issues that parents profess to be under their child's discretion are the ones that cause conflict in their relationships" (p. 184).

I propose that although, as Smetana and her colleagues stated, the parental goal of retaining control is an important factor that can contribute to conflicts, the contribution to conflict of variations among parents in the emphasis they place on the goals of maintaining authority and of enforcing societal conventions should also be examined. That is, researchers still need to investigate the various ways in which conflict emerges in parent–child relationships and more importantly examine how conflict is averted by some dyads. Smetana and colleagues did not examine significant variations in parents' goals that may vary as a function of parenting styles to ascertain the different ways conflicts emerge.

Baumrind's (1991a, 1991b) longitudinal studies during early adolescence reveal that although the emphasis on the parental goal of maintaining authority and enforcing conventions may describe the process that engenders conflict in some families, a different process describes parental child-rearing goals and how parents act to achieve these goals in other families. For example, Baumrind (1991a, 1991b) found that permissive parents hold a child-centered philosophy of noninterference in relation to children's autonomy such that maintaining authority and control and enforcing conventions are not their primary goals. Permissive parents' primary goal is to encourage children's autonomy, which they do not balance with the parenting goals to maintain authority and enforce social conventions (Baumrind, 1991a, 1991b; Baumrind et al., 2010). Baumrind found that the goals of authoritative parents are neither exclusively parent centered (i.e., exerting control) nor child centered (i.e., granting autonomy). Instead, authoritative parents integrate the two types of goals (Baumrind & Thompson, 2002). Authoritarian parents, by contrast with both authoritative and permissive parents and congruent with domain theory, are status oriented and hold the primary goals of instilling obedience to their authority and of requiring conformity to societal conventions. Hastings and Rubin (1999) also found that the primary socialization goal of authoritarian parents included the parent-centered goal of obtaining immediate obedience from their children and not the child-centered goals of teaching self-regulation skills and principles for appropriate behavior that would increase child independence and autonomy. Baumrind (1991a, 1991b) also identified a group of directive parents who had the socialization goal of instilling conformity with societal conventions and a group of parents she called *nonconforming* (Baumrind, 1973), whose goals were to have their children question and critically examine the actions of authority rather than conform or cave to pressure from authority. In sum, Baumrind's studies reveal that only a subgroup of parents (i.e., authoritarian and directive) has the primary aim of enforcing conventions, and only authoritarian parents have as their primary goal maintaining their authority. Domain theorists ascribe these two primary aims and goals to parents as a category.

The view held by domain theorists concerning which socialization goals are primary is centered on the supposition that parent–child relationships are inherently hierarchical, implying that as a category parents have more power than adolescents and want to retain their dominance (Smetana & Asquith, 1994; p. 1159). However, it is complex to assess the power that parents have relative to adolescents when power is defined as social influence (Emery, 1992; Maccoby, 1999), and the extent of power or social influence in relationships has not been studied by domain theorists. Relationship theorists (e.g., Schermerhorn & Cummings, 2008) have proposed that the extent of power in relationships is determined by the party who can exert influence to win conflicts or to gain advantageous outcomes. Children with permissive parents can be said to have greater power than their parents, despite the fact that their parents are the nominal authority figures, because they, not their parents, control the outcome of interactions. For example, Patterson and Fisher (2002) found that there are coercive children who make unreasonable demands on their parents and immobilize and force their parents to defer to their demands. As Patterson and Fisher indicated, in permissive families it is the child who is domineering and coercive and demands immediate compliance from parents without discussion. These parents typically respond by complying with child demands to avoid child anger, temper tantrums, and rejection. These interactive patterns have also been found by Baumrind (1971, 1991a, 1991b) and Baumrind et al. (2010) in permissive families in which parents give in to child and adolescent demands or resistance, retreat from confrontation, and are unable to exert assertive control to ensure a mutually beneficial outcome. When compliance is imperative, permissive parents resort to covert forms of manipulation, such as withdrawal of love and attention, which may or may not be successful in gaining adolescent compliance.

Therefore, permissive parents do not possess much power and control over their children to attempt to retain during adolescence and do not know how to exert the authority that parents who act as leaders of the household possess. Further study is needed to fully understand the range of factors involved in the emergence of conflicts associated with parental goals, variations in parental goals, and variations in instantiation of goals in accord with parenting styles.

CONFLICT EMERGENCE: ADOLESCENTS' DESIRE
FOR AUTONOMY AND SEPARATION FROM PARENTS VERSUS
VARIATIONS IN PARENTAL SUPPORT FOR ADOLESCENTS' NEED
FOR AUTONOMY AND FOR CONTINUED CONNECTION

Domain theorists posit that adolescents' desire to curtail the parameters of parental power so as to gain greater freedom and personal autonomy is central to their resistance to parental authority and the emergence of parent–adolescent conflicts. Smetana (2005) wrote that "adolescent–parent conflicts are, *at their heart* [emphasis added], debates over where to draw the line between parental control and authority and adolescents' autonomy over the self" (p. 75). The empirical evidence for this proposition (Smetana, 1988, 1989) involves the personal justifications adolescents offer to explain why they have conflicts with their parents (e.g., "It should be up to me"; "It's my room"), primarily in response to hypothetical scenarios.

Although domain theorists' proposition points out one cause of parent–adolescent conflicts, their explanation is incomplete in that they examine only adolescents' desire for separation and autonomy. Possible variations in the quality of parents' parenting styles need to be taken into account to determine whether a generalization about all parents is supportable or instead whether some parents do and other parents do not support autonomy.

As Baumrind (1971, 1989, 1991a, 1991b, 2008) found, one of the central socialization aims of authoritative parents is to facilitate autonomy and promote self-reliance. Authoritative parents promote self-reliance and consciously support children's autonomy and individuation not only by acquiescing to developmentally appropriate child demands but also by increasing cognitive insight into cause-and-effect relations and consequences of action by means of reason, explanation, and imparting of knowledge. The authoritative parent also encourages high maturity by setting standards that are attainable with sustained effort and work, by demanding persistence in the face of obstacles or failure, and by acknowledging achievement. Baumrind (1971, 1991a, 1991b) and Baumrind et al. (2010) found that authoritative parents, by the combined means of rational control (i.e., firm control, confrontive discipline) and independence training (starting in the preschool years through adolescence), had children who were individuated, self-reliant, efficacious, and generally competent—outcomes that domain theorists and Baumrind deem as important indicators of optimal development. Interactions with authoritative parents involving tasks that initially appear difficult or arduous provide children and adolescents with the experience of mastery that accompanies goal attainment. These interactions encourage autonomous actions not just in the personal domain, as domain theorists emphasize (Nucci, 2008), to decide relatively superficial matters of clothing, hairstyle, or music but also in the moral and conventional domains involving matters that are more consequential. Therefore, even when authoritative parents apply control, their aim is not simply to prohibit action but to enable competent independent action and self-reliance. As Baumrind indicates in Chapter 1 of this volume, adolescent conflicts with authoritative parents are not fundamentally about adolescents' seeking autonomy from parents because adolescents are consistently encouraged to be self-reliant and supported in their endeavors to individuate and to develop their strengths.

Furthermore, conflicts that emerge with authoritarian and permissive parents also may not represent adolescents' desire for separation and autonomy from parents, as is emphasized by domain theorists (e.g., Smetana, 1995a), so much as adolescents' unmet needs for intimacy, acceptance, and parental understanding. Baumrind (1991a, 1991b) found that authoritarian parents do not acknowledge or praise constructive behavior and achievements, demean the child for failure, are quick to find fault and criticize, do not support reasonable child demands for self-direction, and do not promote cognitive insight necessary for sound decision making when external controls and guidance are absent. The work of many others, including Patterson (1971), Emery (1992), and Greenberger and Chen (1996), confirmed Baumrind's findings that in certain parent–child relationships adolescents may not receive validation, acceptance, and positive attention for constructive behavior but instead consistently receive negative attention, derogation, and criticism not only for transgressions and failures but also for all types of behaviors.

Patterson has found that authoritarian parents indiscriminately respond in a coercive and punitive manner even when the child is compliant and attempting to please the parent and do not show positive attention for constructive behavior. Patterson and Fisher (2002) stated that "no matter what the child does the parent reacts with contempt and criticism" (pp. 65–66). Indiscriminate rejection of child behavior and initiative by the authoritarian parent may hinder the sense of attachment and connection to parents that children and adolescents seek and need. Indeed, Baumrind (1991a, 1991b) found that adolescents whose parents were categorized as authoritarian by observers perceived their parents as uncaring, cold, and disconnected from them as individuals.

Similarly, Greenberger and Chen (1996) found that both early and late adolescents who lacked a sense of connection to their parents, evident in their endorsement of such items as "I find it hard to please my mother" and "I worry that my mother will stop loving me if I don't live up to her expectations," also reported more conflict.

Caughlin and Malis (2004), who examined the ways in which conflicts are actuated, also found that the maladaptive pattern of conflict engagement, namely, demand–withdraw (in which one party makes incessant demands and as the demands increase so does withdrawal by the other party in the dyad), is characteristic of parent–adolescent conflicts consistent with authoritarian parenting contexts. Caughlin and Malis indicated that when parents frequently coerce, nag, and criticize, as authoritarian parents do (Baumrind et al., 2010), the adolescent may withdraw from parents to seek validation from other sources (e.g., peers), which further elicits coercive behaviors from the parent and in turn further withdrawal from the adolescent.

Such conflict exchanges would be explained by domain theorists (e.g., Nucci, 2008) as adolescents' attempts to maintain a personal domain by associating with peers. However, in the context of authoritarian parenting, such conflict exchanges and behaviors may also reflect adolescents' unmet needs for connection to parents, which they attempt to gratify by seeking validation and acceptance from peers. Therefore, parent–adolescent conflicts may not merely represent adolescents' attempts to be free of any kind of parental control but may also involve a particular demand–withdraw conflict pattern or authoritarian parental control that reflects parental rejection of the adolescent that leaves the adolescent with unmet needs for connection and acceptance.

Conflicts with permissive parents may also mark adolescents' unmet needs for connection and acceptance. Baumrind (1991a, 1991b) and Baumrind et al. (2010) found that permissive parents' lack of commitment to parenting and involvement in adolescents' lives is manifested by noncontingent reinforcement and affirmation of the adolescent in ways that are disconnected from the adolescent's developmental needs and the consequences of the adolescent's actions. Permissive parents indiscriminately agree with and affirm the adolescent because they do not want to directly confront the defiant adolescent regarding behaviors that require change. Permissive parenting practices may hinder adolescents' sense of connection to parents because permissive parents appear to lack the involvement and commitment to engage in practices that clearly demarcate praiseworthy and negative behaviors.

Consistent with Baumrind's findings regarding the permissive parent's lack of commitment, indiscriminate affirmation, and tendency to retreat from confrontation with the adolescent are Patterson and Fisher's (2002) findings that permissive parents often react to coercive and unacceptable child behavior in a neutral or even in a positive way and simply give in to whatever it is the child wants. Similarly, Caughlin and Malis's (2004) research on demand–withdraw conflict patterns within the context of permissive parenting reveals that conflicts involve the adolescent wanting to discuss an issue or a problem and the parent withdrawing in any of the following ways: physically withdrawing from contact, becoming silent, ignoring the adolescent, ignoring the problem, or dismissing or minimizing the importance of the matter the adolescent wants to discuss. The more the parent withdraws in these various ways, the more the adolescent demands, blames, and criticizes the parent. Thus, parent–adolescent conflicts may not merely represent adolescents' need for freedom but may also involve permissive parents' insufficient commitment and engagement and reflect adolescents' unmet needs for connection.

In sum, both permissive and authoritarian parenting hinder adolescents' sense of connection to parents because permissive parents indiscriminately affirm, agree, or withdraw, and authoritarian parents indiscriminately criticize or derogate. Both kinds of parents send the message that the parent is rejecting and insufficiently involved to engage in differentiated practices that account for adolescents' individuality.

When adolescents' constructive initiative, choices, and attempts at self-reliance are recognized and supported, as is the case with authoritative parents, adolescents' sense of connection to parents is strengthened. When adolescents' initiative is unrecognized and unsupported, as is the case with permissive parents, or demeaned and obstructed, as is the case with authoritarian parents, adolescents' autonomy is stymied and their sense of connection to parents is hindered. When adolescents' autonomy is constructively supported, as is the case with authoritative parents, so is their sense of connection to parents. For example, Caffery and Erdman's (2000) conceptual review suggested that when adolescents feel a lack of connection to their parents, they engage in risky behaviors that they know their parents will disapprove of, not as a way to individuate or separate from parents but as a way to engage their parents' sympathy and to forge a stronger connection with their parents. Similarly, Fuligni's (1998) cross-sectional and longitudinal data reveal that as adolescents' feelings of cohesion with their mothers increased, their willingness to disagree with their mothers decreased, and their endorsement of maternal authority increased.

Social domain theory emphasizes that conflicts emerge as a result of the opposition between parents' goal of maintaining control and adolescents' goal of attaining freedom. However, when parenting styles are taken into account, a more differentiated range of reasons emerges for the existence and ongoing nature of conflicts. Conflicts may also be debates about adolescents' unmet needs for acceptance and connection to parents and not just a need for freedom and separation from parents. More research is needed to explore from both adolescents' and their parents' perspectives the range of reasons that exists for the emergence of conflicts with parents having different parenting styles.

CONFLICT EMERGENCE: ADOLESCENTS' VIEW OF THE POWER DIFFERENTIAL WITH PARENTS AS UNJUST VERSUS VARIATIONS IN ADOLESCENTS' JUDGMENTS ABOUT THE POWER DIFFERENTIAL WITH PARENTS

A third reason domain theorists (Smetana, 2002) offer for the emergence of parent–adolescent conflicts is that adolescents regard the unequal nature of their relationship with their parents as oppressive and unfair and want to elevate their subordinate status in the family and achieve mutual authority or symmetrical status with parents. Smetana (2002) stated, "An obvious but frequently ignored fact is that, like relationships between men and women in traditional societies, parent–child relationships are hierarchical with parents in dominant positions and children in subordinate roles" (p. 57). Smetana further indicated that adolescents' subordinate position "in hierarchical relationships with parents is fraught with many of the same tensions and contradictions noted by cultural anthropologists focusing on those in subordinate positions [women relative to men] in more traditional cultures" (p. 57). Adolescents' attempt to elevate their subordinate status is said to be reflected in their resistance to parental rules and authority (Nucci, 2008; Smetana, Crean, & Campione-Barr, 2005).

Domain theorists reveal an important factor in parent–adolescent relationships: Adolescents judge and evaluate their parents' requests, demands, and actions, which affect how they behave in relation to their parents. Other researchers (e.g., Hetherington & Kelly, 2002) confirmed that if adolescents (and even young children) judge their relationship with their parents as iniquitous and unfair, they will resist such autocratic imposition of control. However, I propose that it is important to identify and examine variations among adolescents' views of their parents' greater power and resources and their willingness to resist parental authority. Adolescents do not always interpret parental authority as unjust or evaluate all types of parental control as a hierarchical structure that stifles their autonomy in ways similar to the subordination that some women may feel in iniquitous relationships with some men. The different ways that parents exercise their power provide the basis for adolescents' evaluative judgments of the unequal nature of their relationship with their parents and, if and when it occurs, subsequent rebellion or resistance to parental authority.

Evidence for my argument that adolescents do not inherently view the unequal nature of their relationship with their parents as hierarchical and unfair is based on studies that examined (a) adolescents' ideal view of parental power and their own power and (b) the extent to which adolescents accept or reject parental power to construct rules that govern adolescent activities.

Adolescents May Not Regard the Power Differential With Their Parents as Unjust

Feldman and Gehring (1988) found that when asked to represent their conceptions of the ideal power balance with their parents, adolescents in all age groups (11.9–18.2) conferred greater power to their parents than to themselves. Adolescents' ideal preference for parents to possess more power than they do reveals that the natural power differential between parents and adolescents is not seen as unjust and may be preferred to equality.

Adolescents Do Not Resist Parental Power
to Unilaterally Construct Rules

Sorkhabi (2010), using Baumrind's longitudinal data, found that most adolescents do not reject parental authority to make rules, and contrary to Sorkhabi's hypotheses and past research findings by Lamborn, Dornbusch, and Steinberg (1996), conflict frequency was not significantly related to whether parents allowed adolescents to have a say or a role in constructing the rules that affect them. Variations in the ways parents construct rules (i.e., unilateral parent rule construction, bilateral rule construction, unilateral adolescent rule construction) were not significantly related to conflict frequency (except in adolescents' reports about their mothers' rule construction). Sorkhabi and Middaugh (2012) also found that adolescents (10th and 12th graders) having a say in the construction of family rules was not significantly related to conflict frequency or intensity.

The Ways Parents Enforce Rules Contribute to Conflicts More
Significantly Than the Ways Rules Are Constructed

The ways parents regulate adolescent activities may more significantly influence adolescents' willingness to resist parental authority and to perceive the unequal nature of their relationship with their parents as unjust than the mere fact that parents possess more power than adolescents and are the authorities who can construct rules. Given that parents with different parenting styles regulate adolescent activities in qualitatively different ways, Baumrind (1991a, 1991b; see Tables 3 and 5.2, respectively) found that permissive, disengaged, and authoritarian parents were likely to be evaluated by adolescents as unjust, arbitrary, and lacking influence over the adolescent. By contrast, authoritative parents were evaluated by adolescents as just and influential, not as unjust and arbitrary. Consistent with Baumrind's findings regarding variations in adolescents' evaluations of parents with different parenting styles, Chassin et al. (2005) found that adolescents with authoritative parents compared with other parent types experienced the lowest levels of rebelliousness and resistance to control.

Parental authority to construct and enforce rules that govern adolescent activities, which domain theorists (e.g., Nucci, 2008; Smetana, 2002; Smetana et al., 2005) consider a significant aspect of parental authority and power, may not in and of itself be viewed by adolescents as an unjust imposition they must resist. Instead, adolescents appear to accept that by definition the parental role entails the power to make and enforce rules. Future research should examine whether the ways parents enforce rules and apply control, in particular at points of disagreement, manifest in variations in parenting styles, significantly affect variations in conflict and in adolescents' evaluation of the power differential with their parents.

ADAPTIVENESS OF CONFLICTS: ADOLESCENT RESISTANCE AND CONFLICTS AS MEANS THAT FORCE PARENTS TO RELINQUISH CONTROL VERSUS VARIATIONS IN PARENTAL INTERPRETATION OF AND RESPONSE TO ADOLESCENT RESISTANCE AND CONFLICTS

Some researchers have found parent–adolescent conflicts to be maladaptive and related to negative adolescent outcomes of anxiety, depression, inattention, and difficulty with concentration. For example Chung, Flook, and Fuligni (2009), with a large sample of adolescents from different ethnic groups (Asian, Latino, and European American), found that daily or everyday adolescent conflicts with mothers and fathers were related across the adolescent years to anxiety, depression, and emotional distress with more pronounced effects on adolescent girls than boys.

However, social domain theorists (Smetana, 1995a) emphasize that parent–adolescent conflicts are adaptive and have inherent developmental benefits because "conflict forces parents to reevaluate the limits of their authority and the boundaries of adolescents' personal jurisdiction" (p. 178). Reevaluation of parental authority, which is said to lead to the expansion of adolescents' personal domain, is said to occur on a case-by-case basis involving specific issues on which adolescents reject parents' conventional and authority-based views, and parents in turn, faced with adolescent rejection, are compelled to reevaluate and reinterpret their authority and jurisdiction toward an incremental establishment of a more symmetrical relationship.

I propose that although, as domain theorists suggest, conflicts may prompt some parents to reinterpret their conceptions of their authority and adolescent autonomy in ways conducive to the creation of a symmetrical relationship, some parents do not need to be prompted to invite a more equalitarian relationship as adolescents mature, and other parents are unlikely to be forced by adolescent resistance to loosen control. Evidence for my proposition that conflicts per se may not stimulate or force positive change (even any change) comes from a study by Lichtwarck-Aschoff, Kunnen, and van Geert (2009), who found that some parents and middle adolescents, despite having high conflict about a variety of issues in different contexts, continue to respond in the same invariant and rigid ways to their conflicts. However, they found that other parent–adolescent dyads that have very infrequent conflicts are nevertheless sensitive to contextual and topical variations in conflicts, consciously examine why conflicts emerge, and are flexible in how they respond to and resolve conflicts. Therefore, not all parents, even if they experience frequent conflicts about a variety of topics, will be "forced" to change their approach to respond to adolescents in ways that resolve conflicts and accommodate adolescents' developmental needs. Some parents willingly invite a more symmetrical relationship as adolescents mature.

Parental accommodation of adolescent resistance and demands for greater independence depend on at least three factors: (a) whether parents' most essential socialization goal is being threatened by adolescent resistance; (b) whether parents attribute the cause of adolescent resistance to adolescent disposition; and (c) whether parents tolerate behaviors, arguments, or opinions that diverge from or involve rejection of the parental perspective.

Parents' Essential Socialization Goals and Willingness to Accommodate Adolescent Resistance

With respect to the first factor, I propose that parents' willingness to accommodate adolescent demands and resistance may depend on whether parents' essential socialization goal is being challenged. Coplan, Hastings, Lagace-Seguin, and Moulton (2002) found that compared with authoritative mothers, authoritarian mothers' primary socialization aim is to instill obedience and respect for authority, and child behaviors that diverge from this goal stimulate negative emotions in authoritarian parents such as anger and embarrassment across all child-rearing scenarios even when child behaviors were not overtly antisocial or defiant but were unconventional (i.e., shyness). Coplan et al. explained that authoritarian parents feel that they have failed to meet the most important goal they have as parents, which is to instill obedience and respect for authority, and are concerned that people in various social contexts will negatively judge their parenting skills. Therefore, authoritarian parents who place a premium on obedience and believe in hierarchy are more likely to regard adolescent resistance as their failure to have instilled obedience and respect for authority than to reinterpret their goals in ways consistent with a more symmetrical relationship. Coplan et al. did not study the essential goals of permissive or authoritative parents. Hastings and Grusec (1998) did study the different parenting practices that are associated with different parental goals and found that parent-centered goals are associated with power assertion and decreased parental sympathy for the child; child-centered goals with reasoning and a desire to understand the child perspective; and relationship-centered goals with warmth, negotiation, and cooperation as well as increased sympathy for the child. Hastings and Grusec's findings are consistent with Baumrind's (1991a, 1991b) findings.

It is important for future research to identify the essential socialization goals of permissive and authoritative parents and to examine how authoritative and permissive parents respond if or when adolescents seriously challenge their essential socialization goals.

Parental Interpretation of and Willingness to Accommodate Adolescent Resistance

With respect to the second factor, I propose that the ways parents explain child resistance will affect how they respond (Dix & Reinhold, 1991; Grusec, Rudy, & Martini, 1997). Parents explain child behavior by attributing the cause of child behavior to either internal/dispositional or to external/situational factors (e.g., Coplan et al., 2002). Coplan et al. (2002) examined differences between authoritarian and authoritative parents' causal attributions about socially nondisruptive behavior (i.e., shyness), positive behavior (i.e., prosocial behavior), and negative behavior (i.e., defiance). Coplan et al. found that compared with authoritative mothers, authoritarian mothers attributed positive child behavior to external/situational factors and negative child behavior to internal/dispositional factors, a tendency that led Coplan et al. to regard authoritarian mothers as "developmental pessimists." These findings reveal that authoritarian parents are unlikely to interpret adolescent resistance as reflecting a legitimate need for developmentally appropriate autonomy and are likely to impute negative disposition to the adolescent as obstinate and defiant. Such reasoning may activate their use of intrusive and coercive control (Baumrind, 1991a, 1991b; Baumrind et al., 2010; Grolnick, Weiss, McKenzie, & Wrightman, 1996).

Therefore, conflicts per se will not force some parents—namely, authoritarian parents—to reinterpret their authority to form a more symmetrical relationship but will instead motivate them to develop even more entrenched views of their child as obstinate or rejecting. Future research might examine the reasoning of authoritative and permissive parents regarding how they interpret and explain child resistance, the conditions that contribute to dispositional versus situational explanations for positive and negative child behaviors, and the conditions that lead to appropriate autonomy granting versus to disengagement or further coercion.

Parental Tolerance for Disagreement and Accommodation of Adolescent Resistance

With respect to the third factor, I propose that parents' tolerance for disagreement and for child behavior and opinion that departs from parents' beliefs or expectations varies. Not all parents are willing to accommodate adolescents' perspectives at points of disagreement and conflict. Sorkhabi (2010), using Baumrind's Time 3 archival interview data with mothers, fathers, and adolescents, examined variations in the ways parents respond to adolescents at points of conflict when the adolescent disagrees with or opposes the parent and is unwilling to comply. Interview questions were targeted to assess whether parents accommodate adolescents' increased developmental capacity to use reason and explanation by permitting adolescents to explain and argue for their perspective and whether parents alter their initial position to accommodate a cogent argument presented by the adolescent. Sorkhabi found that some parents, consistent with authoritative parenting, not only acknowledge but also are willing to accommodate adolescents' opposing viewpoint by altering their initial position if they hear a convincing argument from the adolescent. However, other parents, consistent with authoritarian parenting, were unwilling to hear adolescents' opposing viewpoint or to alter their initial position. A third group of parents, consistent with permissive parenting, did not effectively engage in reciprocal communication and even admitted that their adolescent is more competently able to use reason and logic than they are. On the basis of reports from mothers, fathers, and adolescents about their mothers and fathers, parents who engaged in authoritative use of reason experienced least conflict compared with parents who engaged in permissive or authoritarian use of reason (Sorkhabi, 2010). Tolerance and acknowledgement of adolescents' perspective reduces conflict frequency. These findings reveal that parents vary in their tolerance for adolescent disagreement and vary in their willingness to acknowledge the valid aspects of adolescents' perspective when such acknowledgment requires parents to alter their own position in some way.

Therefore, not all parents will be forced by adolescent resistance to accommodate adolescents' needs or demands because authoritarian and permissive parents do not engage in reciprocal interaction with the adolescent to accommodate adolescents' perspective. Future research is needed to assess whether conflicts with authoritarian and permissive parents have any adaptive value in terms of compelling them to decenter, recognize their children's needs and perspective, and alter their practices in ways that are developmentally adaptive.

ADAPTIVENESS OF CONFLICTS: DOMAIN SPECIFICITY OF PARENTAL CONTROL AND CONFLICT VERSUS VARIATIONS IN CONTROL APPLIED ACROSS DOMAINS BY AUTHORITARIAN, AUTHORITATIVE, AND PERMISSIVE PARENTS

Social domain theorists represent conflicts as adolescents' attempts to construct a personal domain that is outside of parental jurisdiction. Consistent with this emphasis on adolescent need to establish a personal domain, Smetana

(1997) found that when reasoning about hypothetical scenarios "children and adolescents view any type of parental intervention in the personal domain as inappropriate" and therefore "actively claim events as personal, resisting regulation and challenging adult authority" (p. 184). Consistent with their findings regarding judgments in hypothetical scenarios, domain theorists have found that actual parental regulation of the personal domain is linked to frequent conflicts and to negative developmental outcomes (i.e., low achievement, feelings of psychological control, depression, eating disorders, anxiety; Hasebe, Nucci, & Nucci, 2004; Nucci, 2008; Smetana et al., 2005). Therefore, Nucci (2008) concluded, "Clearly, the personal domain is an area where parents should tread lightly" (p. 84). However, domain theorists have found that when adolescents reason about hypothetical scenarios involving the socially regulated domains (i.e., moral, conventional, prudential), adolescents accept the legitimacy of parental authority in these domains. Nucci (2008) stated, "Children and adolescents across a broad spectrum of cultures . . . maintain that parents have jurisdiction over children's moral, conventional, and prudential behaviors" (p. 84). Consistent with their hypothetical judgments concerning the socially regulated domains, domain theorists have found that adolescents do not resist actual parental authority in these domains and that even overcontrol or restrictive control of the socially regulated domains is not linked to negative developmental outcomes or to frequent conflicts (Hasebe et al., 2004; Nucci, 2008; Nucci et al., 2005; Smetana et al., 2005). For example, Nucci (2008) stated that "adolescents and parents report almost no disputes over issues of morality, basic societal conventions, or clear prudential issues . . . all of which are viewed as within the legitimate sphere of parental authority" (p. 84). Furthermore, domain theorists have posited that adolescents who resist parental jurisdiction in the socially regulated domains constitute a small minority of the adolescent population who belong in a clinical category outside the normative range. Smetana (2005) indicated that "developmentally appropriate resistance occurs over the boundaries of . . . adolescents' personal jurisdiction" (p. 82) and that "as the clinical definitions of conduct disorders and oppositional behavior disorders suggest, defiance may entail adolescent rejection of parental moral and conventional rules, norms, and values, but healthy development does not" (p. 82).

Thus, domain theorists do not account for variations in the quality of parental control in the socially regulated domains or even in the personal domain when they attribute conflict and negative developmental outcomes only to parental regulation of the personal domain and not to the socially regulated domains (Nucci, 2008; Smetana, 2005).

It is necessary to examine the domains of parent–child interactions to fully apprehend the constellation of factors that contribute to the emergence of conflicts and adaptiveness of conflicts. However, the emphasis of domain theorists on differential effects of parental authority across domains and their reliance on hypothetical scenarios for the assessment of parental legitimacy minimize the important features of actual parent–adolescent interactions that attend variations in parents' disciplinary or control styles (Baumrind, 2005). I argue that maladaptive forms of control, such as Barber's (2002) psychological control or Baumrind's (1991a, 1991b; Baumrind et al., 2010) intrusive/coercive control, pertain not only to parental regulation of the personal domain but also to the socially regulated domains. I suggest that adolescents who are not a part of the clinical population may also resist parental control of the socially regulated domains and not resist parental control of the personal domain, depending on the ways parents with different parenting styles regulate across domains. The ways parents actually regulate any domain will significantly affect adolescents' perceptions of the legitimacy of parental authority, the likelihood of conflict or adolescent resistance, and developmental outcomes (Sorkhabi & Middaugh, 2012).

Smetana's (1991, 1995b; Smetana, Yau, & Hanson, 1991) own data on justifications that adolescents offer for intense conflicts over moral and conventional issues reveal that conflicts arise because of the ways parents regulate social as well as personal domains. Intense conflicts arise when parents overcontrol the moral domain by imposing unfair regulations that abrogate adolescents' rights or when parents enforce conventional domain issues arbitrarily by overcontrolling and dictating the details of how and when, for example, chores are to be completed or by unfairly distributing chores among siblings. Although when reasoning about hypothetical scenarios adolescents endorse the legitimacy of parental authority more in the socially regulated domains than in the personal domain, intense conflicts arise in real life in the socially regulated domains (Smetana, 1995b), and adolescents who are not a part of the clinical population resist parental authority in these domains because of the ways parents regulate. Similarly in the personal domain, depending on the quality of the parent–adolescent relationship, which is shaped by the parenting style the parent exercises, adolescents may welcome suggestions from directive, authoritative, democratic, or good-enough parents about personal domain issues such as their choice of clothing and friends (e.g., when they have conflicts with friends or are harassed by peers) rather than feel psychologically controlled (Baumrind et al., 2010), as Hasebe et al. (2004) suggested they would feel.

Similarly, domain theorists depict conflicts over multifaceted issues (i.e., issues that share features of more than one domain), such as the cleanliness of adolescents' rooms, as adolescents' attempts to curtail parental authority to expand their autonomy and their personal domain and indicate that parents should relinquish control in these areas as adolescence progresses. With respect to cleanliness of adolescents' room, conflicts are said to arise because the views of parents and adolescents diverge on the same issue. Adolescents insist that their room is their personal space, and parents in turn insist that they own the entire house, and the adolescent's room is one part of the house. Once again, it is plausible that conflicts emerge not primarily because the issue at hand is multifaceted and parents and adolescents have inherently unbridgeable views on the same issue (as Smetana, 1998, suggested) but because of the way parents demand cleanliness (as I suggest). Conflicts will continue if parents, who are supposed to be developmentally more advanced than adolescents, are unwilling to bridge the gap in understanding between themselves and their child. When parents ignore adolescents' perspective and assert arbitrary control by positing that as the sole owner of the house they will dictate how every square inch of the house will be kept, conflict will arise because the adolescent feels excluded and disregarded, not because the issue is multifaceted. Some parents may take this conflict further and engage in verbal hostility (e.g., "You're a disorganized slob").

Baumrind et al. (2010) found that arbitrary discipline, unqualified power assertion, and verbal hostility are the defining features of authoritarian parenting. However, if parents were to try a noncoercive strategy characteristic of authoritative parents by taking the adolescent's perspective into account, including the adolescent as an important member of the house, and acknowledging the adolescent when the room is clean, the conflict might be easily resolved. When power is arbitrarily imposed without regard for the adolescent, unbridgeable conflict may arise about any issue, not just personal and multifaceted issues. Overall, adolescents' justifications for the existence of conflicts with parents reveal that conflicts are frequent, intense, and unbridgeable (Smetana et al., 1991) whenever, consistent with Baumrind's authoritarian parenting style, parents apply coercive control that is unqualified, arbitrary, and hostile—devoid of connection to adolescents' needs and perspective.

Consistent with Baumrind's findings, other studies (Gerris, Dekovic, & Janssens, 1997; Pratt, Arnold, Pratt, & Diessner, 1999) have found that authoritative parents are more likely than other types of parents to establish intersubjectivity, to display higher levels of perspective taking, and to be more inclusive of the child's perspective, especially when the interests of parent and child initially conflict. Authoritarian and permissive parents' failure to establish intersubjectivity means that on the one hand authoritarian parents do not recognize areas of adolescent competence that render control superfluous, and permissive parents do not recognize areas of adolescent incompetence that render firm control and confrontive discipline necessary (Baumrind et al., 2010).

Much research and theory on adolescence emphasizes the autonomy needs of adolescents and in turn parents' obligation to relinquish control (e.g., Kerr, Stattin, Biesecker, & Ferrer-Wreder, 2003). It is also important to emphasize adolescents' need for parental involvement and understanding and the necessity of continued control exercised by authoritative and directive parents (Baumrind et al., 2010).

CONCLUSION AND FUTURE DIRECTIONS

The social domain framework (Turiel, 1983) provides an important and valuable means to organize and differentiate the range of human activities and the consequences of social actions and decisions. However, social domain framework is a cognitive explanation of social relationships and uses methodology (i.e., hypothetical scenarios) that does not sufficiently account for variations in actual normative parent–child interactions. It is necessary to examine variations in actual parent–child relationships to uncover the range of reasons that exists for the emergence of conflicts and to establish whether all conflicts within the normative range are adaptive. Therefore, socialization research will benefit from integrating domains and parenting styles.

Future research on the differentiated effects of parenting styles is needed to examine the following issues:

1. Can clusters of parenting patterns consistent with parenting styles be identified across domains and the outcomes that are associated with such parenting patterns (Sorkhabi & Middaugh, 2012)? Such research could address the question of domain specificity of parenting put forth not only by social domain theorists but also by Grusec and Davidov (2010), who posited that the form of parenting among domains and the outcomes associated with each domain may be distinct or unrelated to one another.
2. Whether parents use different practices within different domains and how variations in practices among domains are related to outcomes (Sorkhabi & Middaugh, 2012). This research will also address the question and claim made by domain theorists and others (e.g., Grusec & Davidov, 2010; Trickett & Kuczynski, 1986) that parents use different practices in accord with different types of child activities or behaviors.
3. Whether goals of parents with different parenting styles are instantiated in ways consistent with their goals and the outcomes associated with congruence between parental goals and implementation of parental goals.
4. What are adolescents' primary goals and do their goals conflict with their parents' goals depending on their parents' parenting style?

5. How do adolescents view the power differential between themselves and their parents depending on their parents' parenting style?
6. Are variations in adolescents' views of parental power related to adolescent resistance, conflict, and psychosocial outcomes?
7. How do parents with different parenting styles interpret and respond to adolescent resistance?
8. What factors affect whether parents will accommodate adolescent resistance and demands for autonomy and how will they do so?

REFERENCES

Barber, B. K. (Ed.). (2002). *Intrusive parenting: How psychological control affects children and adolescents*. Washington, DC: American Psychological Association. doi:10.1037/10422-000

Baumrind, D. (1971). Current patterns of parental authority. *Developmental Psychology Monographs, 4*(1, Pt. 2), 1–103. doi:10.1037/h0030372

Baumrind, D. (1973). The development of instrumental competence through socialization. In A. Pick (Ed.), *Minnesota symposia on child psychology* (Vol. 7, pp. 3–46). Minneapolis: University of Minnesota Press.

Baumrind, D. (1989). Rearing competent children. In W. Damon (Ed.), *Child development today and tomorrow* (pp. 349–378). San Francisco, CA: Jossey-Bass.

Baumrind, D. (1991a). Effective parenting during the early adolescent transition. In P. E. Cowan & E. M. Hetherington (Eds.), *Advances in family research* (Vol. 2, pp. 111–163). Hillsdale, NJ: Erlbaum.

Baumrind, D. (1991b). The influence of parenting style on adolescent competence and substance use. *The Journal of Early Adolescence, 11*, 56–95. doi:10.1177/0272431691111004

Baumrind, D. (2008). Authoritative parenting for character and competence. In D. Straight (Ed.), *Parenting for character: Five experts, five practices* (pp. 14–30). Portland, OR: Council for Spiritual and Ethical Education.

Baumrind, D., Larzelere, B., & Owens, L. (2010). Effects of preschool parents' power assertive patterns and practices on adolescent development. *Parenting: Science and practice, 10*, 157–201. doi:10.1080/15295190903290790

Baumrind, D., & Thompson, R. (2002). The ethics of parenting. In M. Bornstein (Ed.), *Handbook of parenting: Vol. 5. Practical issues in parenting* (2nd ed., pp. 3–34). Mahwah, NJ: Erlbaum.

Caffery, T., & Erdman, P. (2000). Conceptualizing parent–adolescent conflict: Applications from systems and attachment theories. *The Family Journal, 8*(1), 14–21. doi:10.1177/1066480700081004

Caughlin, J. P., & Malis, R. S. (2004). Demand/withdraw communication between parents and adolescents: Connections with self-esteem and substance use. *Journal of Social and Personal Relationships, 21*(1), 125–148. doi:10.1177/0265407504039843

Chassin, L., Presson, C. C., Rose, J., Sherman, S. J., Davis, M. J., & Gonzalez, J. L. (2005). Parenting styles and smoking-specific practices as predictors of adolescent smoking onset. *Journal of Pediatric Psychology, 30*, 333–344. doi:10.1093/jpepsy/jsi028

Chung, G. H., Flook, L., & Fuligni, A. J. (2009). Daily family conflict and emotional distress among adolescents from Latin American, Asian, and European backgrounds. *Developmental Psychology, 45*, 1406–1415. doi:10.1037/a0014163

Coplan, R. J., Hastings, P. D., Lagace-Seguin, D. G., & Moulton, C. E. (2002). Authoritative and authoritarian mothers' parenting goals, attributions, and emotions across different childrearing contexts. *Parenting: Science and Practice, 2*, 1–26. doi:10.1207/S15327922PAR0201_1

Dix, T., & Reinhold, D. P. (1991). Chronic and temporary influences on mothers' attributions for children's disobedience. *Merrill-Palmer Quarterly: Journal of Developmental Psychology, 37*, 251–271.

Emery, R. E. (1992). Family conflicts and their developmental implications: A conceptual analysis of meanings for the structure of relationships. In C. U. Shantz & W. W. Hartup (Eds.), *Conflict in child and adolescent development* (pp. 270–298). New York, NY: Cambridge University Press.

Feldman, S. S., & Gehring, T. M. (1988). Changing perceptions of family cohesion and power across adolescence. *Child Development, 59*, 1034–1045. doi:10.2307/1130269

Fuligni, A. J. (1998). Authority, autonomy, and parent–adolescent conflict and cohesion: A study of adolescents from Mexican, Chinese, Filipino, and European backgrounds. *Developmental Psychology, 34*, 782–792. doi:10.1037/0012-1649.34.4.782

Gerris, J. R. M., Dekovic, M., & Janssens, J. M. A. M. (1997). The relationship between social class and childrearing behaviors: Parents' perspective taking and value orientations. *Journal of Marriage and the Family, 59*, 834–847. doi:10.2307/353786

Greenberger, E., & Chen, C. (1996). Perceived family relationships and depressed mood in early and late adolescence: A comparison of European and Asian Americans. *Developmental Psychology, 32*, 707–716. doi:10.1037/0012-1649.32.4.707

Grolnick, W. S., Weiss, L., McKenzie, L., & Wrightman, J. (1996). Contextual, cognitive, and adolescent factors associated with parenting in adolescence. *Journal of Youth and Adolescence, 25*(1), 33–54. doi:10.1007/BF01537379

Grusec, J. E., & Davidov, M. (2010). Integrating different perspectives on socialization theory and research: A domain-specific approach. *Child Development, 81*, 687–709. doi:10.1111/j.1467-8624.2010.01426.x

Grusec, J. E., Rudy, D., & Martini, T. (1997). Parenting cognitions and child outcomes: An overview and implications for children's internalization of values. In

J. E. Grusec & L. Kuczynski (Eds.), *Parenting and children's internalization of values* (pp. 259–282). New York, NY: Wiley.

Hasebe, Y., Nucci, L., & Nucci, M. (2004). Parental control of the personal domain and adolescent symptoms of psychopathology. *Child Development, 75,* 815–828. doi:10.1111/j.1467-8624.2004.00708.x

Hastings, P. D., & Grusec, J. E. (1998). Parenting goals as organizers of responses to parent–child disagreement. *Developmental Psychology, 34,* 465–479. doi:10.1037/0012-1649.34.3.465

Hastings, P. D., & Rubin, K. H. (1999). A longitudinal study of the development of mothers' beliefs about preschool-aged children's social behavior. *Child Development, 70,* 722–741. doi:10.1111/1467-8624.00052

Hetherington, E. M., & Kelly, J. (2002). *For better or for worse: Divorce reconsidered.* New York, NY: Norton.

Kerr, M., Stattin, H., Biesecker, G., & Ferrer-Wreder, L. (2003). Relationship with parents and peers in adolescence. In R. M. Lerner, M. A. Easterbrooks, & J. Mistry (Eds.), *Handbook of psychology: Developmental psychology* (Vol. 6, pp. 395–419). New York, NY: Wiley.

Lamborn, S. D., Dornbusch, S. M., & Steinberg, L. (1996). Ethnicity and community context as moderators of the relations between family decision making and adolescent adjustment. *Child Development, 67,* 283–301. doi:10.2307/1131814

Lichtwarck-Aschoff, A., Kunnen, S. E., & van Geert, P. L. C. (2009). Here we go again: A dynamic systems perspective on emotional rigidity across parent–adolescent conflicts. *Developmental Psychology, 45,* 1364–1375. doi:10.1037/a0016713

Maccoby, E. E. (1999). The uniqueness of the parent–child relationship. In W. A. Collins & B. Laursen (Eds.), *Relationships as developmental contexts: Minnesota symposia on child psychology* (Vol. 30, pp. 157–175). Mahwah, NJ: Erlbaum.

Nucci, L. P. (2008). The domains of social reasoning: How we think about right and wrong and why it matters to parents. In D. Streight (Ed.), *Parenting for character: Five experts, five practices* (pp. 76–88). Portland, OR: Council for Spiritual and Ethical Education.

Nucci, L. P., Hasebe, Y., & Lins-Dyer, M. T. (2005). Adolescent psychological well-being and parental control of the personal. In J. Smetana (Ed.), *New directions for child and adolescent development: No. 108. Changing boundaries of parental authority during adolescence* (pp. 17–30). San Francisco, CA: Jossey-Bass. doi:10.1002/cd.125

Patterson, G. R. (1971). *Families: Applications of social learning to family life* (Rev. ed.). Champaign, IL: Research Press.

Patterson, G. R., & Fisher, P. A. (2002). Recent developments in our understanding of parenting: Bidirectional effects, causal models, and the search for parsimony. In M. H. Bornstein (Series Ed.), *Handbook of parenting: Vol. 5. Practical issues in parenting* (2nd ed., pp. 59–88). Mahwah, NJ: Erlbaum.

Piaget, J. (1932). *The moral judgment of the child*. New York, NY: Free Press.

Pratt, M. W., Arnold, M. L., Pratt, A. T., & Diessner, R. (1999). Predicting adolescent moral reasoning from family climate: A longitudinal study. *The Journal of Early Adolescence, 19*, 148–175. doi:10.1177/0272431699019002002

Schermerhorn, A. C., & Cummings, E. M. (2008). Transactional family dynamics: A new framework for conceptualizing family influence processes. In R. V. Kail (Ed.), *Advances in child development and behavior* (Vol. 36, pp. 187–250). San Diego, CA: Elsevier. doi:10.1016/S0065-2407(08)00005-0

Smetana, J. G. (1988). Adolescents' and parents' conceptions of parental authority. *Child Development, 59*, 321–335. doi:10.2307/1130313

Smetana, J. G. (1989). Adolescents' and parents' reasoning about actual family conflict. *Child Development, 60*, 1052–1067. doi:10.2307/1130779

Smetana, J. G. (1991). Adolescents' and mothers' evaluations of justifications for conflicts. In R. L. Paikoff (Ed.), *Shared views in the family during adolescence* (Vol. 51, pp. 71–86). San Francisco, CA: Jossey-Bass.

Smetana, J. G. (Ed.) (1994). Beliefs about parenting: Origins and developmental implications. In *New directions for child development* (No. 66, pp. 21–36). San Francisco, CA: Jossey-Bass. doi:10.1002/cd.23219946604

Smetana, J. G. (1995a). Conflict and coordination in adolescent–parent relationships. In S. Strauss (Series Ed.) & S. Shulman (Vol. Ed.), *Human development: Vol. 7. Close relationships and socioemotional development* (pp. 155–184). Norwood, NJ: Ablex Publishing.

Smetana, J. G. (1995b). Parenting styles and conceptions of parental authority during adolescence. *Child Development, 66*, 299–316. doi:10.2307/1131579

Smetana, J. G. (1997). Parenting and the development of social knowledge reconceptualized: A social domain analysis. In J. E. Grusec & L. Kuczynski (Eds.), *Parenting and children's internalization of values: A handbook of contemporary theory* (pp. 162–192). New York, NY: Wiley.

Smetana, J. G. (1998). Concepts of self and social convention: Adolescents' and parents' reasoning about hypothetical and actual family conflicts. In M. R. Gunnar & W. A. Collins (Eds.), *Minnesota symposia on child psychology: Vol. 21. Development during the transition to adolescence* (pp. 79–122). Hillsdale, NJ: Erlbaum.

Smetana, J. G. (2002). Culture, autonomy, and personal jurisdiction in adolescent–parent relationships. In R. V. Vail & H. W. Reese (Eds.), *Advances in child development and behavior* (Vol. 29, pp. 51–87). New York, NY: Academic Press.

Smetana, J. G. (2005). Adolescent–parent conflict: Resistance and subversion as developmental processes. In L. Nucci (Ed.), *Conflict, contradiction, and contrarian elements in moral development and education* (pp. 69–91). Mahwah, NJ: Erlbaum.

Smetana, J. G., & Asquith, P. (1994). Adolescents' and parents' conceptions of parental authority and adolescent autonomy. *Child Development, 65*, 1147–1162.

Smetana, J. G., Crean, H. F., & Campione-Barr, N. (2005). Adolescents' and parents' changing conceptions of parental authority. In J. Smetana (Ed.), *New directions for child and adolescent development: Changing boundaries of parental authority during adolescence* (pp. 31–46). San Francisco. CA: Jossey-Bass. doi:10.1002/cd.126

Smetana, J.G., Yau, J., & Hanson, S. (1991). Conflict resolution in families with adolescents. *Journal of Research on Adolescence, 1,* 189–206. doi:10.1207/s15327795jra0102_5

Sorkhabi, N. (2010). Sources of parent–adolescent conflicts: Content and form of parenting. *Social Behavior and Personality, 38,* 761–782. doi:10.2224/sbp.2010.38.6.761

Sorkhabi, N. & Middaugh, E. (2012). *Adolescents' perceptions of variation in parental control as exercised by parents with different parenting styles: Outcomes of parent–adolescent conflict, adolescent problem behaviors and disclosure.* Manuscript in preparation.

Trickett, P.K., & Kuczynski, L. (1986). Children's misbehaviors and parental discipline strategies in abusive and nonabusive families. *Developmental Psychology, 22,* 115–123. doi:10.1037/0012-1649.22.1.115

Turiel, E. (1983). *Development of social knowledge: Morality and convention.* Cambridge, England: Cambridge University Press.

III

CLINICAL AND EDUCATIONAL APPLICATIONS

7

WORKING WITH PARENTS OF AGGRESSIVE CHILDREN: TEN PRINCIPLES AND THE ROLE OF AUTHORITATIVE PARENTING

TIMOTHY A. CAVELL, AMANDA W. HARRIST,
AND TAMARA DEL VECCHIO

Baumrind's conceptualization of authoritative parenting describes a pattern of socialization strategies that fits most parents and their typically developing children. It encompasses a particular set of parental goals (e.g., socializing a child to be a competent citizen, facilitating development of self-discipline), values (e.g., communication, child autonomy), and skills (e.g., setting boundaries, conveying acceptance). But is an authoritative parenting style possible for parents who are struggling to discipline or enjoy a child who is highly aggressive? Researchers' understanding of the development of aggressive behavior has become more sophisticated; however, adaptations to Baumrind's framework have not mirrored these changes. Similarly, current models of parent training have failed to fully incorporate the complex nature of aggressive parent–child dyads. In this chapter, we review recent advances in knowledge about parenting and the development of childhood aggression. We offer 10 guiding principles for parent-based interventions that incorporate the contributions of both

DOI: 10.1037/13948-008

Authoritative Parenting: Synthesizing Nurturance and Discipline for Optimal Child Development, Robert E. Larzelere, Amanda Sheffield Morris, and Amanda W. Harrist (Editors)

165

Baumrind's relationship-based typologies and skill-based parent training models and reflect an understanding of the complexity of parenting an aggressive child. We start, however, with the case of Robert:

> Robert is 10 years old and lives with his mother and his two younger half-sisters. At home, Robert refuses to help with chores and screams and whines if he does not get his way. He argues constantly with his sisters, occasionally hitting them, teasing them, and taking things from them. Linda, Robert's mother, works part time at a nursing home and is twice divorced. She feels overwhelmed and is unsure of how to deal with Robert. She is quick to react when he misbehaves, but punishing him does not seem to help. At other times, she does not have the energy to discipline him and believes it's better not to aggravate him. At school, he is known for getting into trouble—breaking rules and fighting with other kids. He even threatened a teacher who made him sit out during recess. He's a capable student but typically unmotivated. Lately, he's been hanging around some older boys, including two who like to smoke cigarettes and talk about being in a gang.

Diagnostically, Robert would likely meet criteria for conduct disorder, childhood onset (American Psychiatric Association, 2000). In cases like Robert's, extant research suggests there is cause for concern. Childhood aggression is quite stable (Loeber, 1990), and Patterson, Forgatch, Yoerger, and Stoolmiller (1998) found that 50% of boys identified as aggressive by age 9 or 10 were arrested by age 14; in turn, 75% of boys arrested by age 14 had three or more arrests by the age of 18. The risks are particularly serious for children who meet what Moffitt (1993) called the *life-course persistent* pattern of offending, which has an early onset, is extreme in its severity, occurs across settings, and is predictive of a later criminality and antisocial personality disorder.

Parents of children like Robert often need guidance on how best to parent in a way that will make a positive difference for them and their family. Such guidance has generally emanated from two sources. One source is research on authoritative parenting, which offers a compelling case for the combination of parental responsiveness and demandingness. It is a pattern commonly used by parents whose children are socially competent and unlikely to show signs of serious behavior problems. A second source is behaviorally based parent training, a frequently recommended and often studied intervention strategy that emerged simultaneously with Baumrind's groundbreaking studies on authoritative parenting (Cavell, 2000).

In this chapter, we explore how these two bodies of work can (a) inform each other, (b) be updated to reflect current research on the role of parenting in the development of childhood aggression, and (c) be integrated to offer a more comprehensive framework for understanding the struggle facing parents of aggressive children. We present this framework in the form of 10 guiding principles.

RECENT ADVANCES IN KNOWLEDGE ABOUT PARENTING AND THE DEVELOPMENT OF CHILDHOOD AGGRESSION

Over the last 25 years, researchers have learned a great deal about aggressive children and the role that parenting plays in the onset and maintenance of childhood aggression. The developmental course of aggressive, antisocial behavior (ASB) has come to be viewed as a dynamic process that involves biological, cognitive, and affective variables interacting with social contextual factors (Cicchetti & Toth, 2009). Prospective longitudinal studies demonstrate that biogenetic risks, maladaptive social cognitions, risky social contexts (e.g., negative parenting, deviant peers), externalizing behavior problems, and delinquent activity are coparticipants in a *developmental cascade*, that is, a series of complex transactions that accumulate outcomes far more intractable than what would be expected from a simple linear, unidirectional, and mediational trajectory (Lansford, Malone, Dodge, Pettit, & Bates, 2010).

An important area of advancement in researchers' understanding of childhood aggression has involved work explicating the contribution of child effects (Lytton, 1990) and the interactive role of nature and nurture in children's development (Collins, Maccoby, Steinberg, Hetherington, & Bornstein, 2000). A meta-analysis (Burt, 2009) estimated that 58% of the variance in child and adolescent conduct problems was accounted for by genetic endowment. An additional portion of variance was accounted for by gene–environment interplay, including the tendency for children with certain biologically based risk factors such as attention-deficit/hyperactivity disorder to evoke negative parenting. Neurodevelopmental/self-regulatory factors also contribute to the levels of aggression children display (Fairchild et al., 2011; Nigg & Huang-Pollock, 2003). Also noteworthy are studies supporting the role of callous/unemotional traits as a predictor of child and adolescent ASB (Frick, Stickle, Dandreaux, Farrell, & Kimonis, 2005). Children high in callous/unemotional traits have been shown to be relatively insensitive to punishment, to hold social-cognitive expectancies that aggression will lead to positive outcomes, and to exhibit elevated levels of externalizing behaviors that are not predicted by parenting effectiveness (Oxford, Cavell, & Hughes, 2003).

A second area of knowledge advancement has documented the influence of competing social contexts on the development of aggression and ASB (see Cavell, Hymel, Malcolm, & Seay, 2007). Some contexts offer positive influence (e.g., schools, 4-H Clubs) but are inaccessible to or overly demanding for children at risk; other contexts offer "success" in antisocial activities (e.g., deviant peers, crime-ridden neighborhoods). Such contexts represent powerful sources of nonparental environmental influences, and efforts to model the role of parenting in the development of ASB cannot ignore these competing influences or the wider social matrix in which parenting resides (Conger & Simons, 1997; Harris, 1995).

A final area of advancement is in researchers' understanding of the dyadic processes that make the parent–child relationship the key context in children's socialization. Much of the work in this area is tied to social learning models of parental influence (and thus behaviorally based parenting interventions), especially that involving the role of coercive exchanges between parent and child (Patterson, Reid, & Dishion, 1992). However, recent studies have expanded researchers' models of parenting and the processes leading to the development of aggression. Newer models have examined attachment-related phenomena, the emergence of conscience, parental emotion socialization strategies, and the level of mutuality or reciprocity that characterizes parent–child interactions. For example, low levels of parent–child mutually responsive orientation (e.g., Kochanska, Aksan, Prisco, & Adams, 2008) and dyadic synchrony (e.g., Harrist & Waugh, 2002) in early childhood have been linked to later poor child self-regulation and aggression.

In the 40+ years since the introduction of authoritative parenting, the science that informs researchers' understanding of parenting and socialization has undergone tremendous change. Conceptual models depicting the developmental course of ASB have also become broader and more complex, as illustrated by the *integrated life-course–social learning* model of socialization and the development of ASB (Cavell et al., 2007), which situates parenting with respect to other socialization forces operating over the course of children's development (Figure 7.1). The model has important implications for parent-based interventions that target aggressive children. Emphasized are robust contributions involving (a) biogenetic risk factors, (b) available social contexts, and (c) children's capacity to access and succeed in those contexts. The parent–child relationship is but one context among many that can influence developing youths, and parents of aggressive children, like most parents, must compete with other, sometimes deviant, contexts for children's time and emotional investment. Aggressive children are doubly disadvantaged: They are less likely to succeed in prosocial contexts (e.g., schools) and are more likely to be drawn to and more successful in deviant contexts. The parent–child relationship, at minimum, should be a context that does not promote ASB. But authoritative parents have to do more than limit ASB if they are to compete well against other less prosocial contexts.

Also recognized in this model is the challenge of monitoring and managing children's involvement in other contexts. Parents who are consistently in the dark about children's whereabouts, companions, and activities are, by definition, poor monitors. However, the direction of causality is not always

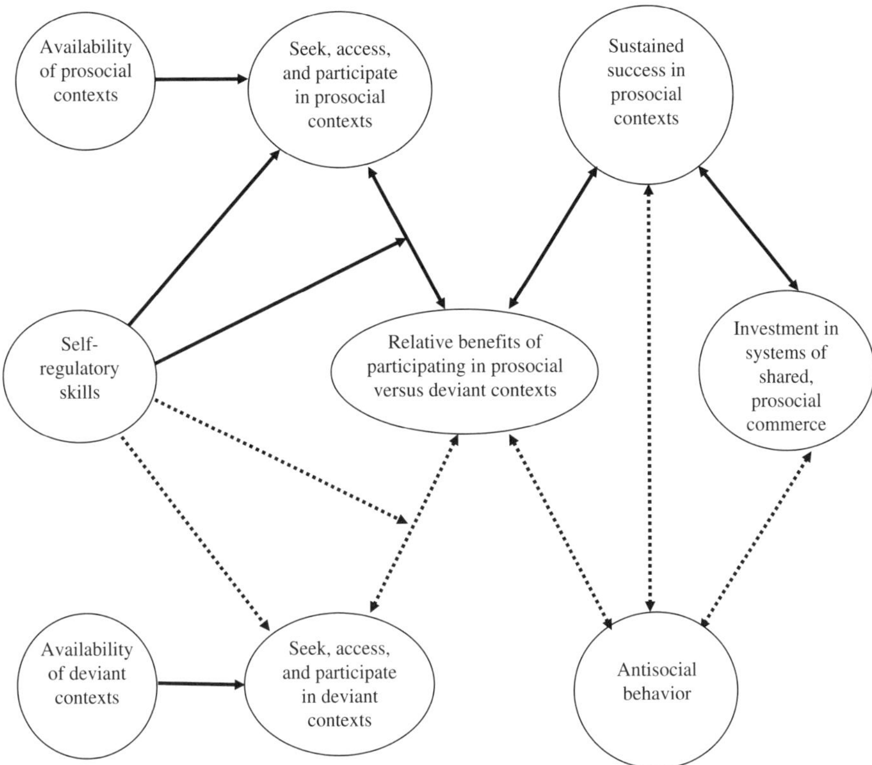

Figure 7.1. Integrated life course–social learning model depicting the relation between socialization processes and the development of antisocial behavior. Moderator effects are indicated by arrows pointing to paths rather than to constructs. Dotted lines indicate inverse relations.

clear: Some children are more difficult to monitor. In fact, it appears the robust relation between parental monitoring and ASB is due in part to children and adolescents actively managing the information they give to parents about the other contexts in their lives (Kerr & Stattin, 2000). Thus, to view monitoring solely as a parenting practice fails to appreciate the level of influence that children and adolescents wield in this process. And some youths are more susceptible to the influence of deviant peers (Vitaro, Brendgen, & Tremblay, 2001). Youths who are aggressive and disliked do not have the luxury to be discriminating about their companions or the kinds of activities (e.g., delinquency, substance use) deemed "necessary" to maintain companionship (Boivin, Vitaro, & Poulin, 2005). For these youths, affiliating with deviant peers is not so much an option as it is a last resort for social interchange, which makes difficult parents' efforts to limit the contexts in which children spend their time and energy.

PARENT MANAGEMENT TRAINING

During the time when Baumrind (1967, 1971) was introducing the concept of parenting style, other researchers were engaged in developing an intervention strategy for parents whose children were defiant, disruptive, or aggressive (Patterson & Brodsky, 1966; Wahler, Winkle, Peterson, & Morrison, 1965). *Parent management training* (PMT) is a summary term used to describe a therapeutic strategy in which parents are trained to use behaviorally based disciplinary skills to manage their children's misbehavior (Kazdin, 1993). PMT is the most widely studied intervention for children with oppositional defiant and conduct disorders (Serketich & Dumas, 1996). It is also one of the most promising (Lundahl, Risser, & Lovejoy, 2006; Maughan, Christiansen, Jenson, Olympia, & Clark, 2005). Long-term outcomes are generally positive (Hood & Eyberg, 2003; Webster-Stratton, 1990), although follow-up assessments following randomized control trials are often limited in length and reveal mixed outcomes (e.g., Hagen, Ogden, & Bjornebekk, 2011). An exception is recent work by Forgatch, Patterson, DeGarmo, and Beldavs (2009) examining outcomes for boys of divorced mothers 9 years post intervention. PMT significantly reduced teacher-reported delinquency and police arrests in this nonclinical sample. Despite lingering questions about long-term outcomes (Eyberg, Edwards, Boggs, & Foote, 1998) or of the use of PMT for disadvantaged or minority populations (Lundahl et al., 2006; Prinz & Miller, 1991), PMT is one of the few empirically supported treatments for children with conduct problems (Eyberg, Nelson, & Boggs, 2008).

Still, PMT's basic assumptions about effective and ineffective parenting have not kept pace with recent advances in researchers' understanding of parenting and its role in the development of aggression, although components addressing parents' role in emotion socialization are evident in some programs (e.g., Forgatch & Patterson, 2010; see also Chapter 8, this volume). PMT approaches the treatment of child aggression from an operant conditioning perspective. A fundamental assumption is that aggression is learned through parent-delivered contingencies that inadvertently reinforce negative behaviors. Coercion theory (Patterson et al., 1992) posits that children learn coercion from parents who themselves are coercive (using behaviors ranging from nattering to physical assault) but who also give in to and thus reinforce children's use of coercion to resist parents' demands. Over time, the coercive cycle establishes coercion as a dominant influence strategy for children who are early starters on a path toward later delinquency. When coercive behavior is generalized to interactions with others, the stage is set for a series of negative cascades, including reinforcement of more varied forms of ASB by deviant peers (Forgatch et al., 2009). Patterson's (1982) seminal work examining moment-to-moment contingencies in the homes of aggressive children offered a solid foundation for PMT interventions designed to alter those contingencies. The emphasis on microsocial parent–child processes was also a sharp contrast to the more molar-level notion of parenting styles.

Patterson's original coercion theory has undergone important revisions since the publication of his 1982 volume. Snyder and Patterson (1995) used the basic tenets of the matching law (Herrnstein, 1974) to reexamine Patterson's (1982) original hypotheses, in particular, the emphasis on between-individuals differences in contingencies governing aggressive behavior. The matching law places greater emphasis on within-individual variation and the context of competing positive and negative contingencies that govern variation. The matching law proposes that the probability of an individual performing a response will generally match the probability of that response being reinforced or punished relative to other responses (Snyder & Patterson, 1995). Equally important for understanding the role of context is the *time allocation* component of the matching law, which posits that "time spent in an environment will also be relative to the rate of reinforcement provided by that environment" (Conger & Simons, 1997, p. 62). The distribution of reinforcing contingencies within a given context (e.g., parent–child interactions) influences whether children perform ASB, but it is the distribution of reinforcing contingencies across social contexts that influences whether children spend time in deviant contexts (Conger & Simons, 1997). Accordingly, it becomes critical to consider the competing value of social contexts that differentially support prosocial versus antisocial activities (Cavell et al., 2007). The implication for parents of aggressive children is that strict limits on misbehavior must be balanced against providing a parent–child relationship that keeps children invested in the family context.

Granic and Patterson (2006) further revised and expanded coercion theory, venturing beyond operant principles to apply dynamic systems principles and methods. Retained was the core premise that coercive interactions drive the emergence and stabilization of child aggression, but important limitations were noted. Among these limitations was the use of unidirectional operant principles to explain interactions better understood in terms of reciprocal or circular causality. Also lacking was an appreciation for relationship patterns or whole systems that reflected more than the behavior of individual members: "The relationship itself has its own features and its own developmental history" (Granic & Patterson, 2006, p. 106). When that history involves repeated coercive interactions between parent and child, future interactions are constrained as "the degrees of freedom along the dyadic trajectory are pruned by developing habits" (p. 105).

A dynamic systems model proposes that patterns of interaction (attractors) vary in intensity, with more intense patterns becoming increasingly resistant to change. Multiple attractors can coexist within a system, thereby creating competing response demands. Within parent–child relationships, dyads move toward some attractors and away from other attractors, depending on contextual variations. However, some attractors are quite powerful in that dyads move quickly toward them and remain stuck in them; such is the case with mutually hostile patterns for parents and aggressive children. Granic and Patterson's (2006) revision of coercion theory also includes cognitive and affective elements that were absent from previous versions. When combined with firmly established attractors, parents' negative attributions and expectations, along with feelings of anger or contempt, can lead to rapid escalation in coercive behavior, often triggered by seemingly benign, minimally aversive actions. Cognitive and emotional aspects of parenting also help differentiate two distinct patterns of coercive parenting: one in which parents are hostile and coercive and one in which parents are overly lax in their response to children's coercion. These patterns are reminiscent of authoritarian and permissive parenting, respectively, but are recognized by Granic and Patterson as leading similarly to growth in children's use of coercion and ASB. Granic and Patterson also noted that adverse environmental contexts, often in concert with difficult child temperament and parental psychopathology, can disrupt parenting practices and give rise to coercive parenting. Over time, adversity produces "an imbalance" between coercive and noncoercive parenting (Patterson, Forgatch, & DeGarmo, 2010, p. 951), limiting the availability of prosocial exchanges as coercion becomes the stronger attractor.

Thus, within a dynamic systems framework, ineffective parenting is not simply the inadvertent reinforcing of child coercion but a rigid returning to coercive dyadic interaction patterns (hostile or permissive) in the face of shifting contexts and competing demands. One can see in this latest revision of coercion theory parallels to the parenting styles first identified by Baumrind (1973). Patterson et al. (2010) suggested that coercive parenting functions as a stop–go mechanism and "family members are essentially coercive or essentially positive in their interactions with each other" (p. 967). Patterns of mutual hostility reduce the likelihood of positive (authoritative-like) parenting that is needed to promote social competence and prosocial development. Aggressive children are similarly drawn into rigid interaction patterns with peers and others outside the family, further limiting their access to and success in prosocial contexts.

As an intervention strategy, the core components of PMT for managing behavior have changed little over the years. Innovations have been limited to changes in delivery format (e.g., group, video modeling) or components added to the core curriculum. The typical PMT curriculum borrows heavily from the toolbox of behavior modification. Positive parenting strategies designed to increase the rate of desirable child behaviors (i.e., praise, attention, rewards) are typically presented first, followed by strategies for decreasing the rate of undesirable behaviors (i.e., ignoring, time out). As research in support of PMT mounted, this set of skills came to be viewed not as borrowed techniques for managing behavior but as the basics of effective parenting (Cavell, 2001; Cavell et al., 2007). Interestingly, parents of nonreferred children seldom use contingent praise, and there is evidence that it is unrelated to the level of child compliance in clinic (Roberts, 1985) and nonclinic families (Griest, Forehand, Wells, & McMahon, 1980). Still, parents whose children behaved aggressively were often viewed as lacking basic parenting skills, and a lack of skills was considered a key contributor to children's aggression. This notion was a good fit for an intervention that focused on skills training.

Related to the skills-deficit hypothesis is the difference between skill acquisition and skill performance. Much of the research linking poor parenting to child misbehavior documents disruptions in the use of effective parenting rather than a lack of effective skills. A classic example of this distinction is found in the study by Green, Forehand, and McMahon (1979). In the initial phase of the study, mothers of referred and nonreferred children were instructed every 30 seconds (through a "bug" in the ear) to give their children specific, nonrepeated, labeled commands. Children with conduct problems were compliant 52% of the time, whereas nonreferred children were compliant 73% of the time. In the next phase, mothers were instructed to make their children "look" compliant or noncompliant, and mothers were free to choose how to do this. Surprisingly, both groups of mothers were able to accomplish both tasks. Mothers became more negative when making their child look noncompliant, and they became more positive when making their child look compliant. The findings suggest that mothers of referred children have in their repertoire the skills necessary to make a child look compliant, but their performance of key parenting practices is disrupted in some way.

Despite considerable support for the efficacy of PMT, some families fail to benefit (e.g., Webster-Stratton, 1990), and there remains room for improving its outcomes with aggressive school-age children. Our premise is that practitioners who work with the parents of aggressive children could benefit from a more up-to-date model of socialization as it applies to aggressive school-age children. Needed is a framework that considers how ASB changes from toddlerhood to late adolescence, how changes in ASB affect the parent–child relationship, and how parenting changes as a result of children's transactional success or failure at various developmental periods. Also needed is a conceptual model that recognizes the chronic nature of childhood aggression (Kazdin, 1993) and the fact that parenting an aggressive child can be a long-term task spanning nearly 2 decades. For children on the early-onset trajectory of ASB, aggression is not a temporary detour from prosocial development, and practitioners would be wise to recognize that socialization is the intervention (Cavell et al., 2007). The short-term goal of child compliance should not detract from the long-term goal of socialization.

An expanded and updated model would also recognize that parenting effectiveness can wax and wane as parents struggle from time to time with external stressors and family transitions. The notion that parents are competing with other socialization forces is also critical. Parenting an aggressive child means managing over time the multiple contexts that influence socialization and competing well when children are drawn to deviant contexts or to peers engaged in appealing but delinquent activities. Finally, a broader conceptual model would emphasize parents' long-term management of the parent–child relationship, for it is the key context in the socialization of aggressive children. In sum, current models of parent training only partly address the inherent complexity or messiness of parenting an aggressive child. In the following section, we offer a conceptual framework that appreciates that complexity, as well as the wholes or patterns of parent–child relationships first introduced by Baumrind (1967, 1971) and recently articulated by Granic and Patterson (2006).

TEN GUIDING PRINCIPLES FOR PARENT-BASED INTERVENTIONS

Our organizing framework is represented by 10 guiding principles (Cavell, 2000, 2001; Cavell & Elledge, 2007; Cavell & Strand, 2003). Collectively, these principles provide an overarching heuristic for working with parents of aggressive children. Metaphorically, this framework is neither new wine nor old wine in new bottles; instead, it is a new way to blend grapes from old proven vines. It is also an attempt to close an important gap: the gap between what is known about parenting and the development of childhood aggression and what is typically recommended to practitioners in the form of PMT. Theoretically, these principles draw from social learning, family systems, and attachment theories and, more specifically, from a strong appreciation for environmental contingencies (Conger & Simons, 1997), genetically endowed individual differences (Scarr, 1992), and children's capacity to affect their own development (Kuczynski, 2003) and from relationship-based models of socialization (Kuczynski & Hildebrandt, 1997; Richters & Waters, 1991). At the heart of these principles is the goal of helping parents of aggressive children blend responsiveness and demandingness (Baumrind, 1971) over the course of a long-term socializing relationship.

Principle 1: The Long-Term Socialization of Aggressive Children Takes Precedence Over the Short-Term Management of Their Behavior

The long-term goal of socializing children into a system of shared prosocial commerce (Richters & Waters, 1991) is important for parents generally and critical for parents of aggressive children (Cavell et al., 2007). This single shift in focus could have tremendous implications for the way practitioners approach the task of working with parents of aggressive children. Childhood aggression tends to have a chronic course (Kazdin, 1993), but few parents of aggressive children will have an articulated long-term socialization plan. They are more likely to seek help with matters that are occurring in the here and now, driven by the complaints of those affected by their child's behavior and by the emotional costs of parenting a child who is hard to manage and hard to like. Parents also miss the mark of socialization when they overestimate their capacity for influencing some child outcomes (e.g., intellectual functioning) while underestimating the value of pursuing the developmentally significant but long-term goal of their child's socialization.

Principle 2: The Parent–Child Relationship Is a Useful Vehicle for Socializing Aggressive Children

We propose that parents of aggressive children are well served when they focus on managing the nature and quality of the parent–child relationship. This recommendation stands in contrast to the dominant theme of PMT, which is managing child behavior. Effectively managing the behavior of aggressive children is important, but how parents respond to child behavior cannot be understood apart from the context of the parent–child relationship (Cavell, 2000, 2001; Kuczynski & Hildebrandt, 1997; Richters & Waters, 1991). Eschewed here is the notion that effective parenting involves merely matching a specific problem behavior with the right behavior modification technique (e.g., Christophersen & Mortweet, 2001). Instead, we are emphasizing the broader temporal context in which these processes occur. As noted by Kuczynski and Hildebrandt (1997), a relationship-based model of socialization "gives a time dimension to parent–child interactions" (p. 236) and helps explain how parent–child dyads adapt to past interactions and how they approach future interactions.

Principle 3: Socializing Relationships Provide Aggressive Children, Over Time, With Emotional Acceptance, Behavioral Containment, and Prosocial Values

Cavell proposed that parents who establish and sustain a relationship that offers all three conditions will be more likely to alter the risk trajectory of their aggressive child. It is not easy to discipline firmly or accept emotionally children who are extremely coercive and combative (Granic & Patterson, 2006), and some parents of aggressive children display behaviors or espouse beliefs that are decidedly antisocial (Pettit, Dodge, & Brown, 1988; Tapscott,

Frick, Wootton, & Kruh, 1996). Parents of aggressive children must find a way to provide these relationship conditions over time in the face of dramatic shifts in children's ASB and the contextual factors influencing ASB.

The notion that good parenting is multifaceted is certainly not new, and Baumrind's (1971) concept of authoritative parenting is but one well-known case in point. PMT programs routinely train parents to use both positive (e.g., praise, rewards) and disciplinary techniques (Eyberg, 1988; Forehand & McMahon, 1981; Webster-Stratton, 1987). However, the implicit model of parenting reflected in PMT is one that trains positive parenting and discipline practices in a piecemeal fashion: Parents are expected to use both, but rarely considered is the challenge of performing both tasks more or less simultaneously over time. The separation of these two tasks is particularly problematic for parents of aggressive children who must restrict their child's use of coercion while not resorting to coercion themselves (Granic & Patterson, 2006).

Principle 4: The Ratio of Emotional Acceptance to Behavioral Containment Is a Key Parameter of the Socializing Relationship

Effective parents can successfully navigate two competing demands: (a) imposing strict limits on coercive behavior and (b) maintaining an emotionally positive parent–child relationship (Baumrind, 1971; Maccoby & Martin, 1983). Such parents give children the opportunity to learn right from wrong without feeling threatened emotionally or relationally. Parents of aggressive children often struggle to meet these competing demands: They pursue one but not the other; they switch back and forth between the two; or they simply give up on both (Patterson et al., 1992; Webster-Stratton & Spitzer, 1996).

Recent studies have converged on the notion that the ratio of positive-to-negative exchanges is an important parameter when distinguishing between functional and dysfunctional interpersonal relationships. Relationships tend to be more stable and adaptive when the proportion of positive emotional exchanges consistently exceeds the proportion of negative exchanges (Dumas, LaFreniere, & Serketich, 1995; Gottman, 1994). Mothers of nondisruptive children express positive maternal affect about 80% of the time (i.e., a 4:1 ratio), whereas mothers of disruptive children express positive affect only 30% of the time (Dumas et al., 1995), parents of young preschool children maintain a 6:1 ratio of positive-to-negative comments (Hart & Risley, 1995), and mothers of nonreferred school-age children tend to initiate only one instruction-compliance exchange for every seven positive social exchanges (Wahler, Herring, & Edwards, 2001). From a matching law perspective, a positive interaction ratio provides dyadic partners with an overall level of reinforcement that lessens the relative value of performing aversive behavior (McDowell, 1982).

In parent–child dyads, most negative exchanges occur when parents try to correct or restrict children's behavior. Parents of aggressive children are thus operating within a kind of disciplinary "quota system" in which efforts to manage child misbehavior are constrained by the need to provide an emotionally positive relationship. Needed is a disciplinary approach that is yoked to the level of positive interactions, one that is forceful enough to counter child ASB but not so forceful that it spoils the affective quality of the parent–child relationship.

Most parents can think of any number of reasons why children should perform this or that prosocial behavior or why children should not engage in various undesirable behaviors. But parents' expectations can exist separately from what is feasible and necessary, given the nature of the parent–child relationship. And parents' expectations will matter little if the affective tone of the parent–child relationship becomes overly harsh and punitive. As noted by Stormshak and colleagues (Stormshak, Bierman, McMahon, Lengua, & Conduct Problems Prevention Research Group, 2000), "punitive discipline is clearly a core parenting deficit and may be the most relevant parenting problem to work on with children and families in clinical settings" (p. 27). Even parents who use empirically supported behavior management techniques will likely find that aggressive children continue to display some level of coercive behavior (Forgatch, 1991; Webster-Stratton, 1990). Waging too strong a disciplinary campaign could reduce the ratio of positive-to-negative exchanges and jeopardize the foundation for socialization (Dumas et al., 1995; Kochanska, 1997; Richters & Waters, 1991; Wahler, 1997). Thus, with this principle, we are endorsing a neo-Baumrindian model integrating supportive relationships and firm discipline into a single coordinated system over time.

Principle 5: Characteristics of the Parent, the Child, and the Ecology Surrounding the Parent–Child Relationship Affect the Degree to Which Socializing Relationships Are Established and Maintained

In theory, parents whose children are generally cooperative and non-coercive operate under the same quota system as parents of aggressive children. That possibility is likely to go unappreciated, however, when children meet most, if not all, of parents' expectations. And if the parents are generally calm and deliberate, the notion that parents are working under a "disciplinary quota" is even less obvious: Parents set high expectations; children meet those expectations; and the parent–child relationship is none the worse for it. But families with aggressive, high-risk children operate under different circumstances. Parents are often inconsistent and emotionally reactive, and children can be uncooperative and coercive. Typically added to this mix are marital strife, economic disadvantage, beleaguered schools, and violent neighborhoods. All these factors make it difficult to foster a positive parent–child interaction ratio, thereby hampering parents' ability to provide an effective socializing relationship.

Principle 6: The Primary Goal of Parent-Based Interventions for Aggressive Children Is Helping Parents Establish and Maintain a Parent–Child Relationship That Offers Minimal Coverage but Maximum Sustainability of the Conditions Necessary for Socialization

The parent–child relationship is a useful vehicle for socialization, but an effective socializing relationship can be an elusive goal for parents of aggressive children. Practitioners must address the following question: How can this parent and this child live peaceably together in a way that does not promote the child's use of antisocial behavior? Complicating matters are various risk factors that can impact the parent, the child, and the child-rearing context. Therefore, practitioners should strive to help parents identify and implement those strategies that provide at least minimum coverage but maximum sustainability of the relationship conditions necessary for socialization. As such, it is important to define the lower boundaries of these conditions.

Principle 7: Behavioral Containment Begins With Strict Limits on Aggressive, Antisocial Behavior

The typical PMT curriculum recognizes the critical importance of firm discipline, but this task has been poorly integrated with the task of balancing positive and negative emotional exchanges. At issue here is not simply how parents discipline but what and when they discipline. In many PMT programs parents are encouraged to punish (e.g., through time out) acts of noncompliance because noncompliance is purportedly a keystone behavior in the development of children's aggression (Loeber & Schmaling, 1985). But for some parent–child dyads, an overly inclusive stance against noncompliance could undermine the affective quality of their relationship (Cavell, 2001). Cavell recommended tailoring disciplinary goals to fit the characteristics of the parent and child involved. Parents who are seldom harsh or overly reactive can pursue a compliance-based disciplinary strategy without undo damage to the relationship, especially if their child was not overly aggressive and defiant. But for parents who are harsh and overly punitive and whose children are prone to using coercion, the need is for a discipline strategy that is both effective and selective. Cavell (2001) drew from work by Patterson et al. (1992) to show that progression from children's use of nonphysical coercion to physical aggression is more robust than the link between noncompliance and aggression. Developmental studies also reveal that children can be noncompliant without being aggressive (Kuczynski, Kochanska, Radke-Yarrow, & Girnius-Brown, 1987) and that some forms of compliance are unrelated to children's internalization of parents' values (Kochanska, Aksan, & Koenig, 1995). Because coercion carries greater developmental significance than noncompliance, effectively containing aggression and other forms of coercion is where discipline should begin, especially for emotionally reactive parents of highly aggressive children.

Principle 8: Emotional Acceptance Begins With an Implicit Message of Belonging

Positive parenting has been traditionally defined in one of two ways. In the behavioral literature, positive parenting has been traditionally represented by parents' contingent use of attention or encouragement (e.g., praise, rewards) when children exhibit prosocial behavior. In the developmental literature, positive parenting is often viewed as responsiveness or warm involvement (Baumrind, 1971; Maccoby & Martin, 1983). Unfortunately, parents of aggressive children struggle in their efforts to be warm and agreeable, and they can find it difficult to be consistent and contingent in their use of positive reinforcement (Wahler & Dumas, 1989).

An alternative strategy is to view positive parenting as *emotional acceptance*, which Cavell (2000) defined as any behavior that fosters in children a sense of autonomy while not threatening their relationship security. Critical here is the distinction between change and acceptance as ways to enhance the quality of close relationships. As Jacobson (1992) observed, a healthy relationship "involves the ability to accept the inherent unsolvability of some relationship problems" (p. 502). Emotional acceptance is akin to what Baumeister and Leary (1995) referred to as a *need to belong*, which they defined as "the need for frequent, nonaversive interactions within an ongoing relational bond" (p. 497). Baumeister and Leary argued that the need to belong is a fundamental human motivation. The value of defining positive parenting in this way is that parents who are ill-equipped for warm involvement or who fail to track and contingently reinforce good behavior can still maintain *a posture of acceptance* (Cavell, 2000), a default mode of interacting in which the need for parental intervention is not assumed and the use of emotional rejection is the exception and not the rule.

In many families, frequent active parent involvement communicates explicit messages of affection or praise. But in families with aggressive children, parental involvement can devolve into negative affectivity and inadvertent messages of emotional rejection. At minimum, parents of aggressive children should steer clear of interactions that lead predictably to overly harsh parenting and unnecessary control attempts. Less could actually be more for conflict-ridden parent–child dyads, and practitioners should consider how to help parents simply be with their children in ways that convey a more implicit or unstated message of belonging. Emotional acceptance, at minimum, should start with this implicit message of belonging, a message that can be achieved through carefully selected interactions and an overall posture of acceptance.

Principle 9: Prosocial Values Begin With Explicit Statements Against Antisocial Behavior

Studies have documented that children are influenced by explicitly endorsed values and behavioral norms of family members (e.g., Bogenschneider, Wu, Raffaelli, & Tsay, 1998; Brody, Flor, Hollett-Wright, & McCoy, 1998). For example, Bogenschneider et al. (1998) found that the relation between paternal monitoring and adolescent substance use was stronger among adolescents whose fathers held more disapproving views of alcohol use. If children's participation in a socializing relationship facilitates the internalization of parental values, then it helps if those values are prosocial. That may not be the case, however, especially for aggressive children whose parents have a greater likelihood of evincing antisocial personality disorder or a history of criminal behavior than parents of other children (Frick & Jackson, 1993; Tapscott et al., 1996). Children prone to ASB also need more than the absence of antisocial norms; they need strong, explicit messages against ASB. Brody et al. (1998) found that family norms against alcohol use that departed even slightly from an abstinence-based message were more likely to be misinterpreted as relaxed standards by children with high-risk temperaments. Therefore, our recommendation is that parents of aggressive children begin their efforts to foster prosocial values by making explicit statements against ASB.

Principle 10: Effective Parent-Based Interventions for Aggressive Children Are Multisystemic

With this principle, the focus is extended beyond the dyad to include other factors that influence children's socialization experiences, many of which are mediated through disruptions in parenting practices or family functioning (Patterson et al., 1992). Marital conflict, divorce, family violence, parental psychopathology, and economic deprivation are common examples of disruptive forces that can distort how families operate. Typically, when these issues are addressed in the context of parenting training, it has been through additional training modules (e.g., communication skills, problem solving, coping) tacked onto the PMT curriculum (Cavell, 2000). This approach creates a rather long list of skills that parents theoretically lack and that practitioners ideally should teach. For example, the Triple P parenting intervention encompasses 40 different parenting skills from nine different domains of functioning (Sanders, Markie-Dadds, & Turner, 2003). Kazdin and Whitley (2003) found support for their added-on parental problem-solving component, but they questioned the value of enhancing PMT outcomes in this way:

> One cannot keep adding components to a treatment that might enhance or indeed actually does enhance therapeutic change. . . . Patient attrition, already high in child, adolescent, and adult therapy (40%–60%) is partially a function of the demands made of the client (Kazdin, Holland, & Crowley, 1997) and duration of treatment (Phillips, 1985). Adding a component to treatment that increases either one of these is quite likely to cause greater attrition so that fewer patients will complete treatment. (p. 513)

A different approach is to recognize that parenting and, therefore, parent-based interventions involve two critical but non-dyadic areas of functioning: *family structure* and *parental self-care*.

Both domains of functioning can have direct bearing on parents' efforts to establish and maintain a socializing relationship. For example, Patterson, DeGarmo, and Forgatch (2004) found that reductions in maternal depression 6 months post PMT treatment predicted continued gains in maternal and child functioning over the next 18 months. The investigators speculated that "perhaps for many, simply being enrolled in a structured program is associated with a reduction in depression (i.e., now there is renewed hope)" (p. 631). Parents who are overwhelmed and continually despondent, who rely on their children for emotional support, or who refuse to accept the role as their family's leader cannot provide aggressive children with the kind of relationship they need to develop into law-abiding citizens. Finding reliable ways to refuel and compelling reasons to reengage in the difficult task of parenting are not luxuries for parents of aggressive children. Similarly, without adequate family structure, parents of aggressive children will fall prey to automatic but less adaptive ways to parent and to cope (Dumas et al., 2005).

CONCLUSION

The parent–child relationship is a particular kind of social context. It involves biological connections, recurring interactions, enduring social roles, culturally laden meaning, and strong emotional investments. All things being equal, these attributes give the parent–child relationship distinct advantages in its competition with other possibly deviant contexts (Maccoby, 1992), and it offers unique protective functions against the emergence and stabilization of ASB (see Masten, 2001). A long-term relationship-based model of socialization has advantages over models that emphasize the short-term management of child misbehavior and gives a time dimension to parent–child interactions (Kuczynski & Hildebrandt, 1997). Parents and children have overlapping histories as well as shared expectations that can significantly affect the quality of their interactions (Granic & Patterson, 2006). For children with early-onset ASB, the parent–child relationship is only one of many available contexts, but it remains a unique resource in the campaign to promote their integration into society. Over 40 years ago, Diana Baumrind introduced the concept of authoritative parenting around the same time that applied, behaviorally based investigators developed interventions for the parents of aggressive children. For too long, these lines of research have proceeded along separate trajectories, neither having much influence on the other. We believe parents of aggressive children are better served when parenting interventions help parents build and sustain a noncoercive relationship that effectively integrates responsiveness and demandingness over the course of children's development.

REFERENCES

American Psychiatric Association. (2000). *Diagnostic and statistical manual of mental disorders* (4th ed., text revision). Washington, DC: Author.

Baumeister, R. F., & Leary, M. R. (1995). The need to belong: Desire for interpersonal attachments as a fundamental human motivation. *Psychological Bulletin, 117,* 497–529. doi:10.1037/0033-2909.117.3.497

Baumrind, D. (1967). Child care practices anteceding three patterns of preschool behavior. *Genetic Psychology Monographs, 75,* 43–88.

Baumrind, D. (1971). Current patterns of parental authority. *Developmental Psychology Monographs, 4*(1, Pt. 2), 1–103. doi:10.1037/h0030372

Baumrind, D. (1973). The development of instrumental competence through socialization. In A. Pick (Ed.), *Minnesota symposia on child psychology* (Vol. 7, pp. 3–46), Minneapolis: University of Minnesota Press.

Bogenschneider, K., Wu, M., Raffaelli, M., & Tsay, J. C. (1998). Parental influences on adolescent peer orientation and substance use: The interface of a parenting practices and values. *Child Development, 69,* 1672–1688. doi:10.2307/1132139

Boivin, M., Vitaro, F., & Poulin, F. (2005). Peer relationships and the development of aggressive behavior in early childhood. In R. E. Tremblay, W. W. Hartup, & J. Archer (Eds.), *Developmental origins of aggression* (pp. 376–397). New York, NY: Guilford Press.

Brody, G. H., Flor, D. L., Hollett-Wright, N., & McCoy, J. K. (1998). Children's development of alcohol use norms: Contributions of parent and sibling norms, children's temperaments, and parent–child discussions. *Journal of Family Psychology, 12,* 209–219. doi:10.1037/0893-3200.12.2.209

Burt, S. A. (2009). Rethinking environmental contributions to child and adolescent psychopathology: A meta-analysis of shared environmental influences. *Psychological Bulletin, 135,* 608–637. doi:10.1037/a0015702

Cavell, T. A. (2000). *Working with parents of aggressive children: A practitioner's guide.* Washington, DC: American Psychological Association. doi:10.1037/10372-000

Cavell, T. A. (2001). Updating our approach to parent training. I: The case against targeting noncompliance. *Clinical Psychology: Science and Practice, 8,* 299–318. doi:10.1093/clipsy.8.3.299

Cavell, T. A., & Elledge, L. C. (2007). Working with parents of aggressive, high-risk children. In J. Briesmeister & C. Schaefer (Eds.), *Handbook of parent training* (3rd ed., pp. 379–423). Hoboken, NJ: Wiley.

Cavell, T. A., Hymel, S., Malcolm, K., & Seay, A. (2007). Socialization and the development of antisocial behavior: Models and interventions. In J. E. Grusec & P. D. Hastings (Eds.), *Handbook of socialization* (pp. 42–67). New York, NY: Guilford Press.

Cavell, T. A., & Strand, P. S. (2003). Parent-based interventions for aggressive, antisocial children: Adapting to a bilateral lens. In L. Kuczynski (Ed.), *Handbook of dynamics in parent–child relations* (pp. 395–420). Thousand Oaks, CA: Sage.

Christophersen, E. R., & Mortweet, S. L. (2001). *Treatments that work with children: Empirically supported strategies for managing childhood problems.* Washington, DC: American Psychological Association. doi:10.1037/10405-000

Cicchetti, D., & Toth, S. L. (2009). The past achievements and future promises of developmental psychopathology: The coming of age of a discipline. *Journal of Child Psychology and Psychiatry, 50,* 16–25. doi:10.1111/j.1469-7610.2008.01979.x

Collins, W. A., Maccoby, E. E., Steinberg, L., Hetherington, E. M., & Bornstein, M. H. (2000). Contemporary research on parenting: The case for nature and nurture. *American Psychologist, 55,* 218–232. doi:10.1037/0003-066X.55.2.218

Conger, R. D., & Simons, R. L. (1997). Life-course contingencies in the development of adolescent antisocial behavior: A matching law approach. In T. P. Thornberry (Ed.), *Advances in criminological theory* (pp. 55–99). New York, NY: Aldine.

Dumas, J. E., LaFreniere, P. J., & Serketich, W. J. (1995). "Balance of power": A transactional analysis of control in mother–child dyads involving socially competent, aggressive, and anxious children. *Journal of Abnormal Psychology, 104,* 104–113. doi:10.1037/0021-843X.104.1.104

Dumas, J. E., Nissley, J., Nordstrom, A., Smith, E. P., Prinz, R. J., & Levine, D. W. (2005). Home chaos: Sociodemographic, parenting, interactional, and child correlates. *Journal of Clinical Child and Adolescent Psychology, 34,* 93–104. doi:10.1207/s15374424jccp3401_9

Eyberg, S. M. (1988). Parent–child interaction therapy: Integration of traditional and behavioral concerns. *Child & Family Behavior Therapy, 10*(1), 33–46. doi:10.1300/J019v10n01_04

Eyberg, S. M., Edwards, D., Boggs, S. R., & Foote, R. (1998). Maintaining the treatment effects of parent training: The role of booster sessions and other maintenance strategies. *Clinical Psychology: Science and Practice, 5,* 544–554. doi:10.1111/j.1468-2850.1998.tb00173.x

Eyberg, S. M., Nelson, M. M., & Boggs, S. R. (2008). Evidence-based psychosocial treatments for children and adolescents with disruptive behavior. *Journal of Clinical Child and Adolescent Psychology, 37*, 215–237. doi:10.1080/15374410701820117

Fairchild, G., Passamonti, L., Hurford, G., Hagan, C. C., von dem Hagen, E. A. H., van Goozen, S. H. M., . . . Calder, A. J. (2011). Brain structure abnormalities in early-onset and adolescent-onset conduct disorder. *The American Journal of Psychiatry, 6*, 624–633. doi:10.1176/appi.ajp.2010.10081184

Forehand, R., & Long, N. (1991). Prevention of aggression and other behavior problems in the early adolescent years. In D. J. Pepler & K. H. Rubin (Eds.), *The development and treatment of childhood aggression* (pp. 317–330). Hillsdale, NJ: Erlbaum.

Forehand, R. L., & McMahon, R. J. (1981). *Helping the noncompliant child: A clinician's guide to present training.* New York, NY: Guilford Press.

Forgatch, M. S. (1991). The clinical science vortex: A developing theory of antisocial behavior. In D. J. Pepler & K. H. Rubin (Eds.), *The development and treatment of childhood aggression* (pp. 291–315). Hillsdale, NY: Erlbaum.

Forgatch, M. S., & Patterson, G. R. (2010). Parent management training—Oregon model: An intervention for antisocial behavior in children and adolescents. In J. R. Weisz & A. E. Kazdin (Eds.), *Evidence-based psychotherapies for children and adolescents* (2nd ed., pp. 159–178). New York, NY: Guilford Press.

Forgatch, M. S., Patterson, G. R., DeGarmo, D. S., & Beldavs, Z. G. (2009). Testing the Oregon delinquency model with 9-year follow-up of the Oregon Divorce Study. *Development and Psychopathology, 21*, 637–660. doi:10.1017/S0954579409000340

Frick, P. J., & Jackson, Y. K. (1993). Family functioning and childhood antisocial behavior: Yet another reinterpretation. *Journal of Clinical Child Psychology, 22*, 410–419. doi:10.1207/s15374424jccp2204_1

Frick, P. J., Stickle, T. R., Dandreaux, D. M., Farrell, J. M., & Kimonis, E. R. (2005). Callous-unemotional traits in predicting the severity and stability of conduct problems and delinquency. *Journal of Abnormal Child Psychology, 33*, 471–487. doi:10.1007/s10648-005-5728-9

Gottman, J. M. (1994). *What predicts divorce?* Hillsdale, NJ: Erlbaum.

Granic, I., & Patterson, G. R. (2006). Toward a comprehensive model of antisocial development: A dynamic systems approach. *Psychological Review, 113*, 101–131. doi:10.1037/0033-295X.113.1.101

Green, K. D., Forehand, R., & McMahon, R. J. (1979). Parental manipulation of compliance and noncompliance in normal and deviant children. *Behavior Modification, 3*, 245–266. doi:10.1177/014544557932007

Griest, D. L., Forehand, R., Wells, K. C., & McMahon, R. J. (1980). An examination of differences between nonclinic and behavior-problem clinic-referred children and their mothers. *Journal of Abnormal Psychology, 89*, 497–500. doi:10.1037/0021-843X.89.3.497

Hagen, K. A., Ogden, T., & Bjornebekk, G. (2011). Treatment outcomes and mediators of parent management training: A one-year follow-up of children with conduct problems. *Journal of Clinical Child and Adolescent Psychology, 40*, 165–178. doi:10.1080/15374416.2011.546050

Harris, J.R. (1995). Where is the child's environment? A group socialization theory of development. *Psychological Review, 102*, 458–489. doi:10.1037/0033-295X.102.3.458

Harrist, A.W., & Waugh, R.M. (2002). Dyadic synchrony: Its structure and function in children's interactions. *Developmental Review, 22*, 555–592. doi:10.1016/S0273-2297(02)00500-2

Hart, B., & Risley, T.R. (1995). *Meaningful differences in the everyday experience of young American children.* Baltimore, MD: Brookes.

Herrnstein, R.J. (1974). Formal properties of the matching law. *Journal of the Experimental Analysis of Behavior, 21*, 159–164. doi:10.1901/jeab.1974.21-159

Hood, K.K., & Eyberg, S.M. (2003). Outcomes of parent–child interaction therapy: Mothers' reports of maintenance three to six years after treatment. *Journal of Clinical Child and Adolescent Psychology, 32*, 419–429. doi:10.1207/S15374424JCCP3203_10

Jacobson, N.S. (1992). Behavioral couple therapy: A new beginning. *Behavior Therapy, 23*, 493–506. doi:10.1016/S0005-7894(05)80218-7

Kazdin, A.E. (1993). Treatment of conduct disorder: Progress and directions in psychotherapy research. *Development and Psychopathology, 5*, 277–310. doi:10.1017/S0954579400004399

Kazdin, A.E., & Whitley, M.K. (2003). Treatment of parental stress to enhance therapeutic change among children referred for aggressive and antisocial behavior. *Journal of Consulting and Clinical Psychology, 71*, 504–515. doi:10.1037/0022-006X.71.3.504

Kerr, M., & Stattin, H. (2000). What parents know, how they know it, and several forms of adolescent adjustment: Further support for a reinterpretation of monitoring. *Developmental Psychology, 36*, 366–380. doi:10.1037/0012-1649.36.3.366

Kochanska, G. (1997). Mutually responsive orientation between mothers and their young children: Implications for early socialization. *Child Development, 68*, 94–112. doi:10.2307/1131928

Kochanska, G., Aksan, N., & Koenig, A.L. (1995). A longitudinal study of the roots of preschoolers' conscience: Committed compliance and emerging internalization. *Child Development, 66*, 1752–1769. doi:10.2307/1131908

Kochanska, G., Aksan, N., Prisco, T.R., & Adams, E.E. (2008). Mother–child and father–child mutually responsive orientation in the first 2 years and children's outcomes at preschool age: Mechanisms of influence. *Child Development, 79*, 30–44. doi:10.1111/j.1467-8624.2007.01109.x

Kuczynski, L. (2003). Beyond bidirectionality: Bilateral conceptual frameworks for understanding dynamics in parent–child relations. In L. Kuczynski (Ed.), *Handbook of dynamics in parent–child relations* (pp. 1–24). Thousand Oaks, CA: Sage.

Kuczynski, L., & Hildebrandt, N. (1997). Models of conformity and resistance in socialization theory. In J. E. Grusec & L. Kuczynski (Eds.), *Parenting and the internalization of values: A handbook of contemporary theory* (pp. 227–256). New York, NY: Wiley.

Kuczynski, L., Kochanska, G., Radke-Yarrow, M. O., & Girnius-Brown, O. (1987). A developmental interpretation of young children's noncompliance. *Developmental Psychology, 23*, 799–806. doi:10.1037/0012-1649.23.6.799

Lansford, J. E., Malone, P. S., Dodge, K. A., Pettit, G. S., & Bates, J. E. (2010). Developmental cascades of peer rejection, social information processing biases, and aggression during middle childhood. *Development and Psychopathology, 22*, 593–602. doi:10.1017/S0954579410000301

Loeber, R. (1990). Development and risk factors of juvenile antisocial behavior and delinquency. *Clinical Psychology Review, 10*, 1–41. doi:10.1016/0272-7358 (90)90105-J

Loeber, R., & Schmaling, K. B. (1985). The utility of differentiating between mixed and pure forms of antisocial child behavior. *Journal of Abnormal Child Psychology, 13*, 315–335. doi:10.1007/BF00910651

Long, P., Forehand, R., Wierson, M., & Morgan, A. (1994). Does parent training with young noncompliant children have long-term effects? *Behaviour Research and Therapy, 32*, 101–107. doi:10.1016/0005-7967(94)90088-4

Lundahl, B., Risser, H. J., & Lovejoy, M. C. (2006). A meta-analysis of parent training: Moderators and follow-up effects. *Clinical Psychology Review, 26*, 86–104. doi:10.1016/j.cpr.2005.07.004

Lytton, H. (1990). Child and parent effects in boys' conduct disorder: A reinterpretation. *Developmental Psychology, 26*, 683–697. doi:10.1037/0012-1649.26.5.683

Maccoby, E. E. (1992). The role of parents in the socialization of children: An historical overview. *Developmental Psychology, 28*, 1006–1017. doi:10.1037/0012-1649. 28.6.1006

Maccoby, E. E., & Martin, J. (1983). Socialization in the context of the family: Parent–child interaction. In E. M. Hetherington (Ed.) & P. H. Mussen (Series Ed.), *Handbook of child psychology: Vol. 4. Socialization, personality, and social development* (pp. 1–101). New York, NY: Wiley.

Masten, A. S. (2001). Ordinary magic: Resilience processes in development. *American Psychologist, 56*, 227–238. doi:10.1037/0003-066X.56.3.227

Maughan, D. R., Christiansen, E., Jenson, W. R., Olympia, D., & Clark, E. (2005). Behavioral parent training as a treatment for externalizing behaviors and disruptive behavior disorders: A meta-analysis. *School Psychology Review, 34*, 267–286.

McDowell, J. J. (1982). The importance of Herrnstein's mathematical statement of the law of effect for behavior therapy. *American Psychologist, 37*, 771–779. doi:10.1037/0003-066X.37.7.771

Moffitt, T. E. (1993). Adolescence-limited and life-course-persistent antisocial behavior: A developmental taxonomy. *Psychological Review, 100*, 674–701. doi:10.1037/0033-295X.100.4.674

Nigg, J., & Huang-Pollock, C. (2003). An early-onset model of the role of executive functions and intelligence in conduct disorder/delinquency. In B. B. Lahey, T. E. Moffitt, & A. Caspi (Eds.), *Causes of conduct disorder and juvenile delinquency* (pp. 227–253). New York, NY: Guilford Press.

Oxford, M., Cavell, T. A., & Hughes, J. N. (2003). Callous/unemotional traits moderate the relation between ineffective parenting and child externalizing problems: A partial replication and extension. *Journal of Clinical Child and Adolescent Psychology, 32*, 577–585. doi:10.1207/S15374424JCCP3204_10

Patterson, G. R. (1982). *Coercive family process.* Eugene, OR: Castalia Press.

Patterson, G. R., & Brodsky, G. (1966). A behavior modification program for a child with multiple problem behaviors. *Journal of Child Psychology and Psychiatry, 7*, 277–295. doi:10.1111/j.1469-7610.1966.tb02253.x

Patterson, G. R., Forgatch, M. S., & DeGarmo, D. S. (2010). Cascading effects following intervention. *Development and Psychopathology, 22*, 949—970. doi:10.1017/S0954579410000568

Patterson, G. R., DeGarmo, D., & Forgatch, M. S. (2004). Systematic changes in families following prevention trials. *Journal of Abnormal Child Psychology, 32*, 621–633. doi:10.1023/B:JACP.0000047211.11826.54

Patterson, G. R., Forgatch, M., Yoerger, K. L., & Stoolmiller, M. (1998). Variables that initiate and maintain an early-onset trajectory for juvenile offending. *Development and Psychopathology, 10*, 531–547. doi:10.1017/S0954579498001734

Patterson, G. R., Reid, J. B., & Dishion, T. J. (1992). *Antisocial boys: A social interactional approach.* Eugene, OR: Castalia Press.

Pettit, G. S., Dodge, K. A., & Brown, M. M. (1988). Early family experiences, social problem solving patterns, and children's social competence. *Child Development, 59*, 107–120. doi:10.2307/1130393

Prinz, R. J., & Miller, G. E. (1991). Issues in understanding and treating childhood conduct problems in disadvantaged populations. *Journal of Clinical Child Psychology, 20*, 379–385. doi:10.1207/s15374424jccp2004_6

Richters, J. E., & Waters, E. (1991). Attachment and socialization: The positive side of social influence. In M. Lewis & S. Feinman (Eds.), *Social influences and socialization in infancy* (pp. 185–213). New York, NY: Plenum Press.

Roberts, M. W. (1985). Praising child compliance: Reinforcement or ritual? *Journal of Abnormal Child Psychology, 13*, 611–629. doi:10.1007/BF00923145

Sanders, M. R., Markie-Dadds, C., & Turner, K. M. T. (2003). Theoretical, scientific and clinical foundations of the Triple P-Positive Parenting Program: A population approach to the promotion of parenting competence. *Parenting Research and Practice Monograph, 1*, 1–21.

Scarr, S. (1992). Developmental theories for the 1990s: Development and individual differences. *Child Development, 63*, 1–19. doi:10.2307/1130897

Schneider, W. J., Cavell, T. A., & Hughes, J. N. (2003). A sense of containment: Potential moderator of the relation between parenting practices and children's externalizing behaviors. *Development and Psychopathology, 15*, 95–117. doi:10.1017/S0954579403000063

Serketich, W.J., & Dumas, J.E. (1996). The effectiveness of behavioral parent training to modify antisocial behavior in children: A meta-analysis. *Behavior Therapy, 27*, 171–186. doi:10.1016/S0005-7894(96)80013-X

Snyder, J.J., & Patterson, G.R. (1995). Individual differences in social aggression: A test of a reinforcement model of socialization in the natural environment. *Behavior Therapy, 26*, 371–391. doi:10.1016/S0005-7894(05)80111-X

Stormshak, E.A., Bierman, K.L., McMahon, R.J., Lengua, L.J., & Conduct Problems Prevention Research Group. (2000). Parenting practices and child disruptive behavior problems in early elementary school. *Journal of Clinical Child Psychology, 29*, 17–29. doi:10.1207/S15374424jccp2901_3

Tapscott, M., Frick, P.J., Wootton, J., & Kruh, I. (1996). The intergenerational link to antisocial behavior: Effects of paternal contact. *Journal of Child and Family Studies, 5*, 229–240. doi:10.1007/BF02237945

Vitaro, F., Brendgen, M., & Tremblay, R.E. (2001). Preventive intervention: Assessing its effects on the trajectories of delinquency and testing for mediational processes. *Applied Developmental Science, 5*, 201–213. doi:10.1207/S1532480XADS0504_02

Wahler, R.G. (1997). On the origins of children's compliance and opposition: Family context, reinforcement, and rules. *Journal of Child and Family Studies, 6*, 191–208. doi:10.1023/A:1025050724559

Wahler, R.G., & Dumas, J.E. (1989). Attentional problems in dysfunctional mother–child interactions: An interbehavioral model. *Psychological Bulletin, 105*, 116–130. doi:10.1037/0033-2909.105.1.116

Wahler, R.G., Herring, M., & Edwards, M. (2001). Co-regulation of balance between children's prosocial approaches and acts of compliance: A pathway to mother–child cooperation? *Journal of Clinical Child Psychology, 30*, 473–478. doi:10.1207/S15374424JCCP3004_04

Wahler, R.G., Winkle, G.H., Peterson, R.F., & Morrison, D.C. (1965). Mothers as behavior therapists for their own children. *Behaviour Research and Therapy, 3*, 113–124. doi:10.1016/0005-7967(65)90015-X

Webster-Stratton, C. (1987). *The parents and children series*. Eugene, OR: Castalia Press.

Webster-Stratton, C. (1990). Long-term follow-up of families with young conduct problem children: From preschool to grade school. *Journal of Clinical Child Psychology, 19*, 144–149. doi:10.1207/s15374424jccp1902_6

Webster-Stratton, C., & Spitzer, A. (1996). Parenting a young child with conduct problems: New insights using qualitative methods. In T.H. Ollendick & R.J. Prinz (Eds.), *Advances in clinical child psychology* (Vol. 18, pp. 1–62). New York, NY: Plenum Press. doi:10.1007/978-1-4613-0323-7_1

8

EFFECTIVE PARENTING PRACTICES: SOCIAL INTERACTION LEARNING THEORY AND THE ROLE OF EMOTION COACHING AND MINDFULNESS

JAMES SNYDER, SABINA LOW, LISHA BULLARD,
LYNN SCHREPFERMAN, MARISSA WACHLAROWICZ,
CHRISTY MARVIN, AND ANDREA REED

Over 40 years ago, Diana Baumrind reported her seminal research on effective parenting practices (Baumrind & Black, 1967). At about the same time, initial efforts were made to develop interventions to promote parents' skillful child-rearing (Hanf, 1968; Patterson & Brodsky, 1966; Wahler, Winkle, Peterson, & Morrison, 1965). Both approaches shared a social learning perspective and emphasized a combination of firm discipline and positive parenting to promote children's compliance, behavior regulation, and social competence. Since that time, several parent training interventions have been derived from a social interaction learning (SIL) perspective, including Parent Management Training—Oregon (PMTO; Forgatch & Rains, 1997), Incredible Years (Webster-Stratton, 2001), Triple P (Sanders, 1999), and Family Check-Up (Dishion & Kavanagh, 2003). The fundamental premise in SIL is that children are socialized during their day-to-day interactions with other significant social figures, including parents. As such, parent training interventions focus on balancing parents' supportive interaction with their

DOI: 10.1037/13948-009
Authoritative Parenting: Synthesizing Nurturance and Discipline for Optimal Child Development, Robert E. Larzelere, Amanda Sheffield Morris, and Amanda W. Harrist (Editors)

189

children with setting clear limits and using effective discipline. These interventions have been clearly established as efficacious and effective preventive and clinical programs to ameliorate child behavior problems and to promote child competence. Research has also demonstrated that enhanced positive parenting practices and diminished coercive discipline mediate the effects of parent training on child outcomes.

BAUMRIND'S CONTRIBUTION TO PARENTING RESEARCH AND INTERVENTIONS

The degree to which the clusters of parenting practices identified by Baumrind nearly 40 years ago presaged subsequent research on parenting and the development of parent training interventions using an SIL perspective is remarkable. Table 8.1 compares the characteristics of effective (authoritative) and ineffective (authoritarian or permissive) parenting identified by

TABLE 8.1
Baumrind's Contribution to Parenting Research and Intervention

Key targets in SIL parent training and research	Baumrind's parenting clusters descriptors
Skillful parenting practices	
Scaffolding	Stimulating environment
Shape skills with praise and attention	Promote child independence
Prompt, cue, instruct	Not described
Warmth and involvement	Not described
Clear rules and limits	Respect authority
Limit setting	Directive
Command → compliance	Obedience
Time out, response cost	Firm enforcement
Contingent and consistent	Flexible and clear parent views
Pinpointing and tracking	Not described
Monitoring	Not described
Problem solving	Verbal exchange
Not described	Willing to express anger and displeasure
Not described	Promotes individuality
Not described	Confidence as a parent
Ineffective parenting practices	
Coercion	Coercion
Nattering	Punitive discipline
Noncontingency	Lack of firm enforcement
Overinclusive attributions	Not described
Noninvolvement	Low independence demands
Not described	Encourages child emotional dependence

Note. SIL = social interaction learning.

Baumrind (1973) with those reported in subsequent SIL research on parenting practices and SIL parenting training. Baumrind's use of multiple methods to assess parenting was also innovative. These methods included observations of parent–child interaction, observer ratings of parenting, and parent reports about parenting practices (Baumrind & Black, 1967). There is again a remarkable congruence between the methods used by Baumrind in the 1960s and those more recently used to assess the contribution of parenting processes to the development of problem behavior (Dishion, Burraston, & Li, 2003).

Two broad dimensions of parenting practices have emerged in research and serve as general targets of SIL parenting interventions, corresponding to Baumrind's original dimensions of warmth/responsiveness and control/demandingness. These two parenting dimensions have both positive and negative exemplars, as shown in Table 8.1. Positive practices are apparent when parents are attentive to and actively engaged with their children, promote child compliance, scaffold learning opportunities, use active tactics to teach social and instrumental skills, use contingent attention to shape those skills, set and enforce clear limits, and encourage constructive verbal exchange and problem solving. Negative practices are apparent when parents set overly strict or arbitrary limits without explanation, use harsh and inconsistent discipline tactics, are angry, are noncontingent, or give in to child problem behavior encounters (Forgatch & Patterson, 2010).

However, Baumrind and other parenting researchers have indicated that the behaviors described in Table 8.1 may not comprehensively define effective parenting. Rather, a higher order, nonlinear combination of these practices or some additional dimension of parenting such as respect (Barber, 1996), attunement (Baumrind, 1991), and validation (Gottman, Katz, & Hooven, 1996) may also be critical features of effective parenting. We suggest that three additional characteristics of effective parenting might be hypothesized. The first is parents' awareness of their child's current *psychological space* (i.e., emotions, thoughts, and needs)—what Baumrind referred to as *attunement*. This awareness extends to parents' own thoughts and feelings—what is often referred to as *mindfulness*, or an "awareness that emerges through paying attention, on purpose, in the present, and non-judgmentally to the unfolding of experience moment by moment" (Kabat-Zinn, 2003, p. 145). Second, attunement and mindfulness are accompanied by parents' validation of the child's thoughts, emotions, and needs—what might be referred to as *support*—avoiding enmeshment or efforts to control how the child should think or feel. As applied to parents' mindfulness, this might be called *acceptance*—avoiding maladaptive fusion with their own thoughts and flooding by their own feelings. Third, these characteristics provide parents with a capacity to articulate their values about parenting and the hopes they have for their child and with the ability to engage and teach their child in an intentional manner consistent with their values. Our hypothesis is that parents' capacity for attunement and validation in relation to their children and mindfulness and acceptance of their own thoughts and feelings promote access to values about parenting and enable the flexible and consistent deployment of the skillful parenting practices listed in Table 8.1. Collectively, these characteristics reflect sensitive and responsive parenting. A model of effective parenting incorporating these three characteristics is shown in Figure 8.1.

The goal of this chapter is to briefly describe and empirically examine two recent developments in parenting research and intervention that may complement and extend current SIL parenting models and that may capture these additional parenting characteristics: emotion coaching; and relational frame theory (RFT) and its intervention derivative, acceptance and commitment therapy (ACT). *Emotion coaching* refers to parents' efforts and skills in accepting, labeling, and validating their children's emotional experiences and expression and in helping children regulate emotional arousal and display and problem solve about the source of those emotions. RFT and ACT, in a complementary fashion, focus on how parents can help their children learn how to accurately label their emotions, to be willing to "have" rather than "control" their emotions and to use their emotions in service of attaining environmental goals.

However, in pursuit of these goals, it is important to recognize that previous research identifying effective and ineffective parenting practices and establishing the efficacy and effectiveness of SIL parent training interventions represents a substantial empirical achievement. In the search for an increasingly sophisticated understanding of effective parenting practices and more powerful parent training interventions, it is also important to ask

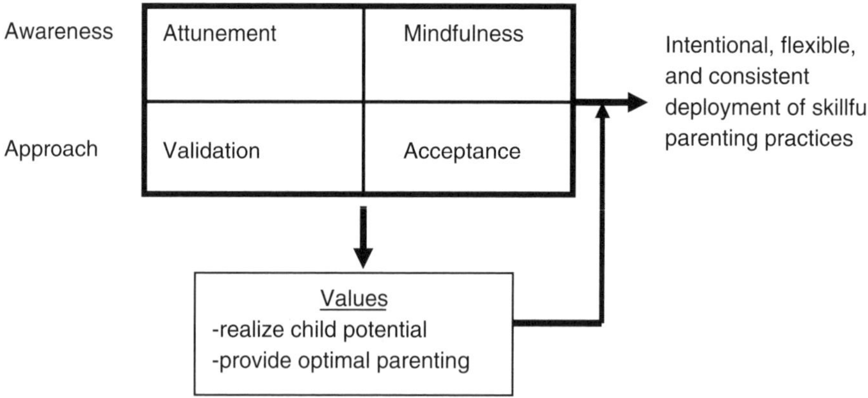

Figure 8.1. Overview of the role of attunement, validation, and intentionality in effective parenting.

whether these new developments provide added empirical value to current models of parenting and parent training.

EMOTION COACHING

Traditionally, research on the parenting practices targeted in parent training derived from an SIL perspective has been relatively silent on emotions and emotion regulation. There has been some recognition of the negative effects of persistent parental displays of dysregulated anger and depressive affect (Silk, Shaw, Forbes, Lane, & Kovacs, 2006) but less description of how parents can effectively respond to children's experience and display of emotions. In contrast, there has been substantial research on emotion in relation to children's development of competence and psychopathology (Silk, Steinberg, & Morris, 2003) and about parents' role in emotion socialization (Gottman, Katz, & Hooven, 1997; Morris, Silk, Steinberg, Myers, & Robinson, 2007).

The fundamental premise of this research is that emotions are natural intraindividual experiential processes that motivate and direct behavior and interindividual social behaviors that are part and parcel of social relationships (Izard, 2002). Emotion experience, arousal, and display are potentially constructive when regulated, expressed in a socially normative way, and used to instigate goal-directed behavior (instrumental competence) and to establish effective social relationships (social competence). However, emotional arousal, experience, and display contribute to the risk for maladjustment and social relational problems when poorly regulated and expressed in a manner that interferes with goal-directed behavior and constructive social processes.

Children's experience, display, and regulation of emotions are shaped by parental behavior just as are compliance, rule following, and instrumental and social skills. Effective parent socialization of child emotions has been called emotion coaching, and ineffective parent socialization has been called *emotion dismissing* (Gottman et al., 1997). Central descriptors of emotion coaching and emotion dismissing behaviors derived from research on parenting are shown in Table 8.2 (Gottman, Katz, & Hooven, 1996; Gottman et al., 1997).

Emotion coaching by parents occurs at two levels. First, as shown in the top of Table 8.2, it entails parents' constructive modeling of awareness, recognition, expression, and regulation of their own emotions to show children how to label, regulate, use, and constructively express emotions. When parents are aware and mindful of their emotions, they create a constructive and emotionally supportive caregiving environment characterized by positive emotion, engagement, and well-regulated parent negative affective

TABLE 8.2

Characteristics of Constructive and Maladaptive Parent Emotion
Socialization Practices

Skillful: emotion coaching	Ineffective: emotion dismissing
Parent modeling and instruction	
Model awareness and expression	Model constriction of emotions
Model regulation and use	Model dysregulation of emotions
Talk about own and child's emotion	Avoid discussion of emotions
Parent responses to child emotion	
Validate, empathize	Ignore
Label	Disparage, criticize
Accept (calmly)	Reciprocate, escalate
Problem solve (source of emotion)	Ask to tolerate, minimize
Practice problem-solving efforts	Distract, fix
Encourage, invite description	Stop commands
Soothe, comfort	Punish
Prompt regulation, self-soothing	Give in (negative reinforcement of dysregulation)

displays. Second, emotion coaching is characterized by parents' constructive responses to children's "hot," online emotional displays. As shown in Table 8.2, these responses include recognition, labeling, and validation of the child's emotions accompanied by efforts to coach regulation and problem solving. Emotion coaching reflects attunement to and validation of the child's emotions. Emotion dismissing responses reflect poor attunement, flooding, and invalidation characterized by disparaging, suppressing, or ignoring child emotion displays and by reciprocating or escalating such displays. Without attunement and validation, parents make few efforts to coach regulatory or problem solving strategies. Parental responses to child emotion displays have been collectively called *emotion-related socialization behaviors* (ERSBs; Eisenberg, Cumberland, & Spinrad, 1998) and reflect parents' relative attunement to and validation of their child's emotions.

Much of the research on emotion socialization has not been integrated with or used to systematically inform parent training interventions derived from an SIL perspective. In fact, comparison of Tables 8.1 and 8.2 indicates there is only modest overlap in the parenting tactics described by the emotion coaching and SIL perspectives. This suggests that the two approaches may not be redundant. One way to ascertain whether they are redundant is to calculate the degree to which standard SIL parenting variables are correlated with emotion coaching variables. If there is not considerable shared variance, it may be useful to more fully incorporate child-focused emotion coaching strategies into SIL parenting research and parent training interventions.

We have initiated empirical efforts to do this by coding mothers' responses (ERSBs) to children's display of negative emotions during ongoing family interactions using a sample of 50 families from a low-socioeconomic-status community in a longitudinal study of 5- to 6-year-old children. The code uses seven mutually exclusive and collectively exhaustive ERSB parent response categories: soothe, problem solve, and empathy/validation (collectively defined as constructive coaching); fix/acquiesce, ignore/move on, and command (collectively defined as minimizing responses); and disparage (with minimizing responses, defined as dismissing responses). The mean frequency and percentage of various parent ERSBs to child displays of anger, sadness, and fear as coded by the Specific Affect Coding System (SPAFF; Gottman, McCoy, Coan, & Collier, 1996) during 2 hours of parent–child interaction are shown in Table 8.3. Most often, parents were observed to simply ignore child emotion displays or to use other minimizing responses. Disparagement was also relatively frequent. Constructive emotion coaching responses to child negative emotions were relatively infrequent. It would appear that constructive ERSB responses are the exception rather than the rule in these families. It is also possible that the use of the SPAFF to delineate child emotion displays may have resulted in an overestimation of the rates at which parents ignore their children's negative emotion displays as an intentional strategy; it is much easier for third-party observers trained in SPAFF coding to identify the occurrence of brief and subtle child negative emotional expressions that would be difficult for parents to ascertain during ongoing interaction.

We have also examined how the rate of these parental ERSBs are related to child adjustment and to observed SIL parenting processes in the same sample of families. As shown in the top of Table 8.4, constructive parent ERSBs during the kindergarten year were associated with fewer child externalizing

TABLE 8.3
Relative Rates of Categories of Observed Parent Emotion-Related
Socialization Behaviors (ERSBs)

| Parent response | Frequency | | % total |
	M	SD	
Empathize, validate	0.12	0.33	0.5
Soothe	0.88	1.42	3.5
Problem solve	0.88	1.54	3.5
Constructive coaching ERSBs	1.88	2.45	7.5
Fix, acquiesce	2.08	3.11	8.4
Command	3.36	4.50	13.6
Ignore, move on	13.28	9.14	53.2
Minimizing ERSBs	18.62	12.82	74.8
Disparage	4.52	5.97	18.0
Dismissing ERSBs[a]	23.14	17.87	92.8

[a]Includes minimizing ERSBs.

TABLE 8.4

Relation of Observed Emotion-Related Socialization Behaviors (ERSBs) to Parenting Practices and Child Outcomes

Parent ERSBs (composite)	Parent-reported externalizing problems					Teacher-reported externalizing problems				
	Fall kindergarten	Spring kindergarten	Fall first grade	Spring first grade	Spring second grade	Fall kindergarten	Spring kindergarten	Fall first grade	Spring first grade	Spring second grade
Constructive	−.40*	−.19	−.28*	−.34*	−.29*	−.23	−.19	−.40*	−.37*	−.57*
Minimizing	.24	.20	.30*	.39*	.26	.28	.31*	.38*	.36*	.61*
Disparaging	.46*	.35*	.50*	.28	.23	.21	.28	.13	.02	.31*

	Observed parenting in kindergarten				Positive peer preference (nominations)	
	Coercive interaction	Poor discipline	Warmth, positive involvement	Poor tracking	Fall kindergarten	Spring kindergarten
Constructive	.08	−.09	.43*	−.23	.42*	.32*
Minimizing	−.08	.05	−.38*	.36*	−.38*	−.36*
Disparaging	.42*	.09	.07	.22	.05	−.27

*p < .05.

behavior problems as reported by parents and by teachers; dismissive ERSBs were associated with more externalizing behavior problems, and these correlations were still apparent at the end of second grade. As shown in the bottom right portion of Table 8.4, constructive parent ERSBs to child negative emotion displays were associated with the frequency of positive peer nominations received by children, and minimizing parent ERSBs were negatively associated with positive nominations. These correlations suggest that the quality of ERSBs provided by parents may affect child behavior problems and social competence. From Baumrind's (1983, 1991) perspective, constructive ERSBs reflect parents' respect for their children's independence and freedom of expression and promote self assertion, individuation, and social competence. In contrast, minimizing and, even more so, disparaging responses are restrictive and intrusive, reflect psychological control, and diminish self regulation and instrumental competence.

A second set of correlational analyses was used to assess whether ERSBs and observed SIL parenting practices were complementary or redundant. As shown in the bottom left portion of Table 8.4, the rate of constructive parental ERSBs to child negative emotion displays was concurrently associated with higher levels of observed parental warmth and involvement, or in the language of Baumrind (1991), responsiveness. The rate of minimizing ERSBs was associated with less warmth and involvement and poor behavior tracking, and the rate of disparaging ERSBs was associated with higher levels of coercive parenting, or in the language of Baumrind (1991), arbitrary, harsh, and nonfunctional demandingness. The correlations between parent ERSBs and standard SIL constructs for skillful and ineffective parenting practices are modest and suggest that emotion coaching may add to and complement the description of parenting practices that have been shown to be associated with child problems and social competence in Baumrind's and other SIL research. Promoting parents' acquisition and application of emotion coaching skills may enhance the efficacy and effectiveness of current SIL parent training interventions.

RELATIONAL FRAME THEORY AND THE ACCEPTANCE AND COMMITMENT THERAPY APPROACH TO PARENTING

Parent training interventions and research on parenting derived from SIL are characterized by a fundamental assumption: It is what the parent does that counts. Parenting behaviors directed toward the child during daily interaction are the proximal and most powerful processes in socialization, and the myriad of internal events such as attributions, intentions, or feelings that parents have during interaction with their children are distal and indirect determinants of overt parent behavior. The primacy of what the parent does relative to what he or she thinks or feels is apparent in SIL research on parenting practices. What parents say they do as parents and their description of their child's reactions are often not very accurate. The correlation of parental reports with observations of parenting is typically modest, and self-reported parenting practices are relatively weak predictors of child outcomes unless those outcomes are also measured by parent report. The primacy of parenting behavior is also apparent in SIL parent training. Parents readily talk about their child's behavior and what "works" or "does not work" in managing that behavior, but talking and getting advice from someone else (even an expert) does not result in much change. One deadly trap in parent training is to spend a lot of time talking with parents about their attributions and discussing how to and not to parent while spending minimal time modeling, role playing, and applying new parenting behaviors in the home environment.

However, some research indicates parents' thoughts and feelings about parenting impact the consistency with which they apply skillful practices (Snyder, Cramer, Afrank, & Patterson, 2005). Some of the most difficult challenges in parent training are to encourage parents to (a) take the time and make the effort to acquire new parenting skills; (b) consistently implement those skills learned rather than reverting to relatively automatic maladaptive and coercive responses; and (c) apply parenting skills when they are depressed, tired, worried, and stressed (Dumas, 2005). Researchers currently do not have a strong theoretical model that translates these research findings into parent training intervention strategies that reduce the negative impact of parents' distress and irritability on the acquisition and daily implementation of skilled parenting practices.

RFT and ACT (Hayes & Wilson, 1999) provide a model to better understand the impact of parents' thoughts and feelings on their parenting and the means to identify tactics for fostering the acquisition and consistent application of effective parenting practices. From an RFT and ACT perspective, thoughts, images, words, and feelings are built-in adaptive responses. These responses are very useful in acting on the external world. Emotions motivate people to take action. Thoughts are useful in setting goals, weighing options, anticipating consequences, and guiding actions. The fact that they are built-in means we keep generating them: We cannot *not* feel or *not* think—these responses are part of our capacity as humans.

Although these continuous streams of ongoing thoughts, images, and feelings are powerful and useful tools for acting effectively on the external world, they can also interfere with doing so. When individuals take their thoughts as literally true or are flooded by their emotions, they may fail to behave in ways consistent with their goals and values because they are intensely fused with those thoughts and emotions. In fusion, thoughts and feelings are given an urgent validity that defines "how things really are," and a premium is placed on managing or acting to dissipate or control them. Given fusion with perceived threat and negative emotion, there is little space for attending to the environment and for intentionally scaffolding and enacting responses that create supportive social relationships. With fusion, there is a very strong self-focus and diminishing attunement to others' needs, goals, thoughts, and emotions. Fusion and the behavior it evokes may be supported by the short-term consequences they generate, including diminution of perceived threat and negative emotions. For example, given provocations by others (threat attributions), anger may seem justified and instigate coercive behavior, which is reinforced by the reduction of other persons' aversive behavior. Notice that this reinforcement promotes fusion with the negative attributions (threats are real) and anger (it is justified and should be expressed) as well as reinforcing the coercive behavior they instigate. The person is "getting things off his chest" and "venting" her anger, and this tactic may dissipate these thoughts and feelings in the short run.

In fusion, negative emotions (anger) and thoughts (negative attributions) are evaluated as unpleasant or bad, and behavior is focused on efforts to dissipate, control, or alter them. However, such tactics may be counterproductive in the long run. Research in RFT indicates that repeated efforts to alter, stop, or control thoughts and feelings actually end up evoking the very thoughts and feelings individuals are trying to diminish or change (Hayes & Gregg, 2001). Anger, for example, is increased and not dissipated by yelling or venting (Olatunji, Lohr, & Bushman, 2007). Trying not to worry often increases the frequency of worries. Fusion and the ensuing persistent efforts to alter, vent, or dissipate internal thoughts and feelings have another substantial long-term cost: They interfere with awareness of the external environment and with an intentional deployment of behaviors needed to achieve more fundamental goals and values—what the person really wants to do if he or she could get rid of negative thoughts or emotions.

Negative thoughts and strong emotions are natural responses. If they cannot be avoided, dissipated, or controlled, what is the constructive alternative? According to RFT and ACT, the constructive alternative is for individuals to become mindful and accepting of their negative thoughts and feelings and to distinguish and distance themselves from thoughts and feelings when those internal responses interfere with behaving in ways consistent with real goals and values. Mindfulness, acceptance, and distancing allow individuals to "step outside" of their negative thoughts and feelings (i.e., to simply notice them or defuse them) and at the same time to intentionally and planfully engage in behaviors consistent with their real values and goals (Hayes, Follette, & Linehan, 2004). More or less constructive and adaptive means of responding to troubling thoughts and feelings from an RFT and ACT perspective are shown in Table 8.5.

TABLE 8.5
A Relational Frame Theory and Acceptance and Commitment Therapy
Approach to Thoughts and Emotions

Constructive/adaptive	Ineffective/maladaptive
Accept/mindful	Fusion
Distance self from thought or feeling	Evaluate as good or bad
Valued action (act on external world)	Focus on control of thought or feeling
Problem solve (about external world)	Dissipate, alter thought or feeling
Plan and implement (about external world)	Avoid, escape thought or feeling
Focus on long-term consequences	Focus on short-term consequences
Intentional	Reactive

How can this RFT and ACT perspective be applied to parenting?
Parents have powerful hopes and dreams for their children. Their real values
are to be loving and supportive and to socialize their children to be competent human beings. Parents' intentions are to behave in ways that foster
their children's physical and psychological health, rule following, social skills,
aptitude for learning, self-regulation, and ultimate independence. Children
are a powerful source of joy and wonder. However, realizing these hopes and
dreams, experiencing joy and wonder, and expressing love and support are
often lost in the day-to-day challenges of parenting and other demands and
stressors. These challenges often engender anger, depression, and distress and
negative attributions about one's child and one's own parenting capacity. If
parents become fused with these negative thoughts and feelings, their capacity to systematically engage in constructive parenting practices consistent
with their genuine goals and values as parents is likely to be diminished.

Two models of parents' fusion with their own thoughts and feelings
might be hypothesized. In the first model (hostile/angry/reactive), shown at
the top of Figure 8.2, parents may engage in negative attributions about their
child's behavior (e.g., "He does it on purpose to push my buttons"), accompanied by anger that is "justified" by the child's persistent and seemingly intentional and provocative negative behavior. These internal parental responses
may cue, accompany, or serve as post hoc reasons for parents' irritability
and reliance on punitive control. Negative attributions, anger, and ensuing
punitive tactics may be reinforced by their short-term success in controlling
the child's behavior. However, research indicates these tactics are met with
countercontrol by the child and result in intermittent negative reinforcement of child coercive behavior (Snyder & Stoolmiller, 2002). This hostile/
angry/reactive parenting response set is also likely to be accompanied by a
failure to recognize and validate the child's needs, thoughts, and feelings; by
inconsistent or noncontingent discipline; and by insufficient scaffolding and

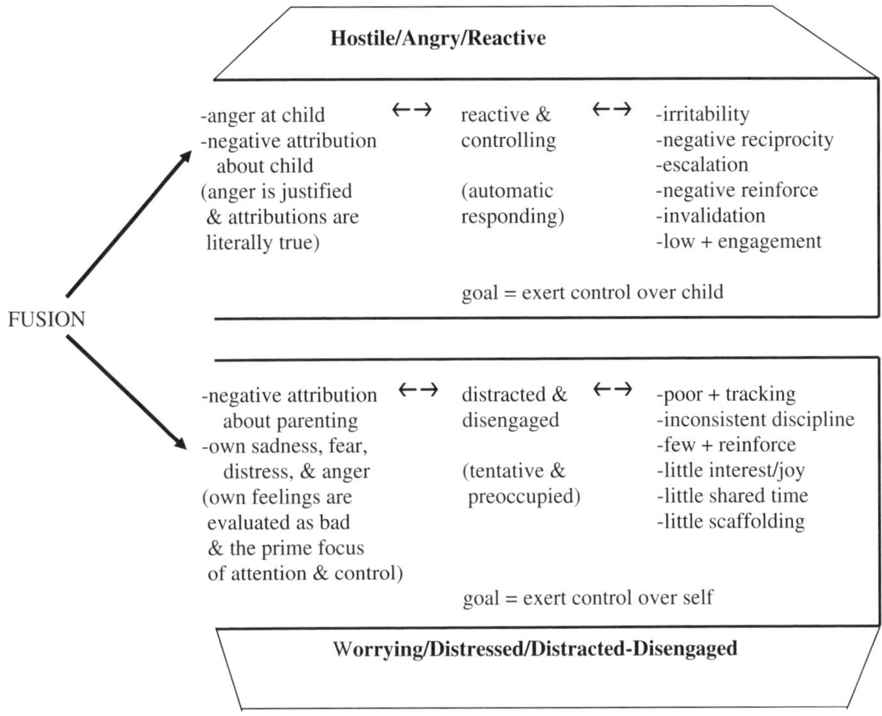

Figure 8.2. Maladaptive parenting attribution–affective response sets.

positive attention to support skillful child behavior, all of which characterize authoritarian parenting (Baumrind, 1967).

The second model (worrying/distressed/distracted-disengaged), shown at the bottom of Figure 8.2, describes parents who are fused with and overwhelmed and flooded by their own worries and sadness and who focus much of their effort on palliative self-care to reduce this distress. This may include a sense of inadequacy as a parent and be expressed as distraction and disengagement from parenting. Functionally, this response set is supported by short-term relief from distress, reduced caregiving demands, and by distress-contingent care from others (Hops, Sherman, & Biglan 1990). It is also associated with poor behavior tracking, few expectations and limits, inconsistent discipline, diminished engagement, a lack of shared joy, and with insufficient scaffolding and contingent reinforcement to promote child skill. These parents are likely to be low both on responsiveness and on demandingness (Baumrind, 1991).

Typically, parenting interventions focus on teaching parents to control or alter their negative emotions (e.g., anger management) and to replace hostile attributions with more adaptive and accurate ways of thinking. From the RFT and ACT perspective, explicit efforts to alter "bad" cognitions and to control negative emotions may be counterproductive; such tactics may engender the very emotions and cognitions targeted for change. In RFT and ACT, a more useful approach is to help parents gain distance from their thoughts and feelings and to get "into" parenting their child in an intentional and responsive manner. This is congruent with constructive emotion socialization practices in which parents model competence in terms of emotion display and regulation, provide a healthy family emotional climate, and intentionally manage their reactions to child negative behavior (Morris et al., 2007). As shown in Figure 8.3, this involves parents' awareness, acknowledgement, and acceptance of their negative thoughts and feelings as responses they have (distancing) rather than fusing with them, allowing parents to identify and engage in parenting behaviors guided by their parenting values. The fundamental notion is that it is possible to have angry or depressed feelings and to have negative thoughts about oneself and one's child and at the same time to engage in parenting practices that emphasize positive engagement, joint attention, and responsiveness and to use noncoercive, contingent limit setting and discipline—or authoritative parenting. A popular term for this approach is *mindful parenting*.

We used structured interviews to assess parental responses to vignettes of challenging child behavior and then probed parents' self-reported cognitive, affective, and behavioral responses to such behavior. Interviews were collected from 267 parents in an at-risk community sample. Open-ended queries about attributions and likely discipline tactics in relation to child mis-

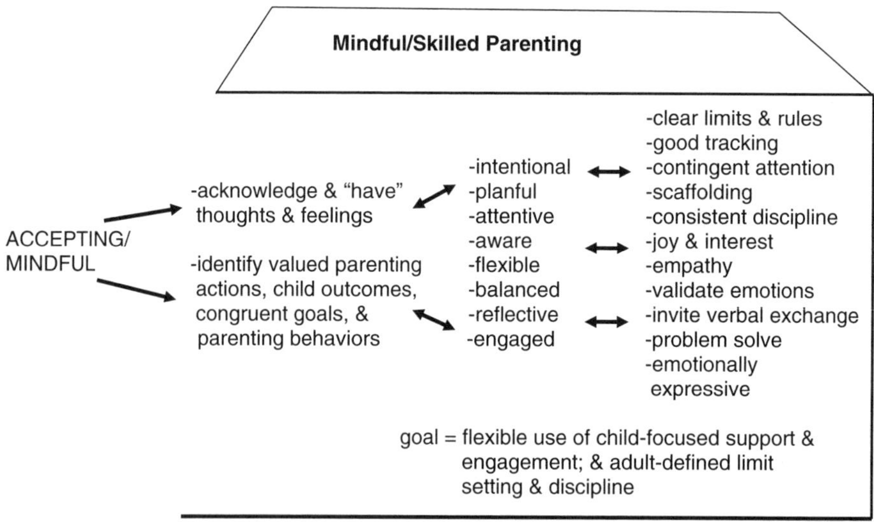

Figure 8.3. A constructive parenting attribution–affective response set.

behavior in the vignettes were coded by observers, and parents then rated the efficacy of their discipline responses and a range of other discipline tactics. These data were used to test the validity of the models in Figures 8.2 and 8.3. Interview variables are shown in the left column of Table 8.6. Factor analysis indicated these variables load onto three parenting attribution–affective response sets related to discipline: firm/contingent, harsh/hostile, and give in/give up. The firm/contingent factor is most closely associated with mindful/skilled parenting responses described in Figure 8.3. Parents who endorse a firm/contingent discipline approach accurately track challenging behavior, distance themselves from negative attributions about the provocative nature of this behavior, modulate their child's distress, engage in problem solving, and apply nonpunitive contingencies.

The two factors labeled *harsh/hostile* and *give in/give up* in Table 8.6 are consistent with the hostile/angry/reactive and the worrying/distressed/distracted-disengaged parenting response shown in Figure 8.2. Parents who endorse a harsh/hostile approach to discipline perceive their children's challenging behavior as provocative or intentional, endorse reactive and power-assertive discipline, and report low agency in dealing with the child's behavior and emotional arousal. This response set is also characterized by endorsement of coercive and harsh discipline tactics. The give in/give up approach

TABLE 8.6

Factor Analysis of Structured Interview Responses:
Parenting Attribution–Affective Discipline Response Sets

Attribution-affective responses	Firm/contingent	Harsh/hostile	Give in/give up
Accurate cue detection	.32		
Hostile attribution	−.76	.68	
Generate problem-solving responses	.38		
High efficacy—manage child negative affect	.50	−.54	
High efficacy—influence child behavior	.40	−.44	
Endorse firm discipline strategies	.54		
Generate high-power responses (command, coerce, consequence)		.62	
Endorse "get tough" discipline strategies		.57	
Generate comforting responses			.78
Endorse "giving in" discipline strategies			.61

to discipline is less well defined by two items describing a noncontingent, warm, and minimalist approach to challenging child behavior: comforting the child, ignoring misbehavior, and capitulating to child demands.

On the basis of the RFT and ACT models shown in Figures 8.1 and 8.2, these attribution-affective approaches should be related to observed parenting. The top section of Table 8.7 provides the correlations of each approach with standard SIL parenting practices derived from observation of parent–child interaction. As hypothesized, the firm/contingent approach was correlated with positive parenting and problem solving. The harsh/hostile approach was positively correlated with observed harsh discipline and inversely correlated with parent teaching skill, positive parenting, and problem solving. The give in/give up approach was inversely correlated with teaching skill. These correlations suggest that parents' self-reported attributions, preferred discipline tactics, and perceived efficacy of those tactics are associated with their observed parenting practices.

The maladaptive RFT and ACT models in Figure 8.2 also involve parents' fusion with their own negative affective states. To test this hypothesis, parent self-reported mood states were correlated with each of the parent attribution-affective factors. As shown at the bottom of Table 8.7, parents' sad affect, anxiety and worry, and anger and hostility were inversely related to the calm/firm approach to discipline. Sadness/depression and anger/hostility were positively related to a harsh/hostile approach, and all three negative parent affective states were positively related to the give in/give up approach. Parents' negative moods are associated with an attribution-affective approach to discipline characterized by a lack of attunement, low sense of efficacy, and endorsement of reactive, punitive, and noncontingent discipline tactics.

TABLE 8.7

Correlations of Structured Interview Factors With Parenting Practices and Parent Self-Reported Affect

	Firm/contingent	Harsh/hostile	Give in/give up
Observed parenting practices			
Harsh discipline	−.12	.35***	.01
Teaching skill	.10	−.22**	−.18*
Positive parenting	.25***	−.28***	−.07
Problem solving	.20**	−.21***	.03
Parent self-reported affect			
Sad/depressed	−.31***	.22***	.27**
Anxious/worried	−.19*	.09	.22**
Angry/hostile	−39***	.41**	.19*

*p < .05. **p < .01. ***p < .001.

Analyses also indicated that calm/firm and harsh/hostile approaches to discipline accounted for additional variance in child externalizing behavior problems above that accounted for by SIL parenting practices. Child externalizing problems in first grade were inversely related to good problem solving ($\beta = -.20$, $p < .05$) and a calm/firm approach to discipline ($\beta = -.18$, $p < .005$) after controlling for kindergarten externalizing problems ($\beta = .57$, $p < .001$). Child externalizing problems in first grade were predicted by observed harsh parental discipline practices ($\beta = .12$, $p < .05$), a harsh/hostile approach to discipline ($\beta = .13$, $p < .05$), and the interaction of harsh discipline practices and harsh/hostile approach ($\beta = .18$, $p < .01$) as well as by kindergarten externalizing problems ($\beta = .54$, $p < .001$). The interaction term indicates the association of observed harsh discipline with child externalizing problems was amplified when parents also endorsed a harsh/hostile approach to discipline. These findings provide some support for an RFT and ACT model and are also congruent with Baumrind's definition of authoritative parenting, which is characterized by a delicate and intentional balance of responsiveness and demandingness attuned to the child's current behavior, affect, and developmental competence (Baumrind, 1991).

Two important aspects of the RFT and ACT model should be emphasized. First, relative to current parent training interventions, an RFT- and ACT-informed approach would use different tactics to help parents who struggle with negative attributions and emotions. The emphasis would be on developing mindfulness, acceptance, and distancing rather than on promoting efforts to dissipate and manage negative attributions and emotions. Mindfulness, acceptance, and distancing should increase readiness for the acquisition of skillful parenting practices and the capacity of parents to consistently implement those practices in everyday interaction with their children. RFT and ACT are compatible with and complement current parenting interventions. Second, RFT and ACT are congruent with emotion coaching. Mindfulness, acceptance, and distancing facilitate parents' modeling of constructive expression and regulation and use of emotions and promote parents' validation, labeling, and problem-solving in response to their children's displays of negative emotions.

EMOTION COACHING AND RELATIONAL FRAME THEORY AND ACCEPTANCE AND COMMITMENT THERAPY IN PARENT TRAINING INTERVENTIONS

Some efforts have been made to develop parenting interventions that explicitly promote constructive emotion socialization practices and to incorporate valuing, mindfulness, and acceptance. Examining the degree to which emotion coaching and ACT are already incorporated into current empirically validated parent training interventions is a first step in designing empirical tests of whether the addition of emotion coaching and ACT components would enhance the efficacy and effectiveness of parent training. The components of a recent parenting intervention derived from an emotion coaching perspective (Havighurst, Wilson, Harley, & Prior, 2009) are shown in Table 8.8 and compared with comparable components of the well-validated PMTO (Forgatch & Patterson, 2010). PMTO primarily focuses on parents' management of their own negative emotions with the assumption that emotion dysregulation interferes with skillful parenting (see self focus in Table 8.8). This is also consistent with the first level of emotion coaching—parental modeling and family affective climate. PMTO is less clear about how parents constructively respond to their children's display of emotions (see child focus in Table 8.8). Constructive ERSBs may be a useful additional skill targeted in SIL parent training.

Parent training interventions have also been developed that primarily focus on parent mindfulness without explicitly addressing other parenting practices (Duncan, Coatsworth, & Greenberg, 2009) or that complement standard empirically validated parent management training with the addition of RFT and ACT principles and exercises (Dumas, 2005). Some RFT and ACT principles are inherent in standard SIL parent training intervention (see comments

TABLE 8.8
Comparison of Targets in Emotion Coaching and Standard Social
Interaction Learning Parent Training Interventions

Emotion coaching targets	PMTO emotion coaching targets
Child-focused emotion-related socialization behaviors	
Attend	Track different emotions
Reflect, label, and empathize	Recognize and label child emotions
Set limits	
Behavior–emotion distinction	
Problem solve	
Prompt, shape regulation strategies	
Safe expression	
Emotion "talk" time	
Parent self-focused	
Awareness and understanding	Recognize, label, and describe own emotions
Beliefs about emotions	Not described
Regulatory strategies	Managing own emotions
Emotion self-care	Emotion and stress
	Describing (objectifying) own emotion
	Effect of parent emotions on children

Note. PMTO = Parent Management Training—Oregon.

TABLE 8.9

The Application of Relational Frame Theory and Acceptance
and Commitment Therapy Principles Inherent in Standard Social
Interaction Learning (SIL) Parent Training Interventions

SIL session content	SIL intervention processes
Hopes and dreams for child (values and goals)	Emphasis on role play, modeling, practice, and at home application (doing rather than saying)
Defining and tracking strengths of parenting and child (focus on external actions)	Use of metaphors, paradox, and reframes (break down literal, fusion)
Parents as teachers, scaffold and use incentives (focus on plans, skills, and results)	Join, listen, connect with story line (reduce countercontrol, resistance)
Recognize own and child emotion (though emphasis on control, accept, mindfulness)	Verbal teaching, experiential activities about parenting skills (doing and experiencing rather than saying)
Problem solving	Not described
Listen and not react to child emotions, thoughts, and experiences; exploring and selecting plans for change (accept, mindfulness, focus on action)	Capitalizes on opportunities for problem solving and conflict management (use "hot" experiences rather than abstract description and discussion)

in parentheses in Table 8.9), though delivered in relatively subtle ways. Little research has tested whether the addition of RFT and ACT exercises to standard parent training increases the range and potency of intervention.

EMOTION COACHING AND RELATIONAL FRAME THEORY AND ACCEPTANCE AND COMMITMENT THERAPY: WHERE DOES ALL OF THIS LEAD?

The SIL model has produced an empirically grounded understanding of effective parenting and a set of intervention tools to promote effective parenting. However, its strong behaviorist roots have resulted in difficulties in incorporating cognitions, emotions, intentions, and values into parenting research and parent training. New theoretical models involving emotion socialization and RFT and new intervention tactics incorporating parent emotion coaching and ACT principles may enhance researchers' understanding of effective parenting practices and serve as platforms to develop increasingly efficacious and effective parenting interventions.

However, the bottom line in searching for new models in research and intervention is empirical. SIL models have substantial empirical support. SIL might be considered the basic model into which new formulations are incorporated. Parent emotion coaching and parent mindfulness are consistent with and may more fully articulate Baumrind's theory of what effective parents do to promote their children's self-regulation, instrumental competence, and social skills. However, in the search for expanded models of parenting, three questions need to be answered. First, can the constructs in expanded models be reliably and validly measured? Second, do the constructs add to the amount of variance in child outcomes that we can explain? Third, does the addition of new targets for change and new tactics in parenting interventions increase the efficacy and effectiveness of existing SIL interventions? Researchers need to balance the basic conservatism of science with an openness to new and creative ideas consistent with the critical contributions of Diana Baumrind.

REFERENCES

Barber, B. K. (1996). Parental psychological control: Revisiting a neglected construct. *Child Development, 67,* 3296-3319. doi:102307/1131780

Baumrind, D. (1967). Child care practices anteceding three patterns of preschool behavior. *Genetic Psychology Monographs, 75,* 43–88.

Baumrind, D. (1973). The development of instrumental competence through socialization. In A. D. Pick (Ed.), *Minnesota symposia on child psychology* (Vol. 7, pp. 3–46). Minneapolis: University of Minnesota Press.

Baumrind, D. (1983). Rejoinder to Lewis's reinterpretation of parental firm control effects: Are authoritative families really harmonious? *Psychological Bulletin, 94,* 132–142. doi:10.1037/0033-2909.94.1.132

Baumrind, D. (1991). The influence of parenting style on adolescent competence and substance use. *The Journal of Early Adolescence, 11,* 56–95. doi:10.1177/0272431691111004

Baumrind, D., & Black, A. E. (1967). Socialization practices associated with dimensions of competence in preschool boys and girls. *Child Development, 38,* 291–327. doi:10.2307/1127295

Dishion, T. J., Burraston, B., & Li, F. (2003). Family management practices: Research design and measurement issues. In Z. Sloboda & W. J. Bukowski (Eds.), *Handbook of drug abuse prevention: Theory, science and practice* (pp. 578–607). New York, NY: Kluwer Academic/Plenum.

Dishion, T. J., & Kavanagh, K. (2003). *Intervening in adolescent problem behavior: A family-centered approach.* New York, NY: Guilford Press.

Dumas, J. E. (2005). Mindfulness-based parent training: Strategies to lessen the grip of automaticity in families with disruptive children. *Journal of Clinical Child and Adolescent Psychology, 34,* 779–791. doi:10.1207/s15374424jccp3404_20

Duncan, L. G., Coatsworth, J. D., & Greenberg, M. T. (2009). A model of mindful parenting: Implications for parent–child relationships and prevention research. *Clinical Child and Family Psychology Review, 12*, 255–270. doi:10.1007/s10567-009-0046-3

Eisenberg, N., Cumberland, A., & Spinrad, T. (1998). Parental socialization of emotion. *Psychological Inquiry, 9*, 241–273. doi:10.1207/s15327965pli0904_1

Forgatch, M. S., & Patterson, G. R. (2010). Parent Management Training –Oregon model: An intervention for antisocial children and adolescents. In J. R. Weisz & A. E. Kazdin (Eds.), *Evidence-based psychotherapies for children and adolescents* (2nd ed., pp. 159–178). New York, NY: Guilford Press.

Forgatch, M. S., & Rains, L. (1997). *Parenting through change* [Parent training manual]. Eugene: Oregon Social learning Center.

Gottman, J. M., Katz, L. F., & Hooven, C. (1996). Meta-emotion philosophy and the emotional life of families: Theoretical models and preliminary data. *Journal of Family Psychology, 10*, 243–268. doi:10.1037/0893-3200.10.3.243

Gottman, J M., Katz, L F., & Hooven, C. (1997). *Meta-emotion: How families communicate emotionally*. Mahwah, NJ: Erlbaum.

Gottman, J. M., McCoy, K., Coan, J., & Collier, H. (1996). *The specific affect coding system (SPAFF) for observing emotional communication in marital and family interaction*. Mahwah, NJ: Erlbaum.

Hanf, C. (1968, November). *Modification of mother controlling behavior during mother–child interaction in a controlled laboratory setting*. Paper presented at the regional meeting of the Association for the Advancement of Behavior Therapy, Olympia, WA.

Havighurst, S. S., Wilson, K. R., Harley, A. E., & Prior, M. R. (2009). Tuning into kids: An emotion-focused parenting program—initial findings from a community trial. *Journal of Community Psychology, 37*, 1008–1023. doi:10.1002/jcop.20345

Hayes, S., Follette, V., & Linehan, M. (2004). *Mindfulness and acceptance: Expanding the cognitive-behavioral tradition*. New York, NY: Guilford Press.

Hayes, S., & Gregg, J. (2001). Functional contextualism and the self. In J. C. Muran (Ed.), *Self-relations in the psychotherapy process* (pp. 291–311). Washington, DC: American Psychological Association. doi:10.1037/10391-012

Hayes, S., & Wilson, K. (1999). *Acceptance and commitment therapy: An experiential approach to behavior change*. New York, NY: Guilford Press.

Hops, H., Sherman, L., & Biglan, A. (1990). Maternal depression, marital discord, and children's behavior: A developmental perspective. In G. R. Patterson (Ed.), *Depression and aggression in family interaction* (pp. 185–208). Hillsdale, NJ: Erlbaum.

Izard, C. E. (2002). Translating emotion theory and research into preventive interventions. *Psychological Bulletin, 128*, 796–824. doi:10.1037/0033-2909.128.5.796

Kabat-Zinn, J. (2003). Mindfulness-based interventions in context: Past, present, and future. *Clinical Psychology: Science and Practice, 10*, 144–156.

Morris, A. S., Silk, J. S., Steinberg, L., Myers, S., & Robinson, L. R. (2007). The role of family context in the development of emotion regulation. *Social Development, 16,* 361–388. doi:10.1111/j.1467-9507.2007.00389.x

Olatunji, B. O., Lohr, J. M., & Bushman, B. J. (2007). The pseudo-psychology of venting in interventions for anger and related conditions: Implications for mental health practice. In T. A. Cavell & K. Malcolm (Eds.), *Anger, aggression and interventions for interpersonal violence* (pp. 119–142). Mahwah, NJ: Erlbaum.

Patterson, G. R., & Brodsky, G. (1966). A behavior modification programme for a child with multiple problem behaviors. *Journal of Child Psychology and Psychiatry, 7,* 277–295. doi:10.1111/j.1469-7610.1966.tb02253.x

Sanders, M. R. (1999). Triple P-Positive Parenting Program: Towards an empirically validated, multilevel parenting and family support strategy for the prevention of behavior and emotional problems in children. *Clinical Child and Family Psychology Review, 2,* 71–90. doi:10.1023/A:1021843613840

Silk, J. S., Shaw, D. S., Forbes, E. E., Lane, T. L., & Kovacs, M. (2006). Maternal depression and child internalizing: The moderating role of child emotion regulation. *Journal of Clinical Child and Adolescent Psychology, 35,* 116–126.

Silk, J. S., Steinberg, L., & Morris, A. S. (2003). Adolescents' emotion regulation in daily life: Links to depressive symptoms and problem behavior. *Child Development, 74,* 1869–1880. doi:10.1046/j.1467-8624.2003.00643.x

Snyder, J., Cramer, D. A., Afrank, J., & Patterson, G. R. (2005). The contribution of ineffective discipline and parent hostile attributions about child misbehavior to the development of conduct problems at home and school. *Developmental Psychology, 41,* 30–41. doi:10.1037/0012-1649.41.1.30

Snyder, J., & Stoolmiller, M. (2002). Reinforcement and coercion mechanisms in the development of antisocial behavior: The family. In J. B. Reid, G. R. Patterson, & J. Snyder (Eds.), *Antisocial behavior in children and adolescents: A developmental analysis and model for intervention* (pp. 65–100). Washington, DC: American Psychological Association. doi:10.1037/10468-004

Wahler, R. G., Winkle, G. H., Peterson, R. F., & Morrison, D. C. (1965). Mothers as behavior therapists for their own children. *Behaviour Research and Therapy, 3,* 113–124. doi:10.1016/0005-7967(65)90015-X

Webster-Stratton, C. (2001). *Leader's guide, the parent and children's series: A comprehensive course divided into four programs.* Seattle: University of Washington.

9

AUTHORITATIVE PARENTING AND PARENTAL SUPPORT FOR CHILDREN'S COGNITIVE DEVELOPMENT

MARY GAUVAIN, SUSAN M. PEREZ, AND HEIDI BEEBE

Authoritative parents provide support for the development of social and emotional skills as well as guidance in the development of mature behaviors (Baumrind, 1973). This parenting style is effective in promoting socioemotional growth because it is responsive to the child's needs without being intrusive or coercive, engages in gradual autonomy granting that allows the child to assume responsibility for decisions when appropriate, and favors reasoning and explanation in providing structure and discipline for the child. Although the contributions of authoritative parenting to social and emotional development have been a main focus of research, as can be seen in many of the chapters in this volume, this parenting style is also ideally suited to supporting cognitive development, both directly through instruction and guidance and indirectly through the influence that authoritative parenting has on child emotional development, which can help to regulate cognitive development across childhood.

DOI: 10.1037/13948-010
Authoritative Parenting: Synthesizing Nurturance and Discipline for Optimal Child Development, Robert E. Larzelere, Amanda Sheffield Morris, and Amanda W. Harrist (Editors)

In this chapter, we discuss the contributions that parents make to children's cognitive development in the context of authoritative parenting. We are particularly interested in the relation between opportunities for cognitive development in parent–child interactions; child characteristics that may be important to this process, such as child emotionality; and parenting behaviors inherent to authoritative parenting. We specifically focus on authoritative parenting behaviors such as warmth and encouragement, responsiveness, and feedback, which can be facilitative of children's independent thinking that may arise when parents guide but do not overly direct their children's activities. We are also interested in efforts by authoritative parents to align their expectations with children's current and developing cognitive and emotional capabilities; such efforts are often referred to as *maturity demands*. We concentrate on the years of early and middle childhood, although some relevant research in the adolescent period is also discussed. Our approach is informed by sociocultural theory, which contends that children's thinking emerges from social experience (Vygotsky, 1987). We begin by discussing the social basis of cognitive development.

THE SOCIAL NATURE OF COGNITIVE DEVELOPMENT

Over the past several decades there has been increasing appreciation of the complex social nature of cognitive development. In this view, the development of thinking is considered an emergent property of the child's social and cultural experiences. The ideas of Russian psychologist Lev S. Vygotsky (1987) and writings and empirical research based on the sociocultural approach to cognitive development (e.g., see Cole, 1996; Göncü & Gauvain, 2012; Rogoff, 1990) have been central to this formulation. In this approach, cognitive development is a social process, that is, it involves other people. Moreover, the social support for this development is wide-ranging and varied. We introduce our discussion of parental contributions to cognitive development by describing these two main tenets of this approach.

Cognitive Development Involves Other People

The sociocultural approach challenges the long-held view that cognitive development is an individual process separate from the social world (Rogoff, 1998). Rather, learning and cognitive development involve other people and the products and processes of the culture in which growth occurs.

Research focused on the individual characterizes cognitive development as the result of maturational forces, experiential learning that is not social, or both of these processes. In contrast, the sociocultural approach focuses on learning that involves other people and the tools, artifacts, and institutions of the culture (Cole, 1996). Social and cultural processes are considered the principal means of cognitive development, and these processes interact with maturational contributions to support, extend, and modify the course of cognitive growth (Gauvain, 2001). Even solitary activities conducted in laboratory settings are imbued with the social context. Human beings design these activities, which rely on social and cultural tools and artifacts, including language and material resources, and make sense to people because of a shared understanding about the world and how to engage with it.

Social Support for Cognitive Development Is Extensive and Varied

Research has shown that social support for cognitive development is wide-ranging and diverse in form. It includes modeling and demonstration, formal instruction, and less formal methods of conveying ideas and ways of thinking to children, such as guided participation, scaffolding, parent–child conversation, and participation in socially organized activities (Gauvain & Perez, 2007; Rogoff, 1998). Instruction aimed at the child's zone of proximal (or potential) development, or the region of sensitivity for learning (Vygotsky, 1978), can be particularly effective in supporting learning. The *zone of proximal development* is the difference between what a child is capable of doing when working alone and what he or she is capable of doing with the aid of a more skilled partner.

When people work together on activities that support learning and cognitive development, the more experienced partner provides assistance that is coordinated with the learning needs of the less experienced partner. In *scaffolding,* for instance, a more knowledgeable partner, such as a parent, adjusts the amount and type of instructional support over the course of the interaction in ways that fit with what the child requires to learn (Wood, Bruner, & Ross, 1976). For example, while solving a problem together, the parent may support the child's learning by shouldering some of the mental demands of the activity, such as keeping track of what still needs to be done. This support, in turn, allows the child to concentrate on the aspects of the problem that are within his or her grasp and to observe the problem-solving behaviors of the parent.

Learning in a social context is a dynamic process. For the child to learn, both the more and less experienced partners must be actively engaged. Whereas the more experienced partner provides support and direction, the less experienced one directs his or her attention and participation in ways that reflect his or her own interests, needs, and capabilities and that mesh with the learning opportunities offered by the partner (Bell, 1968; Odden & Rochat, 2005; Rogoff et al., 2007). Efforts by the less experienced partner are especially important to learning because they communicate how the learner is doing on the task—information that the more experienced partner can use to modify or fine-tune the instruction and support provided.

Parents Provide Much Support for Cognitive Development

A social approach to cognitive development paves an analytical path for examining the role that parents (and other primary caregivers) play in children's intellectual growth (Gauvain & Perez, 2007). Parents are the dominant social learning partners for children early in life, and as children get older parents continue to influence and support children's learning both inside and outside the home (Maccoby, 2007). Children learn from their parents in myriad ways. Parents directly teach their children many things about the world, and children can benefit cognitively from these encounters. Research has demonstrated more advanced performance by children on cognitive tasks, tasks that were initially difficult for the children, after they interacted with their parents on similar tasks (Gauvain & Rogoff, 1989; Rogoff & Gauvain, 1986). Parents also indirectly support children's learning and cognitive development by supporting children's development in other areas, such as emotional development, that intersect with cognitive development and by participating with children in valued community activities in which children are introduced to and get to practice new skills in supportive, organized, and meaningful contexts (Rogoff, 2003).

Several features of the parent–child relationship make it a unique social context for children's learning and cognitive development. Parents possess greater knowledge than their children in many areas of thinking, an arrangement consistent with the social structure described in the notion of the zone of proximal development. Parents and children also differ in the self-regulatory skills they bring to their interactions, which help children control attention and are vital to learning. The sustained nature of family life means that children and parents interact frequently. Repeated interactions offer multiple opportunities for learning, and they provide parents with extensive information about their children's interests and needs. This information can help parents target their guidance and support in meaningful and effective ways. Parents are also socially and emotionally invested in the development of their children's cognitive competence, which means that they are motivated to help their children learn.

The strong emotional bonds that family members have for one another affect both the quantity and quality of parent–child interactions. These bonds may enhance children's learning (Bugental & Goodnow, 1998; Hinde, 1989) perhaps by helping children achieve optimal learning states (Anderson, 2000; Yerkes & Dodson, 1908). However, these strong emotional connections may also undermine social learning opportunities. Gauvain and Perez (2008) observed mother–child interactions on cognitive tasks in dyads that included a chronically noncompliant preschooler or a same-age child in the normative compliance range for the age group. Children in the two groups were matched for IQ, and their performance on a solitary pretest did not differ. Nonetheless, mothers of chronically noncompliant children, relative to mothers of compliant children, expressed more disapproval of their children, and these mothers used more behavioral directives that restricted their children's independent exploration of the task. During the interaction, the noncompliant children were less involved in the task, and they assumed less responsibility for the activity than the compliant children did. These results suggest that the cognitive benefits available in parent–child interactions are not assured and that they may reflect the shared social history of the dyad (Gauvain & DeMent, 1991). That is, the opportunities for learning and cognitive development available to children may be associated with the child's socioemotional development and skills and with the parents' prior experience with the child and their socialization goals. This research suggests that it is important to examine aspects of parent–child interactions and the parent–child relationship that may contribute to different learning outcomes. One aspect that may both contribute to and be informed by children's cognitive and socioemotional development is parenting style. In this light, parenting style may serve as an index of the dynamic nature of learning opportunities in social context.

PARENTING STYLE AND THE DEVELOPMENT OF COGNITIVE COMPETENCE

In her longitudinal research, Baumrind (1967, 1991) found that parents interact with their children in patterned ways that reflect four social psychological dimensions: nurturance, communication, maturity demands, and control. Baumrind used these dimensions to describe three parenting styles. *Authoritative* parents are warm, responsive, and involved yet nonintrusive; set and enforce reasonable limits; and expect appropriately mature behaviors from their children. *Authoritarian* parents are harsh, unresponsive, and rigid and use power-assertive methods of control. *Permissive* parents are affectionate toward their children, but these parents use lax and inconsistent discipline, and they encourage their children to express their impulses freely.

Authoritative parenting is related to positive outcomes including self-esteem, adaptability, internalized control, popularity with peers, and low levels of antisocial behavior (Baumrind, 1973). In contrast, authoritarian and permissive child rearing are associated with negative outcomes. Authoritarian parenting is related to fearfulness and moodiness; vulnerability to stress; and low social competence, self-confidence, and initiative in relations with peers. Permissive parenting is related to impulsive, noncompliant, and aggressive behavior in children. In terms of cognitive competence, the authoritative style is more highly related to the development of a range of cognitive capabilities than are the other two parenting styles (Baumrind, 1967). Even though the children in this research did not differ in IQ across the three parenting styles groups, they differed in other measures of cognitive competence including self-reliance, self-control, a tendency to explore the environment and seek stimulation, academic performance, and positive engagement in activities and with other people.

In the following descriptions, we discuss the four dimensions of parenting style. We also comment on the potential of each for supporting learning and cognitive development during parent–child interactions.

Nurturance

Nurturance includes expressions by parents of positive regard or affection toward the child, responsiveness to the child's needs, and behaviors aimed at safeguarding the child's physical and emotional well-being. Although nurturance by itself does not promote cognitive development, as exhibited in Baumrind's permissive parenting style, it provides a supportive and positive emotional environment for learning. Authoritative parents are responsive to their children's needs, and they use more positive reinforcement, are more accepting of and express more warmth toward their children, and have more sympathy and empathy for their children's experiences than authoritarian parents do. In contrast, the more negative and harsh treatment, including rejection, associated with the authoritarian style offers less support and encouragement for learning (Baumrind, Larzelere, & Owens, 2010).

Research has shown that parental responsiveness to children's attention and interests is associated with the development of cognitive competence in children (Bornstein & Tamis-LeMonda, 1997; Mattanah, Pratt, Cowan, & Cowan, 2005). Although less is known about how parents' affective responsiveness such as warmth contributes to cognitive development, research has revealed that lack of warmth in the form of disapproval and physical intervention in the child's activity is related to poorer independent cognitive performance by the child following collaboration with parents (Gauvain, Fagot, Leve, & Kavanagh, 2002).

Communication

Baumrind (1973) found differences in the three parenting styles in the importance and clarity of parent–child communication. Effective parent–

child communication relies on reason as a means of discipline and uses encouragement to probe the child's feelings and opinions. Baumrind found authoritative parents to use more effective communication with their children. They were more respectful of their children's feelings and views, used reason and explanation to obtain child compliance, and encouraged their children to engage in discussion more than authoritarian or permissive parents did. These communication processes are central to interactions that promote cognitive development. Open and supportive communication of the type associated with authoritative parenting helps parents calibrate their assistance to the child's learning needs and encourages child engagement in the learning process. This form of exchange is also favorable to the establishment of mutual understanding or intersubjectivity (Rommetveit, 1985), which is important to learning in social context (Wertsch, 1985).

Maturity Demands

Maturity demands pertain to the expectations parents have for their child's intellectual, social, and emotional performance and for the child's ability to make independent decisions. Parents with high maturity demands expect their children to perform up to their intellectual, social, and emotional capacity. These parents also encourage and support the development of independent decision making. Authoritative parents may promote child learning because they set reasonable yet obtainable limits for the child's behavior and have appropriate expectations regarding the child's display of independent skills (Baumrind et al., 2010).

Parental Control

Parents differ in how they control or discipline their children. In this regard, Baumrind (1973; see also Chapter 1, this volume) was concerned with how parents regulate and try to induce changes in the child's behavior. She focused on control techniques such as structuring the child's activities and establishing and enforcing house rules. She found that control that clarifies the limits to the child's behavior and provides structure and order in the child's life has positive outcomes for development. In relation to cognitive development, control would include efforts by the parent to modify and direct the child's attempts at mastering a skill or knowledge base and responses to the child's bids for autonomy in making decisions and in planning.

Much of the research on parental control and parenting styles concentrates on corrective actions by parents to discipline the child when he or she misbehaves. This research has little relevance to cognitive development in a social context during interactions without strife. However when discord occurs, especially as a result of child misbehavior, support for child learning may hinge on the parent's skill at providing structure and redirection that help the child engage in and learn from the activity. Whereas too little control, as seen among parents with a permissive style, provides minimal guidance for the learner, too much control, such as that offered by authoritarian parents, may constrain opportunities for cognitive growth. Moreover, when parental direction is disapproving, harsh, or interferes with the child's activity, as has been found among parents who use an authoritarian style, it may dampen the child's interest and persistence in learning. Authoritative parents, with their focus on reasoning and dialogic parent–child communication, tend to use control techniques that rely on skillful engagement with the child. They are also sensitive to the child's point of view, an approach that may be especially useful during cognitive interactions in which children have difficulty engaging in the task at hand.

Summary

Baumrind's model suggests that parenting style may influence the behaviors that parents encourage and demonstrate for their children during collaborative cognitive activity along with the types of emotional connections between parents and children that can support learning. Authoritative parenting appears to be more conducive than authoritarian and permissive parenting to the provision of cognitive support during parent–child interactions. Parents who use an authoritative style that is responsive and nonintrusive and permits the child freedom to explore within reasonable limits may be supportive of the child's learning needs and the child's bids for independence, which, in turn, may facilitate the transfer of responsibility for the activity to the learner when he or she is ready. This is an important feature of social interactions that foster learning and cognitive development. Social contributions to cognitive development are made manifest in the transfer of responsibility from the more to the less experienced partner when the learner is ready and able to engage in new areas of thinking and problem solving.

In support of these conjectures, research has revealed some direct links between authoritative parenting and parents' support for children's learning. In research with preschoolers, authoritative mothers and fathers as compared with nonauthoritative parents were more likely to target their assistance at the child's zone of proximal development when working together on problem-solving tasks, and authoritative parents were also more likely to shift the level of assistance they provided as the child gained competence on a task (Pratt, Kerig, Cowan, & Cowan, 1988). In research with school-age children, authoritative parenting style was associated with more effective scaffolding by parents on children's mathematics homework (Pratt, Green, MacVicar,

& Bountrogianni, 1992). Adolescents with authoritative parents are more responsive to parental influence when making important decisions (Mackey, Arnold & Pratt, 2001). These adolescents allow their parents to act as guides, yet the adolescents are able to secure appropriate levels of autonomy in reaching their own decisions.

In the following sections, we explore the relation between authoritative parenting and parent–child interactions that support leaning and cognitive development. First, we discuss the unique features of parent–child interactions that make them a particularly rich setting for cognitive development. Then we describe our research on the development of planning and decision making that illustrates connections between authoritative parenting and parent–child cognitive interactions that promote learning. We then discuss research from our laboratory on parent–child interactions involving children who have problems learning socially because of difficulty in emotional functioning. This research suggests that parental support and responsiveness to children's learning needs, behaviors that coincide with authoritative parenting, can yield positive benefits for children's learning in these more difficult types of parent–child interactions.

AUTHORITATIVE PARENTING AND COGNITIVE DEVELOPMENT

Parental contributions to cognitive development have been studied in several ways. Some research seeks relations between characteristics of the family, such as parent education, social class, ethnicity, and family practices (e.g. parent–child reading), and the child's academic achievement (Davis-Kean, 2005; Gauvain, Savage, & McCollum, 2000). In other research, a parent and child are observed as they participate together in a cognitive activity or collaborate in reaching a goal. Much of this research is guided by a socio-cultural approach to cognitive development (Vygotsky, 1987), which concentrates on the assistance provided by other people that introduces children to ways of thinking that enable them to function intellectually in their social and cultural context. In this view, social interactions involving children and more experienced partners, such as parents, are especially important to cognitive development. The more experienced partner assists in ways that support the child's engagement in actions that extend beyond his or her current capabilities. In an effective learning situation, this engagement occurs in the child's zone of proximal development (Vygotsky, 1978). As the child gains competence, the more experienced partner gradually withdraws support, and in time, the child comes to function on his or her own in a more advanced intellectual way. During joint cognitive activity, parents use various methods to support their children's cognitive development, for example, a parent may explain or demonstrate how to solve a problem by breaking it into parts and directing the child's attention and effort toward manageable subgoals (Saxe, Guberman, & Gearhart, 1987).

Parent–child interactions have been shown to relate to cognitive development in several areas, including attention, memory, reasoning, problem solving, and planning (Gauvain, 2001). For instance, results have revealed that children can acquire problem-solving and memory skills during parent–child interactions that lead to improved individual performance on similar types of problems following the interaction (Gauvain & Rogoff, 1989; Haden, Ornstein, Eckerman, & Didow, 2001; Landry, Miller-Loncar, Smith, & Swank, 2002; Stright, Herr, & Neitzel, 2009). Furthermore, the contribution of these exchanges transcends the immediate learning context. Longitudinal research has found that children who at 2 years of age have supportive mothers and fathers perform better on mathematics and language assessments at age 5 (Martin, Ryan, & Brooks-Gunn, 2007). Other research has found that parents who use scaffolding methods have children who are motivated to succeed academically (Mattanah et al., 2005) and have more autonomy when entering school (Stright et al., 2009). Taken together, this research shows that the parent–child relationship is an important social context for the development of cognitive skills. It also suggests that parenting practices associated with the authoritative parenting style may be particularly beneficial in this regard.

Authoritative Parenting and the Development of Planning Skills

Research from our laboratory supports the assertion that parental support for children's learning is consistent with an authoritative parenting style. First, we discuss research on parental involvement and support for the development of children's planning skills from early childhood to midadolescence. This study used longitudinal data from Baumrind's (1966, 1973, 1991) Family Socialization and Developmental Competence Research Program (FSP). Then we describe results from our longitudinal study of how parents support the development of children's skill at decision making (Gauvain & Perez, 2005). Both of these studies suggest links between parent–child cognitive interactions and parental nurturance, communication, maturity demands, and control, the four social psychological dimensions of authoritative parenting advanced by Baumrind (1967, 1991). Last, we turn to an examination of parent–child interactions involving children with emotional difficulties (Perez & Gauvain, 2005, 2009), interactions that may not offer children many learning opportunities. In this discussion, we concentrate on the cognitive benefits these children obtain when their parents provide support consistent with a responsive authoritative style.

Children's Planning in the Family Setting

Does authoritative parenting relate to children's participation in family discussions about forthcoming activities and events? Such participation may support the development of future-oriented thinking and planning skills, both of which are important to mature social and cognitive functioning (Kopp, 1997). Gauvain and Huard (1999) analyzed data from the FSP (Baumrind, 1966, 1973, 1991), a longitudinal project that included children at 4, 9, and 15 years of age and their parents. Home observations provided a form of ethnographic data useful for investigating how parenting style and parent–child interactions relate to opportunities for children to participate in conversations that involved the anticipation and planning of future action. The family is an ideal social setting for the development of future-oriented thinking because the family regularly organizes or plans future activities.

We used a subset of the FSP data set that included 68 families (27 girls). These families had two parents living in the home at the outset of the study, and they participated in home observations at all three time periods, namely, early and middle childhood and midadolescence. Home observations occurred during late afternoons and early evenings and usually included dinnertime. We coded Baumrind's home observation records for planning-related discussions, with the coders blind to the family's parenting style. We identified any family discussion that pertained to a future-oriented activity and coded the content of these discussions and who initiated and participated in them. For instance, a discussion of a forthcoming family vacation was recorded as follows: "Mother starts a discussion about the family's summer vacation. Mother, father, and child discuss the vacation, including details about when they leave and how long they will be gone." Future-oriented talk was also identified in temporal terms, as pertaining to a near or short-term goal (that same afternoon or evening) or a distant or long-term goal (further in the future).

Results indicated that parenting style was a predictor of child participation in planning-related discussions over time. Children of authoritative parents had higher rates of planning initiations in adolescence than children of parents with an authoritarian style, who had the lowest rates. Analysis of the content of parent-initiated future talk showed that authoritarian parents were more directive when discussing their children's future behaviors, whereas authoritative parents were more likely to make suggestions and remind their children of future behaviors. These styles differentially predicted initiations by adolescents of future-oriented talk with more suggestions and reminders by parents related to adolescents initiating more plans.

The roles of scaffolding, modeling, and other forms of social transmission were not directly assessed. However, some insight into these processes was available. The consistently high rates of future talk in authoritative families in early and middle childhood suggest that modeling was occurring. Open-ended forms of interaction, such as reminders and suggestions, were more common in families in which parents used an authoritative style, and these forms are consistent with laboratory assessments of scaffolding. These findings suggest that certain types of interactional exchanges between parents and children associated with the authoritative parenting style are supportive of the development of planning skills in the family context.

Parent–Child Decision Making About What Children Do After School

Gauvain and Perez (2005) investigated relations between parenting style and children's opportunities to decide on activities in and around the home. We examined relations among parents' emphasis on maturity demands, warmth, and control and how parents organize and support their children in deciding on activities outside of school. Consistent with assumptions about parenting styles, we predicted that maturity demands would relate to opportunities for children to develop decision-making skills and that a climate of warmth or responsiveness would augment this process. We also expected that parents who place high emphasis on control and are low in responsiveness would provide fewer opportunities for children to learn about and practice decision making.

Mothers and children ($N = 149$) participated annually over a 3-year period beginning when the children were 7 years of age. During a laboratory visit, mothers completed two questionnaires: Your Child's Daily Activities, which assessed children's participation in organized and informal activities outside of school and children's and parents' involvement in deciding on these activities, and the Child-Rearing Practices Report (Block, 1965). The Child-Rearing Practices Report, which is based on Baumrind's (1973) conceptualization, taps three dimensions of parenting: (a) maturity demands defined as expectations regarding age-appropriate behavior and responsibilities; (b) warmth defined as affection, support, and concern for the child's well-being; and (c) control defined as strict enforcement of rules.

The results showed relations between parental support for the development of decision-making skills and the authoritative parenting style. Parents' emphasis on maturity demands was positively related to children's participation in activities and to the parent and child deciding together on these activities. Parental warmth was positively related to the parent and child deciding on the child's participation in activities. Parental control was negatively related to children's participation in activities and positively related to the parent alone deciding on this participation.

These patterns indicate that parenting practices that are responsive to children's needs, include appropriate maturity demands, and are low in control offer more opportunities for children to decide on their own activities. In contrast, lower levels of warmth and maturity demands along with high emphasis on control lead to fewer such opportunities. We also found that over the 3 years of the study, children with parents who engaged in more supportive practices were more likely to assume responsibility for their own decision making about activities as they got older than were children whose parents used alternative practices. This is consistent with Baumrind's (1991) view that authoritative parents foster the development of autonomy.

Together, these two studies demonstrate connections between authoritative parenting practices and opportunities for children to develop planning and decision-making skills in the family context during parent–child interactions. These results suggest that authoritative parenting (i.e., supportive and presents age-appropriate expectations for children) provides a family climate that is conducive to the development of skills at planning and future-oriented decision making.

Child Emotional Functioning and Children's Learning During Parent–Child Interactions

The dynamic learning process during social interaction between parents and children occurs within the context of an emotionally significant dyadic relationship (Hinde, 1989). Parents' approaches to instruction are likely influenced by both their socialization goals for children and the aforementioned shared social history that parents and children have with one another. Parents with a tendency toward authoritative parenting may be more likely to engage in the types of cognitive support known to benefit children's learning. However, this support may vary according to the child's own characteristics and how those characteristics interact with parenting practices. We are especially concerned with variations related to children's emotional development. It is our tenet that parenting practices contribute to both child emotional and cognitive development. In turn, child emotional functioning may contribute to parent–child cognitive interactions and the child's opportunities for learning from the interaction.

Parenting Style and Emotional Development

In what ways might parenting style contribute to children's emotional development? Baumrind's (1991) research demonstrated that authoritative parenting was associated with children's display of greater social and emotional competence from childhood through adolescence. Recent findings (Baumrind et al., 2010) indicated that adolescents whose parents were classified as authoritative in preschool were more competent and well-adjusted in comparison with adolescents whose parents were classified as authoritarian. Verbal hostility and psychological control were particularly detrimental to adolescent outcomes.

Several processes may underlie such associations. For example, research indicates that parent–child discourse, modeling of emotion, reactions to children's displays of emotion, and teaching about emotion, influence children's development of emotional competence (Denham, 1998; Halberstadt & Eaton, 2003; Harris, 2000; Parke, 1994; Saarni, 1999). Parents vary in their reactions to individual differences in children's emotions. Research has indicated that mothers who are sensitive and responsive tend to manage children's behavior (e.g., soothe child when distressed) and the environment (e.g., provide distraction and assistance, minimize situational demands) in ways that facilitate the development of self-control and emotion regulation skills (Thompson & Meyer, 2007), processes that are consistent with Baumrind's construct of authoritative parenting. Conversely, when parents are less sensitive and more controlling, they may exacerbate children's regulatory difficulties by increasing situational demands (Manzeske & Stright, 2009). On the other hand, maternal control that is in the context of warm and responsive parenting may facilitate social and emotional development, particularly for children with regulatory difficulties (Blandon, Calkins, & Keane, 2010).

Child Emotion and Parent–Child Cognitive Interaction

In what ways might child emotional functioning contribute to parent–child cognitive interactions and children's learning opportunities? Emotional experience and expression relate to children's capacity to interact socially and to engage in cognitive tasks. Children who tend to become highly emotionally aroused and express more negative emotions are perceived by teachers and peers as having poor social competence (e.g., Eisenberg et al., 1995). Additionally, negative emotion is associated with less effective processing of information (Cummings & Davies, 1995), with a deactivation of the frontal areas of the brain associated with higher order cognitive functioning (Davis, Bruce, & Gunnar, 2002), and with the ability to regulate attention (Fox & Calkins, 2003). Thus, children's emotional competence may play a significant role in their opportunities to develop cognitive skills during interaction with parents.

Parents who are sensitive to their child's emotional functioning (e.g., authoritative parents) may be more likely to adjust their cognitive guidance or modify their control efforts to the needs of the child (see Baumrind, Chapter 1, this volume). Our research (Perez & Gauvain, 2005, 2009) has demonstrated that mothers of children high in emotional intensity and negative emotionality issued more directives to children while working on a joint planning task. These relations were found despite the absence of child displays of emotional intensity during the mother–child planning interaction. Although on the surface instructional behaviors that are directive and controlling may seem antithetical to the types of guidance previously shown to facilitate children's learning, it is not necessarily clear what type of instructional strategy would work best for children displaying emotional difficulties. Perhaps these mothers sensitively respond to children's needs by providing more structure, that is, needed structure, for children who experience difficulty in regulating their emotions and behavior. Further research is needed to examine whether we can distinguish between instructional approaches that may be directive and controlling but also provide nurturance or are at least absent of rejection and hostility.

RECONCILING PARENTING STYLE WITH THE SOCIOCULTURAL APPROACH TO COGNITIVE DEVELOPMENT

Although Baumrind's view of parenting style and the sociocultural approach to cognitive development focus on different aspects of child development, there are several commonalities across these views. They share some philosophical origins (see Baumrind, Chapter 1, this volume; Daniels, Cole, & Wertsch, 2007) as well as an emphasis on the dynamic and social nature of child development and the importance of sensitive and responsive partners in fostering development.

Despite these commonalities, it is difficult to connect these two areas of research completely. First, they differ in their concern with parents and parent behavior. In parenting style research, the theoretical focus is explicitly on parents. In contrast, parents are often included in studies of guided learning for reasons of convenience rather than because of any clearly stated theoretical position on the role of parenting in cognitive development. Second, the two approaches use different levels of analysis. Much of the sociocultural research on cognitive development uses a microanalytic approach, with interactions arranged by researchers to investigate cognitive change in a specific type of learning context. Research on parenting style is concerned with the socialization process more generally and with the behavioral tendencies of family members that transcend the situations observed. Thus, although these two areas of research include parent–child dyads, they focus on different psychological processes and outcomes and they are guided by different assumptions about continuity and context.

Domain-specific views of socialization (Grusec & Davidov, 2010; Grusec & Goodnow, 1994) offer some rapprochement by trying to account for variation in parent–child processes across different areas of socialization. Yet even here the issue of how guided learning fits into child socialization remains. It is clear that child learning is inherent to socialization. But exactly what and who this learning entails, how it occurs, and how often it needs to occur remain open questions. We contend that socialization efforts by parents during cognitive collaboration with their children reflect a range of factors and not just tendencies toward particular parenting styles. For instance, our research on dyadic processes involving children with emotional difficulties suggests that the child, through active participation in learning, regulates parental scaffolding and support for learning. Thus, authoritative parenting alone does not determine the support that parents provide for children's learning and cognitive development.

Studies of learning in naturalistic contexts, such as those described by Rogoff and colleagues (2003, 2007), get closer to the socialization process than do studies that concentrate on processes like scaffolding in laboratory settings. On this point, it is instructive to look at research that has compared mothers and others (e.g., teachers, trained experimenters) in dyadic interactions designed to promote scaffolding. Mothers performed more of the problem-solving behaviors for children than teachers did, thus restricting children's opportunities to participate in aspects of the activity that are known to promote learning (Wertsch, Minick, & Arns, 1984). In other research, mothers were compared with a trained experimenter as they collaborated with preschoolers on a puzzle (Pacifici & Bearison, 1991). Mothers responded in ways that were sensitive to their children's learning needs, but they did so at less than the ideal rate in terms of contingent and consistent responding. Children who worked with mothers showed improvement from the pretest to the posttest but not as much improvement as children who worked with the experimenter. Finally, other research suggests that children's everyday experiences with scaffolding differ from what has been observed in the laboratory. Home observations found that young children initiated more than 75% of the interactions that led to scaffolding (Carew, 1980), a pattern quite different from laboratory observations in which scaffolding opportunities are arranged by researchers and mothers typically assume responsibility for the interaction and learning that occur. Interactions in the home also involved many social partners, such as mothers, fathers, siblings, and grandparents, who contribute differently to children's learning.

These studies suggest that cognitive support in the context of the parent–child relationship is an important avenue for future research. However, to contribute to our understanding of socialization, this research will require a theory that describes children's learning in the context of an ongoing socioemotional relationship embedded in a cultural context that imbues parents with values, beliefs, and a set of practices pertaining to what and how children learn.

The sociocultural approach is concerned with both the social and cultural basis of human development, which includes how parental beliefs derived from culture penetrate parenting practices and, by extension, contribute to child development and learning (Harkness et al., 2010). This approach questions the claim that authoritative parenting is optimal for child development regardless of cultural context. Research that points to the authoritative style as the most beneficial for development comes largely from Western samples, principally European American families. Research in non-Western communities and certain ethnic communities in the United States suggests that other parenting approaches may be as beneficial for child development in these settings, although this view is not without controversy (Chao & Tseng, 2002; Sorkhabi, 2005; see also Sorkhabi & Mandara, Chapter 5, this volume).

Our review is limited in addressing this issue. We did not examine cross-cultural data on parent–child interactions, children's learning, and parenting style because there is scant research on these topics in non-Western and more traditional societies. Also, the research that exists has not attempted to tie the observations to dimensions of parenting as described in the parenting style literature. Processes of authoritative parenting, although not uniquely Western, may be more common in Western cultures and reflect, or perhaps stem from, cultural institutions and other factors such as formal schooling and Western ideals (Maccoby, 2007). Because no overarching theory of socialization exists that captures the diversity of learning processes that children experience in social context even in Western cultures, describing and attempting to unify these ideas awaits further study. The direction proposed by Edwards, Sheridan, and Knoche (2010) that aims to describe parent engagement in a way that is applicable across diverse cultural settings seems promising in this regard. These researchers defined parent engagement along three dimensions of parent behaviors: parental warmth and sensitivity, support for the child's emerging autonomy, and active participation in learning. These dimensions, which are consistent with authoritative parenting, are predictive of the child's socioemotional and cognitive development and adjustment to school (National Institute of Child Health and Human Development, Early Child Care Research Network, 2002).

CONCLUSIONS AND NEW DIRECTIONS

The main conclusion we draw from our examination of parenting style and children's cognitive development is that, at least in Western cultural contexts, authoritative parenting is more conducive than authoritarian and

permissive parenting to the provision of cognitive support during parent–child interactions. Parents who are authoritative, that is who are nonintrusive and permit the child freedom to explore within reasonable limits, are responsive to the child's learning needs as well as to the child's bids for independence. Such parental behaviors may facilitate the transfer of responsibility for the activity to the learner when he or she is ready, the process that underlies learning in the zone of proximal development (Vygotsky, 1978). Thus, in Western cultural settings, parenting practices associated with the authoritative parenting style appear to foster the type of social learning context that may facilitate the development of cognitive skills in everyday experience, including guided learning.

This said, there is still much work to be done to build a clear bridge between authoritative parenting and the social foundations of cognitive development. Perhaps the biggest barrier is our understanding of cognitive development from a human relational point of view. Over the past 3 decades, sociocultural theory has advanced research in cognitive development by describing the social and cultural nature of human intellectual development. Yet the human relational substrate of this process has received little research attention. Children do not just learn from others, they learn from others whom they know, often very well. And in many instances their partners in learning are people with whom they have significant emotional bonds. Current models of cognitive development, even those that stress the social and cultural context, are far from capturing the richness and complexity of this process. We hope that this chapter shows that insights may be found by examining links across seemingly very different approaches to the development of cognitive competence in social context.

REFERENCES

Anderson, J. R. (2000). *Cognitive psychology and its implications* (5th ed.). New York, NY: Worth.

Baumrind, D. (1966). Effects of authoritative parental control on child behavior. *Child Development, 37*, 887–907. doi:10.2307/1126611

Baumrind, D. (1967). Child care practices anteceding three patterns of preschool behavior. *Genetic Psychology Monographs, 75*, 43–88.

Baumrind, D. (1973). The development of instrumental competence through socialization. In A. Pick (Ed.), *Minnesota symposia on child psychology* (Vol. 7, pp. 3–46). Minneapolis: University of Minnesota Press.

Baumrind, D. (1991). Effective parenting during the early adolescent transition. In P. E. Cowan & E. M. Hetherington (Eds.), *Advances in family research* (pp. 111–163). Hillsdale, NJ: Erlbaum.

Baumrind, D., Larzelere, R. E., & Owens, E. B. (2010). Effects of preschool parents' power assertive patterns and practices on adolescent development. *Parenting: Science and Practice, 10,* 157–201. doi:10.1080/15295190903290790

Bell, R. Q. (1968). A reinterpretation of the direction of effects in studies of socialization. *Psychological Review, 75,* 81–95. doi:10.1037/h0025583

Blandon, A. Y., Calkins, S. D., & Keane, S. P. (2010). Predicting emotional and social competence during early childhood from toddler risk and maternal behavior. *Development and Psychopathology, 22,* 119–132. doi:10.1017/S0954579409990307

Block, J. H. (1965). *The children-rearing practices report.* Berkeley: University of California, Institute of Human Development.

Bornstein, M. H., & Tamis-LeMonda, C. (1997). Maternal responsiveness and infant mental abilities: Specific predictive relations. *Infant Behavior & Development, 20,* 283–296. doi:10.1016/S0163-6383(97)90001-1

Bugental, D. B., & Goodnow, J. J. (1998). Socialization processes. In W. Damon (Series Ed.) & N. Eisenberg (Vol. Ed.), *Handbook of child psychology: Vol. 3. Social, emotional, and personality development* (5th ed., pp. 389–462). New York, NY: Wiley.

Carew, J. V. (1980). Experience and the development of intelligence in young children at home and in day care. *Monographs of the Society for Research in Child Development, 45*(6–7, Serial No. 187).

Chao, R., & Tseng, V. (2002). Parenting of Asians. In M. H. Bornstein (Ed.), *Handbook of parenting: Vol. 4. Social conditions and applied parenting* (2nd ed., pp. 59–93). Mahwah, NJ: Erlbaum.

Cole, M. (1996). *Cultural psychology: A once and future discipline.* Cambridge, MA: Harvard University Press.

Cummings, E. M., & Davies, P. T. (1995). The impact of parents on their children: An emotional security perspective. *Annals of Child Development, 10,* 167–208.

Daniels, H., Cole, M., & Wertsch, J. V. (2007). *The Cambridge companion to Vygotsky.* Cambridge, England: Cambridge University Press.

Davis, E. P., Bruce, J., & Gunnar, M. R. (2002). The anterior attention network: Associations with temperament and neuroendocrine activity in 6-year-old children. *Developmental Psychobiology, 40,* 43–56. doi:10.1002/dev.10012

Davis-Kean, P. E. (2005). The influence of parental education and family income on child achievement: The indirect role of parental expectations and the home environment. *Journal of Family Psychology, 19,* 294–304. doi:10.1037/0893-3200.19.2.294

Denham, S. A. (1998). *Emotional development in young children.* New York, NY: Guilford Press.

Edwards, C. P., Sheridan, S. M., & Knoche, L. (2010). Parent–child relationships in early learning. In E. Baker, P. Peterson, & B. McGraw (Eds.), *International encyclopedia of education* (Vol. 5, pp. 438–443). Oxford, England: Elsevier.

Eisenberg, N., Fabes, R. A., Murphy, B., Maszk, P., Smith, M., & Karbon, M. (1995). The role of emotionality and regulation in children's social functioning: A longitudinal study. *Child Development, 66,* 1360–1384. doi:10.2307/1131652

Fox, N. A., & Calkins, S. D. (2003). The development of self-control of emotion: Intrinsic and extrinsic influences. *Motivation and Emotion, 27,* 7–26. doi:10.1023/A:1023622324898

Gauvain, M. (2001). *The social context of cognitive development.* New York, NY: Guilford Press.

Gauvain, M., & DeMent, T. (1991). The role of shared social history in parent–child cognitive activity. *The Quarterly Newsletter of the Laboratory of Comparative Human Cognition, 13,* 58–66.

Gauvain, M., Fagot, B. I., Leve, C., & Kavanagh, K. (2002). Instruction by mothers and fathers during problem solving with their young children. *Journal of Family Psychology, 16,* 81–90. doi:10.1037/0893-3200.16.1.81

Gauvain, M., & Huard, R. D. (1999). Family interaction, parenting style, and the development of planning: A longitudinal analysis using archival data. *Journal of Family Psychology, 13,* 75–92. doi:10.1037/0893-3200.13.1.75

Gauvain, M., & Perez, S. M. (2005). Parent–child participation in planning children's activities outside of school in European American and Latino families. *Child Development, 76,* 371–383. doi:10.1111/j.1467-8624.2005.00851_a.x

Gauvain, M., & Perez, S. M. (2007). The socialization of cognition. In J. E. Grusec & P. D. Hastings (Eds.), *Handbook of socialization: Theory and research* (pp. 588–613). New York, NY: Guilford Press.

Gauvain, M., & Perez, S. M. (2008). Mother–child planning and child compliance. *Child Development, 79,* 761–775. doi:10.1111/j.1467-8624.2008.01156.x

Gauvain, M., & Rogoff, B. (1989). Collaborative problem solving and children's planning skills. *Developmental Psychology, 25,* 139–151. doi:10.1037/0012-1649.25.1.139

Gauvain, M., Savage, S., & McCollum, D. (2000). Reading at home and at school in the primary grades: Cultural and social influences. *Early Education and Development, 11,* 447–463. doi:10.1207/s15566935eed1104_5

Göncü, A., & Gauvain, M. (2012). Sociocultural approaches to educational psychology: Theory, research, and application. In K. R. Harris, S. Graham, & T. Urdan (Eds.), *APA educational psychology handbook, Vol. 1: Theories, constructs, and critical issues* (pp. 125–154). Washington, DC: American Psychological Association. doi:10.1037/13273-006

Grusec, J. E., & Davidov, M. (2010). Integrating different perspectives on socialization theory and research: A domain-specific approach. *Child Development, 81,* 687–709. doi:10.1111/j.1467-8624.2010.01426.x

Grusec, J. E., & Goodnow, J. J. (1994). The impact of parental discipline methods on the child's internalization of values: A reconceptualization of current points of view. *Developmental Psychology, 30,* 4–19. doi:10.1037/0012-1649.30.1.4

Haden, C. A., Ornstein, P. A., Eckerman, C. O., & Didow, S. M. (2001). Mother–child conversational interactions as events unfold: Linkages to subsequent remembering. *Child Development, 72,* 1016–1031. doi:10.1111/1467-8624.00332

Halberstadt, A. G., & Eaton, K. L. (2003). A meta-analysis of family expressiveness and children's emotion expressiveness and understanding. *Marriage & Family Review, 34,* 35–62. doi:10.1300/J002v34n01_03

Harkness, S., Super, C. M., Bermudez, M. R., Moscardino, U., Rha, J.-H., Mavridis, C. J., . . . Zylicz, P. O. (2010). Parental ethnotheories of children's learning. In D. F. Lancy, J. Bock, & S. Gaskins (Eds.), *The anthropology of learning in childhood* (pp. 65–81). Walnut Creek, CA: AltaMira Press.

Harris, P. L. (2000). Understanding emotion. In M. Lewis & J. M. Haviland-Jones (Eds.), *Handbook of emotions* (2nd ed., pp. 281–292). New York, NY: Guilford Press.

Hinde, R. A. (1989). Ethological and relationships approaches. *Annals of Child Development, 6,* 251–285.

Kopp, C. (1997). Young children: Emotion management, instrumental control, and plans. In S. L. Friedman & E. K. Scholnick (Eds.), *The developmental psychology of planning: Why, how, and when do we plan?* (pp. 103–124). Mahwah, NJ: Erlbaum.

Landry, S. H., Miller-Loncar, C., Smith, K., & Swank, P. (2002). The role of early parenting in children's development of executive processes. *Developmental Neuropsychology, 21*(1), 15–41. doi:10.1207/S15326942DN2101_2

Maccoby, E. E. (2007). Historical overview of socialization research and theory. In J. E. Grusec & P. D. Hastings (Eds.), *Handbook of socialization: Theory and research* (pp. 13–41). New York, NY: Guilford Press.

Mackey, K., Arnold, M. L., & Pratt, M. W. (2001). Adolescents' stories of decision making in more and less authoritative families: Representing the voices of parents in narratives. *Journal of Adolescent Research, 16,* 243–268. doi:10.1177/0743558401163001

Manzeske, D. P., & Stright, A. D. (2009). Parenting styles and emotion regulation: The role of behavioral and psychological control during young adulthood. *Journal of Adult Development, 16,* 223–229. doi:10.1007/s10804-009-9068-9

Martin, A., Ryan, R. M., & Brooks-Gunn, J. (2007). The joint influence of mother and father parenting on child cognitive outcomes at age 5. *Early Childhood Research Quarterly, 22,* 423–439. doi:10.1016/j.ecresq.2007.07.001

Mattanah, J. F., Pratt, M. W., Cowan, P. A., & Cowan, C. P. (2005). Authoritative parenting, parental scaffolding of long-division mathematics, and children's academic competence in fourth grade. *Journal of Applied Developmental Psychology, 26,* 85–106. doi:10.1016/j.appdev.2004.10.007

National Institute of Child Health and Human Development, Early Child Care Research Network. (2002). Early child care and children's development prior to school entry. Results from the NICHD Study of Early Child Care. *American Educational Research Journal, 39,* 133–164. doi:10.3102/00028312039001133

Odden, H., & Rochat, P. (2005). Observational learning and enculturation. *Educational and Child Development, 21*, 39–50.

Pacifici, C., & Bearison, D. J. (1991). Development of children's self-regulations in idealized and mother–child interactions. *Cognitive Development, 6*, 261–277. doi:10.1016/0885-2014(91)90039-G

Parke, R. D. (1994). Progress, paradigms, and unresolved problems: A commentary on recent advances in our understanding of children's emotions. *Merrill-Palmer Quarterly, 40*, 157–169.

Perez, S. M., & Gauvain, M. (2005). The role of child emotionality in child behavior and maternal instruction on planning tasks. *Social Development, 14*, 250–272. doi:10.1111/j.1467-9507.2005.00301.x

Perez, S. M., & Gauvain, M. (2009). Mother–child planning, child emotional functioning, and children's transition to first grade. *Child Development, 80*, 776–791. doi:10.1111/j.1467-8624.2009.01297.x

Pratt, M. W., Green, D., MacVicar, J., & Bountrogianni, M. (1992). The mathematical parent: Parental scaffolding, parenting style, and learning outcomes in long-division mathematics homework. *Journal of Applied Developmental Psychology, 13*, 17–34. doi:10.1016/0193-3973(92)90003-Z

Pratt, M. W., Kerig, P., Cowan, P. A., & Cowan, C. P. (1988). Mothers and father teaching 3-year-olds: Authoritative parenting and adult scaffolding of young children's learning. *Developmental Psychology, 24*, 832–839. doi:10.1037/0012-1649.24.6.832

Rogoff, B. (1990). *Apprenticeship in thinking: Cognitive development in social context.* New York, NY: Oxford University Press.

Rogoff, B. (1998). Cognition as a collaborative process. In W. Damon (Series Ed.), D. Kuhn, & R. S. Siegler (Vol. Eds.), *Handbook of child psychology: Vol. 3. Cognition, perception, and language* (pp. 679–744). New York, NY: Wiley.

Rogoff, B. (2003). *The cultural nature of human development.* New York, NY: Oxford University Press.

Rogoff, B., & Gauvain, M. (1986). A method for the analysis of patterns illustrated with data on mother–child instructional interaction. In J. Valsiner (Ed.), *The role of the individual subject in scientific psychology* (pp. 261–290). New York, NY: Plenum Press.

Rogoff, B., Moore, L., Najafi, B., Dexter, A., Correa-Chávez, M., & Solís, J. (2007). Children's development of cultural repertoires through participation in everyday routines and practices. In J. E. Grusec & P. D. Hastings (Eds.), *Handbook of socialization: Theory and research* (pp. 490–515). New York, NY: Guilford Press.

Rogoff, B., Paradise, R., Arauz, R. M., Correa-Chávez, M., & Angelillo, C. (2003). Firsthand learning through intent participation. *Annual Review of Psychology, 54*, 175–203. doi:10.1146/annurev.psych.54.101601.145118

Rommetveit, R. (1985). Language acquisition as increasing linguistic structuring of experience and symbolic behavior control. In J. V. Wertsch (Ed.), *Culture, communication, and cognition* (pp. 183–204). Cambridge, England: Cambridge University Press.

Saarni, C. (1999). *The development of emotional competence*. New York, NY: Guilford Press.

Saxe, G. B., Guberman, S. R., & Gearhart, M. (1987). Social processes in early number development. *Monographs of the Society for Research in Child Development, 52* (2, Serial No. 216), 3–162. doi:10.2307/1166071

Sorkhabi, N. (2005). Applicability of Baumrind's parent typology to collective cultures: Analysis of cultural explanations of parent socialization effects. *International Journal of Behavioral Development, 29*, 552–563. doi:10.1177/0165025050500172640

Stright, A. D., Herr, M. Y., & Neitzel, C. (2009). Maternal scaffolding of children's problem solving and children's adjustment in kindergarten: Hmong families in the United States. *Journal of Educational Psychology, 101*, 207–218. doi:10.1037/a0013154

Thompson, R. A., & Meyer, S. (2007). Socialization of emotion regulation in the family. In J. J. Gross (Ed.), *Handbook of emotion regulation* (pp. 249–268). New York, NY: Guilford Press.

Vygotsky, L. S. (1978). *Mind in society: The development of higher psychological processes*. Cambridge, MA: Harvard University Press.

Vygotsky, L. S. (1987). *The collected works of L. S. Vygotsky: Vol. 1. Problems of general psychology* (N. Minick, Trans.). New York, NY: Plenum Press.

Wertsch, J. V. (1985). *Vygotsky and the social formation of mind*. Cambridge, MA: Harvard University Press.

Wertsch, J. V., Minick, N., & Arns, F. J. (1984). The creation of context in joint problem solving. In B. Rogoff & J. Lave (Eds.), *Everyday cognition: Its development in social context* (pp. 151–171). Cambridge, MA: Harvard University Press.

Wood, D., Bruner, J. S., & Ross, G. (1976). The role of tutoring in problem solving. *Journal of Child Psychology and Psychiatry, 17*, 89–100. doi:10.1111/j.1469-7610.1976.tb00381.x

Yerkes, R. M., & Dodson, J. D. (1908). The relationship of strength of stimulus to rapidity of habit formation. *The Journal of Comparative Neurology & Psychology, 18*, 459–482. doi:10.1002/cne.920180503

IV
CONCLUSION

10

NEW DIRECTIONS IN AUTHORITATIVE PARENTING

CAROLYN S. HENRY AND LAURA HUBBS-TAIT

Within the family and the broader social context, how can parents best socialize their children in ways that balance freedom and control, promoting positive child development? As Diana Baumrind's pioneering work on parenting styles approaches a fifth decade, the authors in this volume consolidate the conceptual and empirical legacy of authoritative parenting to generate new directions for authoritative parenting across the theory-research-application spectrum. In this chapter, we highlight these new directions in conceptualization, methods, and practice pertaining to authoritative parenting that hold the promise for increasing positive child development.

DOI: 10.1037/13948-011

Authoritative Parenting: Synthesizing Nurturance and Discipline for Optimal Child Development, Robert E. Larzelere, Amanda Sheffield Morris, and Amanda W. Harrist (Editors)

237

On the basis of concern that the proliferation of research on authoritative parenting includes the taking of liberties in applying the key concepts, Baumrind (see Chapter 1, this volume) calls for a return from a "definitional drift" to the "original meaning" of authoritative parenting. In this section, we highlight Baumrind's conceptualizations of authoritative parenting, responsiveness, and demandingness as well as the extension of these concepts and the differentiation of new insights into authoritative parenting by authors in this volume (see Table 10.1 for a summary).

Authoritative Parenting

Baumrind (1966; see also Chapter 1, this volume) conceptualized *authoritative parenting* as an indivisible synthesis of responsiveness (or warmth and acceptance of a child as an autonomous person) and demandingness (or monitoring and sufficient power-assertive confrontive control; see Table 10.1), each of which was regarded until then as a distinguishing feature, respectively, of permissive or authoritarian parents. Baumrind's (Chapter 1) typological approach conceptualized authoritative parenting as "responsive and demanding, confrontive and autonomy supportive, affectionate and power assertive" (p. 13). Over time, scholars who remained mindful of this synthesis emphasized the unique dimensions of authoritative parenting (e.g., Chapters 2 and 3) as well as variable-centered approaches consistent with one or both dimensions (Baumrind et al., 2010). Nonetheless, *dimensions* now refer both to the overall constructs of responsiveness and demandingness and distinctions within these constructs.

Parenting Style as Emotional Climate

In this volume, contributors discuss three variations in the conceptualization of Baumrind's parenting styles as providing an emotional climate (Darling & Steinberg, 1993) that underlies and transcends parenting techniques. First, similar to other scholars (e.g., Hastings & Grusec, 1998), authors in this volume (Baumrind [Chapter 1]; Cavell, Harrist, & Del Vecchio [Chapter 7]; Morris, Cui, & Steinberg [Chapter 2]; Snyder et al. [Chapter 8]) underscore parental goals and values as part of the emotional climate of parenting style. Sorkhabi (Chapter 6) conceptualizes different parenting goals among Baumrind's parenting styles: (a) Authoritarian parenting is a *parent-centered approach* (or climate) focused on instilling child respect for parental authority supported by parental power assertion to gain child compliance; (b) permissive parenting is a *child-centered approach* with the goal of fostering child autonomy, with little emphasis on socializing children toward social convention; and (c) authoritative parenting is an *integrated child-centered and parent-centered approach* with the goal of child socialization toward self-reliance, autonomy, and social competence. Although not addressed by Sorkhabi, uninvolved parenting can be classified as *parent centered* in that it focuses on parents' needs rather than child socialization (Chapter 8). Parental responses to child noncompliance may reflect these goals: Authoritarian parents feel anger, embarrassment, or failure as a parent, whereas parents using other styles presumably do not, although Sorkhabi emphasizes that research on other styles is needed.

Second, authors in this volume identify abstract, metalevel, or higher order nonlinear constructs that undergird the emotional climate of authoritative parenting (respect, Barber & Xia [Chapter 3]; authority, Baumrind [Chapter 1]; quality of parent–child relationships, Cavell et al. [Chapter 7]; parental beliefs and feelings about emotions, Morris et al. [Chapter 2]; sense of self and orientation to parents' children, Snyder et al. [Chapter 8]). Snyder et al. propose parents' *mindfulness* of their own thoughts and feelings complements *awareness* of (or attunement; Baumrind, 1991) the child, and parental *acceptance* and differentiation of their thoughts, feelings, and needs facilitate an approach characterized by respect (Barber, 1996) for and validation (Gottman, Katz, & Hooven, 1996) of the child's thoughts and emotions. Parents' capacity to share values and reach goals for the self and the child is increased by mindfulness and acceptance (Snyder et al., Chapter 8). Baumrind (see Chapter 1) discusses parents' authority as occurring within the context of social convention (a metalevel construct) accompanied by higher resources, knowledge, experience, and strength of parents in relation to children (see also Kucyznski, 2003).

Respect or positive regard for the specific child as a developing person (Chapter 1) is a widely recognized higher order construct of authoritative parenting. Conceptualizations of regard (Chapter 1), respect as part of parental acceptance (Chapter 8), respect as a universal need in children (Chapter 5), parental psychological control as disrespect (Chapter 3), and authoritative parenting within ongoing parent–child relationship (Chapter 7) illustrate the salience of respect in authoritative parenting. In contrast, Barber and Xia (Chapter 3) explain how intrusiveness reflects parental disrespect, violating the child's self as parents seek control over private matters (e.g., diaries, preferences, friends).

Despite variations extending the breadth (e.g., integration with ongoing parent–child family systems, broader systems such as culture, parent management training [PMT], and bidirectionality) and depth (dimensions within responsiveness and demandingness) of the concept, there is clear consensus

TABLE 10.1

Summary of Authoritative Parenting, Responsiveness,
and Demandingness in This Volume

Authors (Chapter)			
Baumrind (1)	Barber & Xia (3)	Cavell et al. (7)	Gauvain et al. (9)
Authoritative parenting			
Synthesis of responsive and demanding, confrontive and autonomy supportive, affectionate and power assertive	Focuses on parenting dimensions of parental support and control (psychological and behavioral); focuses on adolescents	Quality parent–child relationships reflecting goals, values, and skills of parents; high ratio of acceptance to behavioral containment	Responsive; non-intrusive; promote autonomy and decision making; discipline through reason, structure, and redirection
Responsiveness			
Warmth, acceptance, support for child's autonomy	Support, nurturance, attending to and valuing the child, lack of intrusion	Ongoing emotional acceptance of child, emotion coaching	Affection, warm, responsive, and involved, scaffolding, support, and concern for the child's well-being
Demandingness			
Goal-oriented, firm (or confrontive) behavioral control (direct), monitoring	High noncoercive behavioral control, appropriate exercise of parental authority	Behavioral containment, discuss applications with aggressive children	Reasonable limits, maturity demands, use structure, redirection

Larzelere et al. (4)	Sorkhabi & Mandara (5)	Morris et al. (2)	Snyder et al. (8)	Sorkhabi (6)
Authoritative parenting				
Effective power assertion strategies in the context of reasoning and nurturance	Promotes a balance in communion and agency, which may differ in individualist and collectivist cultures	Moderate control and high warmth, taking into account child effects and the broader context	Mindful/skilled parenting involving both the child and the self as parent	Integration of parent-centered and child-centered goals
Responsiveness				
Nurturing, negotiation, respect for child's decisions	Attending to universal child needs to feel loved and accepted, may vary by culture	Emotion-related warmth or responsiveness toward child emotions	Involvement and warmth, flexible use of child-focused support and engagement, attunement	Promote self-reliance and autonomy, respond to developmentally appropriate child demands
Demandingness				
Reasoning supported by hierarchical, sequentially applied power-assertive strategies; takes into account child effects	Children firmly guided using behavioral control, may vary by culture	Firm authoritative control (flexible and not overly intrusive)	Adult-defined limit setting and discipline	Rational control (firm control and confrontive discipline) based on achievable maturity demands and independence training

regarding the value of Baumrind's conceptualization of authoritative parenting. In the next sections, we address the conceptualization of and new directions in responsiveness and demandingness (see Table 10.1).

Responsiveness

Responsiveness is characterized by warmth and support that includes embracing each child as a unique individual with specific needs, desires, and potential to be cultivated (Chapter 1). Authoritative responsiveness concepts in this volume include warmth, support, nurturance, involvement, affection, emotional expressiveness, concern, awareness, attunement, engagement, attention to child needs, valuing the child (including independence and agency), scaffolding, promoting self-reliance, respecting a child's decisions, awareness, reciprocity, emotion coaching, socialization of positive affect, and absence of intrusive behaviors (see Table 10.1 for specific authors). New directions in responsiveness include responsiveness within the ongoing emotional climate of parent–child relationships and broader systemic contexts (Chapters 2, 3, and 7), identifying specific manifestations of low responsiveness (Chapter 8), cultural specificity or generalizability in the expression and interpretation of responsiveness (Chapter 5), and responsiveness as part of parenting interventions (Chapters 7 and 8) with recognition of both parent and child characteristics (Chapters 2, 8, and 9).

Responsiveness is widely accepted as a continuum that is positively anchored by such features as support (Baumrind et al., 2010; Rollins & Thomas, 1979), warmth (Baumrind, 1966; Baumrind et al., 2010), or affection (Aunola & Nurmi, 2004). Gauvain, Perez, and Beebe (see Chapter 9, this volume) introduce important findings on cognitive development that illustrate that the impact of authoritative parenting and responsiveness on child cognition parallels their impact on emotional and social development. Parental warmth is linked to independent child cognitive performance and also to planning—particularly to planning activities at home.

Researchers show less agreement about the negative anchor of responsiveness. Low responsiveness emphasizes obedience and respecting authority in authoritarian parenting and low investment in the child in uninvolved parenting. Snyder et al. (Chapter 8) greatly advance the conceptualization of low responsiveness by proposing two maladaptive parenting attribution-affective response sets. The hostile/angry/reactive response set is outwardly focused: reactive, irritable, and invalidating, with anger and negative attributions focused on the child. The worrying/distressed/distracted-disengaged response set is inwardly focused: sad, fearful, and distracted, with anger and negative attributions focused on the self. Snyder et al. propose that these two response sets discriminate authoritarian (or harsh/hostile) from uninvolved (or give in/give up) low responsiveness. Give in/give up differs from harsh/hostile parenting through greater anxiety and different patterns of parenting practices, suggesting the importance of this distinction for future work on the etiology and consequences of low responsiveness. On the basis of Snyder et al.'s work, it is important to revisit the progenitor of responsiveness, Schaefer's (1965) acceptance-versus-rejection factor, and dissect that factor into component dimensions: high to low acceptance (or warmth) and high to low rejection (or punitiveness, intrusiveness).

Demandingness

Demandingness, a fundamental aspect of authoritative parenting, involves control attempts by parents to influence child behaviors or internal states that occur as part of parenting style (Rollins & Thomas, 1979). Demandingness is a continuum of control wherein positive and effective parenting at the high end orients and trains children toward parents' goals, values, or desires and the broader social order while fostering child autonomy (Chapters 1, 2, and 3). Effective demandingness balances freedom and control in parent–child relationships to promote the development of a child's sense of self within the social order (Chapters 1, 2, and 3).

Authors in this volume generally embrace Baumrind's conceptualization that authoritative and authoritarian parenting styles are both high in demandingness, with the former involving monitoring and other confrontive control techniques (or firm control) and the latter characterized by coercive or harsh control techniques. However, there are some variations in emphasis on qualitative or quantitative aspects of demandingness across chapters. First, psychological control, a form of coercion, is an element of the authoritarian but not the authoritative style (Baumrind et al., 2010; see also Chapter 3, this volume). Second, Morris et al. (Chapter 2) describe moderate (rather than high as conceptualized by Baumrind) demandingness as a defining feature of authoritative parenting. A third possibility, which has some potential to bridge Baumrind's and Morris et al.'s conceptualizations, is Larzelere, Cox, and Mandara's (Chapter 4) proposal that parental demandingness techniques are part of a dynamic process involving interactions between the parent and the child. These authors posit that parents use progressively higher degrees of power-assertive demandingness techniques in sequences of interactions when children are not responsive to parental demands. In sum, authors in this volume (Barber & Xia [Chapter 3]; Baumrind [Chapter 1]; Cavell et al. [Chapter 7]; Gauvain et al. [Chapter 9]; Larzelere et al. [Chapter 4]; Morris et al. [Chapter 2]; Snyder et al. [Chapter 8]; Sorkhabi [Chapter 6]; Sorkhabi & Mandara [Chapter 5]; see Table 10.1) generally conceptualize authoritative demandingness as high control (see also Morris et al. [Chapter 2], who propose authoritative parenting as involving moderate control) characterized by goal-oriented firm (or confrontive) and flexible behavioral control; developmentally appropriate expectations and limits consistent with family and societal context and the maturity level of the child; and using reasoning, structuring, or scaffolding supported as needed by hierarchically organized, sequentially applied power assertion to provide guidance.

A turning point in the study of demandingness was the conceptualization of two central dimensions: behavioral control and psychological control (Steinberg, Elmen, & Mounts, 1989). *Psychological control* is intrusive, often indirect, control consistent with an authoritarian parenting style increasing the risk for internalized behavior problems in children (Barber, 1996; see also Chapters 2 and 3, this volume). *Behavioral control* involves attempts to regulate the behavior of children in accordance with family and societal goals (Chapter 3). Authoritative behavioral control involves direct firm control (e.g., clear expectations and consequences, reasoning, monitoring) that fosters positive child development (Chapters 1, 2, and 3). In contrast, authoritarian behavioral control is direct, harsh, and often excessive, increasing the risk for externalized behavior problems (Barber, 1996).

Morris et al. (Chapter 2) review research on aspects of parental demandingness (or control): monitoring (parental knowledge, parental solicitation, child disclosure), psychological control, and behavioral control (or discipline) designed to provide "an environment that minimizes negative and maximizes positive behavior" (p. 38). Barber and Xia (Chapter 3) review the research on psychological control since Barber's (1996, 2002) landmark publications. Emerging themes in psychological control include distinguishing two forms of parental conditional regard (encouraging dependency and encouraging achievement); coercive control (intrusiveness and independence-dampening behavior) as a bridge between psychological control and parenting typologies (Baumrind et al., 2010; see also Chapter 1, this volume); perceived disrespect; and identifying new dimensions of psychological control including the violation of privacy, ridiculing, embarrassing, excessive expectations, and comparisons with others.

Responsiveness and Demandingness: Discrete Dimensions?

Authors in this volume (Barber & Xia [Chapter 3]; Baumrind [Chapter 1]) provide insights regarding moving beyond the parenting style verses parenting practices debate as they grapple with delineating the dimensions of demandingness (Barber & Xia [Chapter 3]; Morris et al. [Chapter 2]) and responsiveness (see Table 10.1). First, Barber and Xia raise the possibility that despite the similarities, research on parental demandingness may not map directly onto Baumrind's parenting styles. Psychological control, for example, involves the intersection of high demandingness and harsh responsiveness, which places it conceptually within Baumrind's authoritarian typology (Chapter 3). Psychological control violates the sense of self, may be seen as disrespectful, and heightens the risk for problematic child or adolescent developmental expression (Chapters 2 and 3). Like authoritarian parenting, this intrusive parenting dimension encompasses both high demandingness and low responsiveness. Thus, research is needed regarding the overlap of the demandingness dimension of authoritarian parenting and psychological control (Barber & Harmon, 2002) and also the low responsiveness characteristic of authoritarian parenting.

Second, authors in this volume show that both responsiveness and demandingness may be involved in the discussion provided previously about dissecting the positive (warmth, support, affection; Morris et al. [Chapter 2]) and negative (hostility, punitiveness, intrusiveness; Snyder et al. [Chapter 8]) dimensions of responsiveness. Evaluating their impact along with that of psychological and behavioral control may be another productive future direction for research (see also Bean, Barber, & Crane, 2006). In a meta-analysis of the association between parenting and delinquency, Hoeve et al. (2009) confirmed the importance of psychological control and behavioral control (monitoring) and issued a similar call for a separation of the positive and negative aspects of responsiveness because of the stronger link to delinquency of parental hostility, rejection, and neglect than warmth, acceptance, and affection.

A third aspect of emotion in relation to parenting style in this volume involves Cavell et al.'s (Chapter 7) proposal that parental acceptance of the child as a person is fundamental to effective parenting. Morris et al. (Chapter 2) propose that parenting style serves as the "emotional foundation of the parent–child relationship" (p. 41) and plays a critical role in the emotion socialization of children (e.g., emotion regulation), interfacing with the emotion regulation of the parent. Authoritative parents accept the emotions of their children, recognize how addressing emotions and firm control complement each other (Chapter 2), respond to child emotions, and teach children ways to deal with emotions (e.g., "It is OK to be angry, but it is not OK to hit your sister"; p. 43). Snyder et al. (Chapter 8) note that both self-emotions and child emotions are central to understanding authoritative parenting. Further investigation of issues such as emotion-related parenting, emotion socialization, and regulation (Chapter 2); mindfulness (Chapter 8); respect (Chapter 3); and parent–child dyads as both cognitively and emotionally significant relationships (Chapter 9) may illuminate both parental and child interpretations of emotions associated with responsiveness and demandingness.

AUTHORITATIVE PARENTING AS A BRIDGE ACROSS APPROACHES TO PARENTING

To provide an overview of the range of ways authors in this volume connect parenting style to parenting dimensions and broader contexts, we summarize three blueprints for bridges that make these connections in the sections that follow.

Parenting Styles and Parenting Dimensions

The first blueprint develops out Darling and Steinberg's (1993) framework for relations between styles and practices as set forth by Baumrind (1966, 1971). Barber and Xia (Chapter 3) note that one way to examine typologies is by looking at the interactive and additive effects of behavioral control practices and other aspects of parenting (e.g., psychological control, support). Other authors elaborate and extend the framework of parenting style as emotional climate, proposing that parenting practices interface with family and broader social systems (Chapters 2 and 7). Gauvain et al. (Chapter 9) identify authoritative parenting style as the emotional climate that nurtures cognitive development, particularly in children with emotional difficulties, through scaffolding and other practices. Echoing the work of other scholars (e.g., Morris, Silk, Steinberg, Myers, & Robinson, 2007), these authors see authoritative parenting as critical to the socialization of cognitive development of children with greater emotional intensity.

Authoritative Parenting and Parent Management Training Intervention

The second blueprint integrates aspects of PMT interventions with authoritative parenting style through greater consideration of relationships and context over time (see Chapters 4, 7, and 8, this volume). Cavell et al. (Chapter 7) and Snyder et al. (Chapter 8) sketch bridges between the microlevel aspects of parenting demandingness practices taught in PMT interventions and research on authoritative parenting and emphasize conceptualizing parenting techniques as occurring in the contexts of ongoing parent–child relationships, family systems, and broader contexts. Larzelere et al. (Chapter 4) use Bell's control theory (Bell & Harper, 1977) to conceptualize how increasing parental power-assertive techniques (or PMT demandingness techniques) emerge through sequences of parent–child interactions in which parents exert increasing power assertion when reasoning or less power-assertive techniques do not result in child compliance. Cavell et al. (Chapter 7) advocate for approaching parenting interventions in the contexts of ongoing parent–child relationships, family systems, and broader contexts.

Cultural and Developmental Context of Parenting Styles

The third blueprint for bridges is the cultural and developmental context of parenting styles that is currently better articulated for cultural than developmental contexts. Sorkhabi and Mandara (Chapter 5) provide an insightful review of the cultural specificity (i.e., collectivist vs. individualist, cultural dominance of demandingness styles, differences in children's interpretations of control across cultures) and cultural equivalence perspectives on authoritative parenting. These authors conclude that (a) authoritative parenting relates to positive developmental outcomes across cultures and (b) the reduced risk for negative outcomes associated with authoritarian parenting for Asian American and African American compared with European American youth does not mean it is optimal for any group. Alternatively, Sorkhabi and Mandara propose adding the directive parenting style (Baumrind et al., 2010) to the four existing parenting styles (authoritative, authoritarian, permissive, and uninvolved) to address the controversy between the perspectives of authoritative parenting as culturally specific (to European American families) or culturally equivalent. Analogous to authoritative parenting, the directive parenting style and practices foster positive child outcomes and fit within the contexts of non-European American families. The specific integration of cultures around the world with parenting style remains an important area for future research (see Chapters 5 and 9).

The developmental context of parenting style is mentioned by several authors as an area for further development. Analogous to the relations between parenting style and cultures, some aspects of parenting styles and dimensions are developmentally invariant (i.e., equivalent across time), and some are developmentally salient and even may be critical. Authors in this volume conclude that (a) nurturance and support consistently are linked to positive outcomes across time (Cavell et al. [Chapter 7]; Morris et al. [Chapter 2]; Snyder et al. [Chapter 8]) and (b) psychological control (Barber & Xia [Chapter 3]; Morris et al. [Chapter 2]) and harsh parenting (Cavell et al. [Chapter 7]; Snyder et al. [Chapter 8]) are detrimental to most child and adolescent outcomes, including cognitive performance (Gauvain et al. [Chapter 9]).

Barber and Xia (Chapter 3) use advances in social domain theory about the importance of the personal domain to underscore how psychological control violates the development of identity and autonomy across development but also leave open the possibility that both of these may be more crucial during adolescence than at other periods of development. Adolescence may involve particular vulnerability to psychological control as well as parent–adolescent conflict, particularly for children who have experienced authoritarian or permissive parenting styles that have not nurtured the development of the personal domain (Chapter 6). Although not yet fully articulated, the construct of *disrespect* and the integration of social domain theory with psychological control (Smetana et al.; 2005; see also Chapters 3 and 6) suggest the possibility of developmental cascades with aspects of psychological control having increasingly negative outcomes over time, which may culminate in adolescence with repercussions lasting into adulthood.

CONCEPTUAL HERITAGE AND OTHER THEORETICAL ROOTS OF EMERGING APPROACHES

Baumrind (Chapter 1) provides a detailed account of the conceptual (Marx's dialectical materialism; Montessori's theory of education; the group dynamics perspective of Kurt Lewin, her academic grandparent) and social ideological (Lakoff's strict and nurturant parents, balancing freedom and control) heritage of authoritative parenting. In Table 10.2, we summarize Baumrind's authoritative parenting construct and the other theoretical roots of the emerging perspectives discussed in this volume. We wish to alert readers that our use of unorthodox groupings of some of the theoretical roots reflects both efficiency and our attempts to address conceptual overlap.

BIDIRECTIONAL APPROACHES: THE CLASSIC QUESTION OF PARENT EFFECTS, CHILD EFFECTS, OR BOTH

This volume revisits and expands the classic debate among parenting scholars regarding the relative importance of parent effects, child effects, and bidirectionality in parent–child interaction. We briefly review these perspectives, providing examples from this volume of the increased breadth and depth in the study of bidirectionality in relation to authoritative parenting.

Research emerging from Baumrind's legacy often emphasizes the parent effects (or "social mold"; Hartup, 1978) tradition, addressing how authoritative parenting (or the dimensions of responsiveness and demandingness) relates to child outcomes based on the relative resource and responsibility difference between parents and children (Chapter 1). Authors in this volume (see Table 10.1) extend Baumrind's conceptualization through a greater integration of parental variables (biological, emotional/affective, and cognitive, Cavell et al. [Chapter 7]; Morris et al. [Chapter 2]; mental health and training in parenting, Snyder et al. [Chapter 8]; and fathers as well as mothers, Morris et al. [Chapter 2]) into authoritative parenting.

Morris et al. (Chapter 2) note child effect perspectives (Bell, 1968; Bell & Harper, 1977) as a central trend in parenting research in the past 3 decades. Child temperament is one widely discussed child effect involving reactivity

TABLE 10.2

Authoritative Parenting: Summary of Conceptual Heritage and Other Roots
of Emerging Perspectives in This Volume

	Authors (Chapter)								
	Baumrind (1)	Barber & Xia (3)	Cavell et al. (7)	Gauvain et al. (9)	Larzelere et al. (4)	Sorkhabi & Mandara (5)	Morris et al. (2)	Snyder et al. (8)	Sorkhabi (6)
Conceptual heritage									
Theoretical									
Dialectical materialism (Marxism)	*								
Educational theories (Montessori)	*								
Group dynamics movement (Lewin)	*								
Social ideology									
Strict and nurturant parent metaphors (Lakoff)	*								
Balance of freedom and control (Baumrind)	*	*	*	*	*	*	*	*	*
Other roots of emerging perspectives									
Bidirectional approaches	*	*	*	*	*	*	*	*	*
Systemic approaches								*	
Family systems		*	*				*		
Ecological (Bronfenbrenner and others)			*				*		
Dynamic systems			*				*		

(*continues*)

TABLE 10.2

Authoritative Parenting: Summary of Conceptual Heritage
and Other Roots of Emerging Perspectives in This Volume   *(Continued)*

	Authors (Chapter)								
	Baumrind (1)	Barber & Xia (3)	Cavell et al. (7)	Gauvain et al. (9)	Larzelere et al. (4)	Sorkhabi & Mandara (5)	Morris et al. (2)	Snyder et al. (8)	Sorkhabi (6)
Other roots of emerging perspectives									
Behavioral/social learning approaches									
Operant learning			*		*			*	
Social interaction/ social learning/ coercion			*		*			*	
Parent training/ Bell's control theory					*				
Relational frame theory								*	
Other approaches									
Attachment			*						
Social-domain theory		*					*		*
Self-determination theory		*					*		
Sociocultural theory (Vygotsky and others)				*					
Multidisciplinary cultural perspectives						*	*		

and regulation with implications for authoritative parenting (Chapter 3). Earlier work on the role of *receptive* (willing or committed compliance) versus *situational* (based on parental power assertion) child compliance (Maccoby & Martin, 1983) can now be interpreted as showing that parenting styles (Chapter 2) or practices (Chapter 4) that result in child compliance may vary, in part, on the basis of child temperament, which is both biological and social psychological in nature (Chapter 2). Child qualities that interact with authoritative parenting addressed in this volume include gender; genetics, biological sensitivity, and other biological factors (for a review, see Chapter 2); developmental level (Chapters 2, 3, 6, and 7); psychopathology (aggression, conduct disorders, and oppositional defiant disorder; Chapters 4, 7, and 8); emotion regulation (Chapters 2 and 9); and management of information about activities (Chapters 1, 2, and 3).

Bidirectionality in parent–child relationships occurs in specific sequences of interaction and as part of ongoing parent–child relationships (for reviews, see Kucyznski, 2003; see also Chapter 2, this volume). Baumrind (Chapter 1) conceptualizes the roles of "parents and children as reciprocal, not equal" (p. 18) as parents strive to socialize their children to encourage "self-confident, autonomous behavior" (or agency) as well as "reasonable compliance" with parental directives in the context of the child's uniqueness and social conventions. Some authors in this volume depart from Baumrind's conceptualization using four approaches to bidirectionality: (a) dyadic synchrony or the mutual response orientation between parents and children in the contexts of short-term interactions, long-term parent–child relationships, and broader ecological systems (Cavell et al. [Chapter 7]; Morris et al. [Chapter 2]); (b) cross-cultural variation in reciprocity whereby individuals in collectivist cultures focus on the good of the whole and those in individualistic societies focus on obligation (Sorkhabi & Mandara [Chapter 5]); (c) applying Bell's control theory (Bell & Harper, 1977) to conceptualize how parents may draw on a portfolio of progressively power-assertive consequences in sequences of interactions with children, depending on child responsiveness to maturity demands (Larzelere et al. [Chapter 4]); and (d) internal parent and child interpretations of parental styles and practices (whether shared or different), which may provide critical insight into parent–child interactions (Barber & Xia [Chapter 3]; Sorkhabi & Mandara [Chapter 5]; Sorkhabi [Chapter 6]).

BEYOND BIDIRECTIONALITY: SYSTEMIC APPROACHES

Three systemic approaches proposed in this volume hold potential to advance the study of authoritative parenting. *Family systems perspectives* focus on the intertwined nature of overall family systems and family subsystems (e.g., parent–child, marital, or sibling) with the recognition that the qualities of individuals and broader contexts interface with relationship patterns (Henry, 1994; Henry, Huey, Robinson, & Neal, 2006; Henry, Sager, & Plunkett, 1996; Houltberg, Henry, & Morris, 2012). In this volume, authors (Barber & Xia [Chapter 3]; Morris et al. [Chapter 2]) call for increased investigation of bidirectional parent–child relationships as part of overall family systems.

Ecological systems approaches (Bronfenbrenner, 1989) focus on individual development within multiple systems. Authors in this volume advocate for increased emphasis on investigating authoritative parenting while taking into account the biological (biogenetic and psychophysiologic), emotional/affective, and cognitive or developmental systems or capabilities of children and parents (Barber & Xia [Chapter 3]; Cavell et al. [Chapter 7]; Gauvain et al. [Chapter 9]; Larzelere et al. [Chapter 4]; Morris et al. [Chapter 2]; Sorkhabi [Chapter 6]); ongoing parent–child relationships and broader family dynamics (e.g., overall family system, subsystems such as marital or sibling or multigenerational family systems, Cavell et al. [Chapter 7]; Morris et al. [Chapter 2]; Snyder et al. [Chapter 8]); extrafamilial relationships (e.g., peers, teachers), ecological contexts (e.g., neighborhoods, peers, culture, media), and diverse cultural roots (Cavell et al. [Chapter 7]; Gauvain et al. [Chapter 9]; Morris et al. [Chapter 2]; Sorkhabi & Mandara [Chapter 5]).

Through *dynamic systems perspectives*, child development (cognitive, emotional, behavioral, and physical) emerges through interactions with attractions (e.g., relationships, activities, emotional styles) in the larger system (Thelen & Smith, 1996). Dynamic systems perspectives hold potential in the study of authoritative parenting (Chapter 7), including epigenetic factors. The relative influence of a specific parenting style, for example, might differ for children based on genetic factors (Chapter 2). Alternatively, a child might be attracted to responsive parenting with firm control over harsh control, although the attraction varies according to child qualities (e.g., temperament, Chapter 2; child emotionality, Chapter 9).

BEHAVIORAL AND SOCIAL LEARNING APPROACHES

The historical connections of authoritative parenting to operant learning (with a mechanistic rather than contextualist worldview) stem from the integration of PMT with parenting styles (see Chapter 4, 7, and 8, this volume). Three notable advances in this integration are evident in this volume. First, Cavell et al. (Chapter 7) propose a *life course–social learning* model of socialization involving eight core assumptions including the following: (a) Prevention and intervention relating to child and adolescent aggression entails consideration of biogenetic factors, available social contexts, and capacity of the child for access and success in the social contexts, and (b) parents are responsible for facilitating child contextual involvement, encouraging involvement in prosocial contexts and limiting access to contexts that encourage or condone antisocial behavior. A unique feature of this model is the integration of ideas relating to the life course (or longer term) and social learning approaches within ecological contexts.

Second, Larzelere et al. (Chapter 4) use Baumrind's authoritative parenting and Bell's control theory (Bell & Harper, 1977) to advocate for attention to bidirectional sequences of parent and child interactions to examine how parents' demandingness techniques may increasingly become more power assertive when children are low in responsiveness to parental expectations. This approach integrates two very important and relatively independent streams of research on the positive effects of (a) disciplinary reasoning on child outcomes in nonclinical populations and (b) PMT approaches for clinically referred populations.

Third, Snyder et al. (Chapter 8) integrate ideas from social learning and *relational frame theory* (emphasizing the integration of overt behavior with emotion and cognition—particularly memory and language; Hayes, 2004) with Baumrind's parenting styles. This approach allows Snyder et al. to identify important attribution-affective response sets that differentiate parenting types that hold potential for modifying traditional parent interventions.

OTHER APPROACHES

Cavell et al. (Chapter 7) credit attachment theory (as well as social learning and family systems) with being the conceptual roots of responsive parent therapy, emphasizing quality parent–child relationships as foundational to effective parenting. We have taken the liberty of grouping social domain theory (a structural developmental theory; Chapters 3 and 6) with self-determination theory (Chapters 2 and 3) because both highlight the importance of self and other in developmental process and/or outcome. Advances in social domain theory about the importance of the personal domain are used by Barber and Xia (Chapter 3) to underscore how psychological control violates the development of identity and autonomy across development. As noted previously, there is some consensus that adolescence may be a particularly vulnerable time for the negative impact of psychological control on the basis of vulnerability to intrusiveness or exploitation of self and identity (Chapter 3) and parent–adolescent conflict, particularly for children who have experienced parenting styles that have not nurtured the development of the personal domain (Chapter 6).

Barber and Xia (Chapter 3) view current applications of self-determination theory as an important new direction in psychological control. Self-determination theory (Deci & Ryan, 2000) proposes an innate capacity to explore one's context and grow toward autonomy. Thus, a fruitful avenue of investigation may be to examine specific aspects of authoritative parenting that foster the integration of family and societal goals with the sense of self.

NEW DIRECTIONS IN METHODOLOGY

New directions in methodology have not only developed from classic methods implemented by Diana Baumrind but also include methods emerging from pressures of interdisciplinary endeavors, research costs, and time. In this section, we discuss multiple approaches to the study of authoritative parenting (typologies, dimensions, variable centered); measurement challenges posed by interdisciplinary research; and other methodological considerations, such as ecological validity, congruence of theory and method, including fathers or multiple respondents in addition to mothers, using multiple methodologies, longitudinal design, diversity in race and ethnicity, and family structures.

Typologies Versus Dimensions Versus Variable-Centered Approaches

Reflecting the historical and current study of authoritative parenting, Baumrind (see Chapter 1) contrasts methods to embrace with those to eschew. Embraced methods include naturalistic observations of children and parents and observer ratings (including Q sorts) of those observations, comprehensive interviews, and field experiments ("experimental procedures . . . to elicit children's responses to parents' disciplinary efforts," p. 25). Eschewed methods include experimental methodologies, laboratory settings, self-reports or questionnaires, and variable-centered approaches. The most recent report of data from the Family Socialization Project (Baumrind et al., 2010) confirms that Baumrind's parenting typology—the three traditional patterns of authoritative, authoritarian, and permissive parenting as well as the four more recently derived patterns of democratic, directive, good enough, and disengaged parenting—was and is grounded in those three methods. In addition, Baumrind et al. (2010) derived a variable-centered approach from these other three methods that yielded such variables as responsive, confrontive discipline; unqualified power assertion; psychological control; promotion of conformity and obedience; arbitrary discipline; verbal hostility; and physical punishment.

As research on parenting styles increasingly differentiated from Baumrind's typological taproot to branches specifying dimensions (e.g., Barber, 1996;

Darling & Steinberg, 1993; Maccoby & Martin, 1983; Morris et al., 2007; Rollins & Thomas, 1979) and domains or variables within dimensions (Chapters 2 and 3), an emphasis on self-report and questionnaire methodologies (Chapters 2 and 3) emerged, although observational methods continue to be implemented, in part, as a means of assessing questionnaire validity (e.g., Coolahan, McWayne, Fantuzzo, & Grim, 2002). Some of the methodological shift may be explained by (a) the shift in emphasis on the age of the child being parented (Chapter 3) from preschool children (e.g., Baumrind, 1966, 1971) to older children and adolescents and (b) the shift to research questions based on theoretical models emphasizing adolescents' (Steinberg et al., 1989) or parents' (Chapter 2) interpretations of parenting style, responsiveness, or demandingness, which are critical to understanding developmental expression (Chapters 3 and 5). Barber and Xia review key approaches to measuring psychological control emphasizing self-report, which emerged in the past decade and shows promise for future studies. Also, recent research on preschool and early elementary school children rests on questionnaire methodologies for measuring parenting style (Coolahan et al., 2002). The preponderance of questionnaire methodologies was evident as we searched the PsycINFO database in June 2011 for 2000–2011 peer-reviewed publications. The search terms parenting style*[1] and observation yielded 84 articles, whereas the terms parenting style* and questionnaire yielded 387 articles, and the terms parenting style* and self-report yielded 154 articles. Finally, the use of questionnaires may reflect benefits in cost and time as well as a desire for quick responses to public health issues (e.g., how parenting relates to obesity).

Interdisciplinary Research as Case Study of Measurement Challenges

The decades-long focus on the measurement of parenting style in basic and applied developmental and family research is documented across all chapters in this volume. Since 1995, parenting style has increasingly become the focus of interdisciplinary teams of researchers and practitioners addressing child health issues such as obesity (Birch & Fisher, 1995; Blissett & Haycraft, 2008; Hubbs-Tait, Kennedy, Page, Topham, & Harrist, 2008). Research links child obesity, emotional eating, and other child health issues to parenting style (Rhee et al., 2006; Topham et al., 2011). Baumrind's conceptualization of parenting style has been extremely influential in the development of the measurement of feeding styles (e.g., Hughes, Power, Fisher, Mueller, &

---

[1] This describes the phrase that was typed into the database to search for articles. When one types in, for example, "parenting style*" this garners resources including the term *parenting style* as well as other phrases containing this word followed by other terms.

Nicklas, 2005) and convincing researchers across disciplines to evaluate parenting style in relation to practices in specific domains of socialization (e.g., feeding, smoking, alcohol).

Other Methodological Considerations

Baumrind (Chapter 1) reminds readers of her emphasis on "inferential and ecological validity," which involves examining real-life experiences of participants in their natural settings, reflecting these real-life situations in broader contexts (p. 23). With the range of theoretical approaches and methodologies used to study aspects of authoritative parenting, it is critical for researchers to employ methods that best address specific research questions. Using multiple methodologies and respondents yields both observer and participant perspectives on authoritative parenting. Authors in this volume show that achieving the promise of promoting positive child development in the next wave of authoritative parenting research may entail longitudinal innovative methods (Baumrind, Chapter 1]); racial/ethnic and cultural diversity in samples (Sorkhabi & Mandara [Chapter 5]); including fathers, mothers, and interparental relationships in varying family structures (Cavell et al. [Chapter 7]; Morris et al. [Chapter 2]); and increasing the scope of biological and broader contextual variables (Morris et al. [Chapter 2]).

NEW DIRECTIONS IN PRACTICE

The current volume provides an important step forward in linking authoritative parenting to both developmental expression in children and adolescents and—when insufficient, impaired, or impeded—to parent–child intervention. The paramount value of authoritative parenting to professional practice is documented by theoretically based research on the association of authoritative parenting with competence and well-being in children and adolescents (Chapter 1). Authors in this volume advance existing PMT approaches by adapting them to include principles of authoritative parenting.

A wealth of parenting approaches (Chapter 7) are available to build parental capacity (knowledge and skills) to be consistent with authoritative parenting—either designed for parents in general or focused on specific groups of parents (e.g., new parents, parents of adolescents, parents of children at risk or with particular conditions; Smith, Perou, & Lesesne, 2002). Although parent education approaches emphasize strengthening parent–child relationships as well as increasing knowledge and skills, PMT traditionally focused on social learning approaches to prepare parents to control behavior through operant conditioning techniques (Chapter 7). As eloquently described by authors in this volume, relationship quality between parents and children is fundamental to authoritative parenting style and practices (Barber & Xia [Chapter 3]; Cavell et al. [Chapter 7]; Morris et al. [Chapter 2]; Snyder et al. [Chapter 8]) as well as positive child emotional, behavioral, and cognitive development (Gauvain et al. [see Chapter 9]; Morris et al. [see Chapter 2]).

At about the same time as Baumrind did her work on parenting styles (see Chapters 7 and 8), PMT emerged as the most empirically validated parenting intervention for parents of children with externalizing problem behaviors such as aggression, oppositional defiant disorder, or conduct disorder (Chapter 7). Parents and children with externalizing behavior problems are at risk for coercive cycles in which parent practices and child behavior problems escalate (Patterson, 1982). Authors in this volume (Cavell et al. [Chapter 7]; Larzelere et al. [Chapter 4]; Snyder et al. [Chapter 8]) provide valuable insights for enhancing parenting interventions through the integration of research findings about authoritative parenting style and practices within PMT.

Recommendations for Parent Intervention Based on Authoritative Parenting

This section highlights new directions in authoritative parenting that have the promise to strengthen parent intervention by addressing time and context, responsiveness, demandingness, and values in parent intervention.

Parent Intervention With Time and Context Dimensions

A shortcoming of traditional PMT programs is that using operant-conditioning-based interventions to gain short-term compliance may not translate into internalization of the parents' socialization goals by children (Chapter 7). In contrast, consistent with recent trends in parenting research (for a review, see Chapter 2), Cavell et al. (Chapter 7) advocate parent intervention guided by a "relationship-based model of socialization" (p. 175) in which authoritative demandingness is viewed in the context of ongoing parent–child relationships characterized by acceptance of the child. Effective parenting requires awareness of both the self and the uniqueness of a specific child (Chapter 8) as individuals interacting with each other as part of an ongoing relationship system within broader systems (Chapters 2 and 7). Authoritative parenting occurs across the life cycle, although parental effectiveness may vary when families experience specific transitions or stressor events (Chapter 7). In turn, the reciprocity between parents and children may evolve and change as the child, parent, and family grow and change over time.

Cavell et al. (Chapter 7) share a framework and principles for parenting intervention for aggressive children focused on long-term child socialization that fosters an "implicit message of belonging" (p. 179) to the child. Examples of these principles include seeking a favorable "ratio of emotional acceptance to behavioral containment" (p. 176, ranging from 4:1 to 8:1); integrating "supportive relationships and firm discipline into a single, coordinated system over time" (p. 177); recognizing that child, parent, and ecology are central to child socialization; and emphasizing multisystemic treatment rather than targeting specific child behaviors.

Address Parental Responsiveness, Demandingness, and Prosocial Values

Parent intervention that addresses authoritative parenting style requires addressing both responsiveness and demandingness and the higher order construct of prosocial values as critical to long-term effectiveness (see Chapters 2, 7, and 8). Thus, an important new direction in parent intervention combines successful traditional PMT approaches focusing on demandingness with greater emphasis on the emotional side of parent–child relations.

Emotion Coaching

Authors in this volume (Cavell et al. [Chapter 7]; Morris et al. [Chapter 2]; Snyder et al. [Chapter 8]) recommend teaching parents to use emotion coaching (Gottman et al., 1996) to become attuned to and attend to the child's feelings to provide child socialization while fostering emotional closeness, showing empathy, and validating the child's feelings; help the child label the feelings; and establish limits for appropriate ways to problem solve and guide the child in generating and evaluating possible solutions to produce one that addresses both feelings and associated problems. Emotion coaching facilitates positive parent–child relations and emotion socialization (or development of children's emotion regulation and problem solving; Morris et al., 2007).

Relational Frame Theory and Acceptance and Commitment Therapy

Snyder et al. (see Chapter 8, this volume) challenge a cardinal rule of PMT—parents benefit more from "modeling, role playing, and applying new parenting behaviors in the home environment" (p. 198) than from addressing feelings and information. These authors provide the example of a parent who feels anger toward a child and feels justified in using coercive behavior to obtain short-term child compliance. Yet, long-term success may be undermined by inadequate attention to emotions in the self and the child.

As an alternative, acceptance and commitment therapy (an application of relational frame theory) addresses the feelings that motivate parents toward effective parenting and thoughts critical to goal setting, generating and weighing alternatives and consequences, and being mindful of rather than fusing with the emotion (Chapter 8). Accepting one's emotions or negative attributions about the self or child can allow a parent to distance him- or herself from negative feelings and make a plan to engage in behavior consistent with his or her underlying values and goals (Chapter 8). Parallel to Sorkhabi's (Chapter 6) work linking the essential goals of parenting to parenting style and parents' feelings, Snyder et al. (Chapter 8) associate parents' specific feelings states with parenting styles: Emotional reactivity and anger fosters hostile/angry/reactive (or authoritarian) parenting; a felt need to gain self-control fosters worrying/distressed/distracted-disengaged (or neglectful) parenting; and awareness of one's own feelings while engaging and supporting children combined with limit setting and discipline fosters mindful, skilled (or authoritative) parenting.

Hierarchically Organized Portfolio of Demandingness Techniques

Guided by Bell's control theory (Bell & Harper, 1977), Larzelere et al. (Chapter 4) advocate integrating PMT intervention and parenting research to recognize sequences of parent–child interactions as central to parental control. Demandingness involves a hierarchically organized portfolio of increasingly power-assertive techniques and consequences, which parents deploy on the basis of child characteristics and behavior. Parents set lower and upper limits of acceptable behavior, which, when violated, invoke specific forms of power assertion (Chapter 4). Consistent with Baumrind (Chapter 1), this approach to PMT makes explicit the unfolding of power-assertive techniques by parents as they take into account child responses to parental expectations and directives. This approach clarifies that disciplinary reasoning may be sufficient with children who tend to comply with parental demands.

Develop Parenting Theoretical Models for Intervention Addressing Subjective and Cultural Factors

Snyder et al. (Chapter 8) describe specific challenges to effective parenting interventions that may reflect a need for theoretical models addressing subjective aspects of parenting: resistance to committing time and effort to improve parenting, "automatically" reverting to former parenting skills rather than skills learned in intervention, and difficulties in applying effective skills when under stress. Sorkhabi and Mandara (Chapter 5) review research showing that although authoritative parenting is cross-cultural, further investigation is needed regarding whether directive parenting may promote child competence as well as or better than authoritative parenting for some racial and ethnic groups (e.g., collectivist groups). In this volume, authors propose greater attention to both parents' and children's subjective interpretations of parenting within their cultural contexts to advance research and intervention

(Barber & Xia [Chapter 3]; Cavell et al. [Chapter 7]; Morris et al. [Chapter 2]; Sorkhabi & Mandara [Chapter 5]; Snyder et al. [Chapter 8]).

CONCLUSION

The enduring value of parenting styles is placing patterns of parental practices (responsiveness and demandingness) within ongoing parent–child relationships (Chapter 2 & 7). This chapter provides a consolidation of new directions in conceptualization, methodologies, and professional interventions involving authoritative parenting. Beginning with Baumrind's chapter (Chapter 1), which incorporates developments in authoritative parenting over nearly 50 years, and continuing throughout subsequent chapters in this volume, the potential of authoritative parenting to foster positive outcomes cascading across aspects of development is resoundingly clear. Several themes that hold outstanding promise are highlighted in the paragraphs that follow.

Authors in this volume provide valuable updates on the ongoing dialectical process of developing and extending Baumrind's (Chapter 1) original conceptualization of authoritative parenting and the orthogonal dimensions of responsiveness and demandingness (see Table 10.1). Parenting style can be conceptualized as an emotional climate (Darling & Steinberg, 1993) representing variation in the essential goal of parenting (Sorkhabi [Chapter 6]) reflected through higher order constructs (respect, Barber & Xia [Chapter 3]; parental authority, Baumrind [Chapter 1]; ongoing parent–child relationships, Cavell et al. [Chapter 7]; mindfulness, Snyder et al. [Chapter 8]) embedded within broader contexts (Cavell et al. [Chapter 7]; Sorkhabi & Mandara [Chapter 5]; Morris et al. [Chapter 2]) such as culture. New directions in this volume involve the continued conceptual refinement and investigation of aspects of demandingness (Barber & Xia [Chapter 3]; Larzelere et al. [Chapter 4]; Morris et al. [Chapter 2]) and responsiveness (Cavell et al. [Chapter 7]; Gauvain et al. [Chapter 9]; Morris et al. [Chapter 2]; Snyder et al. [Chapter 8]). Snyder et al. (Chapter 8) provide valuable insights for further investigation regarding the potential detrimental effects of a range of possible manifestations of low responsiveness. Chapters provide three blueprints for showing aspects of parenting: parenting styles and parenting dimensions, authoritative parenting and parenting management intervention, and the cultural and developmental contexts of parenting style. Emerging approaches (bidirectional approaches, systemic approaches, behavioral and social learning, and other approaches, see Table 10.2) complement the conceptual heritage of authoritative parenting.

Baumrind's (Chapter 1) emphasis on ecologically valid methods encourages naturalistic observations of children and parents, observer ratings, interviews, and field experiments over experimental methodologies, laboratory settings, self-report questionnaires, and variable-centered approaches. Self-report questionnaire data methodology has emerged to investigate parent and child interpretations of parenting (Chapters 2, 3, 5, and 6). Methodologies consistent with theoretical approaches and addressing the diversity in cultures and family structures are needed to investigate how authoritative parenting relates to a range of cognitive, emotional, and biological variables (Chapters 1, 2, 3, 5, and 9).

In this volume, Cavell et al. (Chapter 7), Larzelere et al. (Chapter 4), and Snyder et al. (Chapter 8) advance the integrating of authoritative parenting with PMT intervention. Snyder et al. advocate for the development of theoretical models to guide parent interventions that include subjective parent–child relationship factors (e.g., mindfulness, attunement). Cavell et al. emphasize parental acceptance in ongoing high-quality parent–child relationships as part of the foundation of parent interventions. Larzelere et al. recommend that both research and practice reflect the bidirectionality of parental demandingness and child responsiveness to parental expectations. In sum, Baumrind's pioneering conceptualization of and research on authoritative parenting has emerged into bridges across parenting that encompass parenting styles, parenting practices, parent intervention, and sociocultural approaches. Authors in this volume show the potential for further development of authoritative parenting through expanded (a) integration of concepts from a range of theoretical foundations; (b) research methodologies; (c) awareness of the interface with parents' goals and values, ongoing parent–child relationships, family systems, and social contexts (including culture); and (d) awareness of the importance of the subjective aspects of parenting (e.g., a child's interpretations of parenting behaviors and the parent's emotions). Readers are encouraged to use this chapter and the whole volume to reflect on both enduring aspects and new opportunities in conceptualizing, researching, and intervening to enhance the field of authoritative parenting.

REFERENCES

Aunola, K., & Nurmi, J.-E. (2004). Maternal psychological control moderates the impact of affection on children's math performance. *Developmental Psychology, 40*, 965–978. doi:10.1037/0012-1649.40.6.965

Barber, B. K. (1996). Parental psychological control: Revisiting a neglected construct. *Child Development, 67*, 3296–3319. doi:10.2307/1131780

Barber, B. K. (Ed.). (2002). *Intrusive parenting: How psychological control affects children and adolescents.* Washington, DC: American Psychological Association. doi:10.1037/10422-000

Barber, B. K., & Harmon, E. (2002). Violating the self: Parental psychological control of children and adolescents. In B. K. Barber (Ed.), *Intrusive parenting: How psychological control affects children and adolescents* (pp. 15–52). Washington, DC: American Psychological Association. doi:10.1037/10422-002

Baumrind, D. (1966). Effects of authoritative parental control on child behavior. *Child Development, 37,* 887–907. doi:10.2307/1126611

Baumrind, D. (1971). Current patterns of parental authority. *Developmental Psychology Monographs, 4*(1, Pt. 2). doi:10.1037/h0030372

Baumrind, D. (1991). The influence of parenting style on adolescent competence and substance use. *The Journal of Early Adolescence, 11,* 56–95. doi:10.1177/0272431691111004

Baumrind, D., Larzelere, R. E., & Owens, E. B. (2010). Effects of preschool parents' power assertive patterns and practices on adolescent development. *Parenting: Science and Practice, 10,* 157–201. doi:10.1080/15295190903290790

Bean, R. A., Barber, B. K., & Crane, D. R. (2006). Parental support, behavioral control, and psychological control among African American youth: The relationships to academic grades, delinquency, and depression. *Journal of Family Issues, 27,* 1335–1355. doi:10.1177/0192513X06289649

Bell, R. Q. (1968). A reinterpretation of the direction of effects in studies of socialization. *Psychological Review, 75,* 81–95. doi:10.1037/h0025583

Bell, R. Q., & Harper, L. V. (1977). *Child effects on adults.* Hillsdale, NJ: Erlbaum.

Birch, L. L., & Fisher, J. (1995). Appetite and eating behavior in children. *Pediatric Clinics of North America, 42,* 931–953.

Blissett, J., & Haycraft, E. (2008). Are parenting style and controlling feeding practices related? *Appetite, 50,* 477–485. doi:10.1016/j.appet.2007.10.003

Bronfenbrenner, U. (1989). Ecological systems theory. In R. Vasta (Ed.), *Six theories of child development* (pp. 185–246). Greenwich, CT: JAI Press.

Coolahan, K., McWayne, C., Fantuzzo, J., & Grim, S. (2002). Validation of multidimensional assessment of parenting styles for low-income African families with preschool children. *Early Childhood Research Quarterly, 17,* 356–373. doi:10.1016/S0885-2006(02)00169-2

Darling, N., & Steinberg, L. (1993). Parenting style as context: An integrative model. *Psychological Bulletin, 113,* 487–496. doi:10.1037/0033-2909.113.3.487

Deci, E. L., & Ryan, R. M. (2000). The "what" and "why" of goal pursuits: Human needs and the self-determination of behavior. *Psychological Inquiry, 11,* 227–268. doi:10.1207/S15327965PLI1104_01

Gottman, J. M., Katz, L., & Hooven, C. (1996). Parental meta-emotion philosophy and the emotional life of families: Theoretical models and preliminary data. *Journal of Family Psychology, 10,* 243–268. doi:10.1037/0893-3200.10.3.243

Hartup, W. W. (1978). Perspectives on child and family interaction: Past, present, and future. In R. M. Lerner & G. B. Spanier (Eds.), *Child influences on marital and family interaction: A life-span perspective* (pp. 23–46). New York, NY: Academic Press.

Hastings, P. D., & Grusec, J. (1998). Parenting goals as organizers of responses to parent–child disagreement. *Developmental Psychology, 34*, 465–479. doi:10.1037/0012-1649.34.3.465

Hayes, S. C. (2004). Acceptance and commitment therapy, relational frame theory, and the third wave of behavioral and cognitive therapies. *Behavior Therapy, 35*, 639–665. doi:10.1016/S0005-7894(04)80013-3

Henry, C. S. (1994). Family system characteristics, parental behaviors, and adolescent family life satisfaction. *Family Relations, 43*, 447–455. doi:10.2307/585377

Henry, C. S., Huey, E. L., Robinson, L. C., & Neal, R. A. (2006). Adolescent perceptions of family system functioning and parental behaviors. *Journal of Child and Family Studies, 15*, 308–318. doi:10.1007/s10826-006-9051-z

Henry, C. S., Sager, D. W., & Plunkett, S. W. (1996). Adolescents' perceptions of family system characteristics, parent–adolescent dyadic behaviors, adolescent qualities, and adolescent empathy. *Family Relations, 45*, 283–292. doi:10.2307/585500

Hoard, D., & Shepard, K. N. (2005). Parent education as parent-centered prevention: A review of school related outcomes. *School Psychology Quarterly, 20*, 434–454. doi:10.1521/scpq.2005.20.4.434

Hoeve, M., Dubas, J., Eichelsheim, V. I., van der Laan, P. H., Smeenk, W., & Gerris, J. M. (2009). The relationship between parenting and delinquency: A meta-analysis. *Journal of Abnormal Child Psychology, 37*, 749–775. doi:10.1007/s10802-009-9310-8

Houltberg, B. J., Henry, C. S., & Morris, A. S. (2012). Family interactions, exposure to violence, and emotion regulation: Perceptions of children and early adolescents at-risk. *Family Relations, 61*, 283–296.

Hubbs-Tait, L., Kennedy, T. S., Page, M. C., Topham, G. L., & Harrist, A. W. (2008). Parental feeding practices predict authoritative, authoritarian, and permissive parenting styles. *Journal of the American Dietetic Association, 108*, 1154–1161. doi:10.1016/j.jada.2008.04.008

Hughes, S. O., Power, T. G., Fisher, J. O., Mueller, S., & Nicklas, T. (2005). Revisiting a neglected construct: Parenting styles in a child-feeding context. *Appetite, 44*, 83–92. doi:10.1016/j.appet.2004.08.007

Kucyznski, L. (2003). Beyond bidirectionality: Bilateral conceptual frameworks for understanding dynamics in parent–child relations. In L. Kucyznski (Ed.), *Handbook of dynamics in parent–child relations* (pp. 1–24). Thousand Oaks, CA: Sage.

Maccoby, E. E., & Martin, J. A. (1983). Socialization in the context of the family: Parent–child interaction. In P. H. Mussen (Series Ed.) & M. E. Hetherington (Ed.), *Handbook of child psychology: Vol. 4. Socialization, personality, and social development* (pp. 1–101). New York, NY: Wiley.

Morris, A. S., Silk, J. S., Steinberg, L., Myers, S. S., & Robinson, L. R. (2007). The role of the family context in the development of emotion regulation. *Social Development, 16*, 361–388. doi:10.1111/j.1467-9507.2007.00389.x

Patterson, G. R. (1982). *A social learning approach to family intervention: Vol. 3. Coercive family practice*. Eugene, OR: Castalia Press.

Rhee, K. E., Lumeng, J. C., Appugliese, D. P., Kaciroti, N., & Robert H. Bradley. R. H. (2006). Parenting styles and overweight status in first grade. *Pediatrics, 117*, 2047–2054. doi:10.1542/peds.2005-2259

Rollins, B. C., & Thomas, D. L. (1979). Parental support, power, and control techniques in the socialization of children. In W. R. Burr, R. Hill, F. I. Nye, & I. I. Reiss (Eds.), *Contemporary theories about the family: Vol. 1. Research based theories* (pp. 317–364). New York, NY: Free Press.

Schaefer, E. S. (1965). Children's reports of parental behavior: An inventory. *Child Development, 36*, 413–424. doi:10.2307/1126465

Smetana, J. G., Crean, H. F., & Campione-Barr, N. (2005). Adolescents' and parents' changing conceptions of parental authority. In J. G. Smetana (Ed.), *Changing boundaries of parental authority* (pp. 31–46). San Francisco, CA: Jossey-Bass.

Smith, C., Perou, R., & Lesesne, C. (2002). Parent education. In M. Bornstein (Ed.), *Handbook of parenting* (pp. 389–410). Mahwah, NJ: Erlbaum.

Steinberg, L., Elmen, J. D., & Mounts, N. S. (1989). Authoritative parenting, psychosocial maturity, and academic success among adolescents. *Child Development, 60*, 1424–1436. doi:10.2307/1130932

Thelen, E., & Smith, L. B. (1996). *A dynamic systems approach to the development of cognition and action*. Cambridge, MA: MIT Press.

Topham, G. L., Hubbs-Tait, L., Rutledge, J. M., Page, M. C., Kennedy, T. S., Shriver, L. H., & Harrist, A. W. (2011). Parenting styles, parental response to child emotion, and family emotional responsiveness are related to child emotional eating. *Appetite, 56*, 261–264. doi:10.1016/j.appet.2011.01.007

INDEX

Manipulation, 37–38, 67
Marital couple subsystem, 47
Marxist approach, 14–15
Mason, C. A., 122
Matching law, 171
Maturity demands, 212, 217
McFadyen-Ketchum, S., 48
McHale, J., 47
McLoyd, V. C., 121
McMahon, R. J., 173
McNeely, C. A., 127–128
Meaning, 24
Measurement
    of behavioral control, 79
    with interdisciplinary research,
        255–256
    of parental monitoring, 75–76, 79
    of psychological control, 255
Memories, 97–98
Mental health evaluation, 25
Methodologies
    for authoritative parenting research,
        254–256
    for control system analyses, 96–97
    for patterns of parental authority,
        22–24
Microenvironments, 24
Middaugh, E., 148
Mindfulness, 191–192, 329
Mindful parenting, 202–207
Misbehavior
    and cognitive development, 217–218
    parent responses to, 90–93
    reasoning–power assertion synthesis
        for, 103–106
Mize, J., 36
Moffitt, T. E., 166
Moment-to-moment contingencies,
    170–171
Monitoring. *See* Parental monitoring
Montessori, Maria, 14, 15
Moral domain, 153–154
Moral internalization theory, 91–92
Morris, A. S., 252, 258
Morris, S. Z., 105
Mothers, 47, 226
Moulton, C. E., 150
Mounts, N. S., 114–115
Multisystemic interventions, 180–181
Murray, C. B., 118–119, 124–126

Nation, M., 77
Need to belong, 179
Negative emotions, 199, 205
Negative outcomes, 149
Neill, A. S., 18
Noncompliance, 21–22, 178–179
Nonconforming parents, 142
Nonlinear relationships, 77–81, 239
Nonphysical punishment, 100–101
Nonstrategic control, 72–73
Normative conflicts, 139–140
Nucci, L. P., 65, 66, 73, 153
Nurturance, 216, 241–, 247
Nurturant parent metaphor, 17–18
Nurturing, 241

Obedience, 18
Olson, S. F., 46
Operant conditioning perspective, 170
Optimal functioning, 63
Outcomes
    negative, 149
    with parenting style, 215–216
    with parent training, 170, 173–174
Owens, E., 17

Parent–adolescent conflict, 137–140
Parental authority
    with adolescents, 137–139
    adolescent's view of, 146–149
    in parenting prototypes, 12–13
    patterns of, 21–24
Parental monitoring
    and adolescent delinquency, 37
    of adolescents, 40
    and antisocial behavior, 168–169
    and authoritative parenting, 240,
        243–244
    and behavioral control, 75–77
    scales for, 79
Parent–child relationship
    with adolescent children, 11,
        137–140
    with aggressive children, 175
    and antisocial behavior, 168
    as bidirectional process, 44, 251
    in cognitive development, 214–215,
        219–220, 226

ABOUT THE EDITORS

Robert E. Larzelere, PhD, is a professor of human development and family science at Oklahoma State University. He has done research on parental discipline of young children for over 30 years and has collaborated with others to improve the methods used to support social scientific conclusions more generally. His research focuses particularly on comparing the emphasis on consistent consequences in some scientific perspectives on parenting with the emphasis on gentle verbal correction predominant in other scientific perspectives. He recently collaborated with Diana Baumrind to clarify the long-term effects of authoritative parenting and the specific types of power assertion that differentiate it from authoritarian parenting. He benefited from postdoctoral research training from Drs. Murray Straus and Gerald Patterson.

Amanda Sheffield Morris, PhD, is a professor of human development and family science at Oklahoma State University. She is a developmental scientist with research interests in parenting, emotion regulation, and developmental psychopathology. Her research focuses on the role of emotion regulation in child and adolescent adjustment and the ways in which children learn successful regulation skills. She was mentored by Drs. Laurence Steinberg and

Nancy Eisenberg in her doctoral and postdoctoral work at Temple University and Arizona State University.

Amanda W. Harrist, PhD, is an associate professor of human development and family science at Oklahoma State University. Her research centers on the development of children's social competence, specifically the early social antecedents of children's competence and maladjustment exhibited in preschool and the early years of school, and the role that social cognition plays as a mediator. To this end, she has explored the relation of children's behavior in the peer group to early family interactions (parent–child and marriage), observed both naturalistically and in the laboratory. She also is interested in interventions for children at risk in early social settings and has pursued this through several funded projects, most recently in the Families & Schools for Health Project, a longitudinal study of the family and rural school contexts of child obesity. She worked with Drs. Gregory Pettit, Kenneth Dodge, and John Bates while at the University of Tennessee.